PURCHASING MANAGER'S DESK BOOK OF PURCHASING LAW

1991 Supplement

Purchasing Manager's Desk Book of Purchasing Law
1991 Supplement

James J. Ritterskamp, Jr.

PRENTICE HALL
Englewood Cliffs, New Jersey 07632

Prentice-Hall International (UK) Limited, *London*
Prentice-Hall of Australia Pty. Limited, *Sydney*
Prentice-Hall Canada, Inc., *Toronto*
Prentice-Hall Hispanoamericana, S.A., *Mexico*
Prentice-Hall of India Private Limited, *New Delhi*
Prentice-Hall of Japan, Inc., *Tokyo*
Simon & Schuster Asia Pte. Ltd., *Singapore*
Editora Prentice-Hall do Brasil, Ltda., *Rio de Janeiro*

© 1991 *by*
PRENTICE-HALL
Englewood Cliffs, NJ 07632

All rights reserved. No part of this
book may be reproduced in any form or
by any means, without permission in
writing from the publisher.

10 9 8 7 6 5 4 3 2

Library of Congress Cataloging-in-Publication Data

Ritterskamp, James J.
 Purchasing manager's desk book of purchasing law. 1991 supplement
/ James J. Ritterskamp.
  p.   cm.
 Includes index.

 1. Sales—United States. 2. Contracts—United States.
I. Ritterskamp, James J. Purchasing manager's desk book of purchasing
law. II. Title.
KF915.R58 1987 Suppl.
 346.73′072—dc20
 [347.30672]   90–42196
                                                              CIP

ISBN 0-13-741240-1

PRENTICE HALL
BUSINESS & PROFESSIONAL DIVISION
A Simon & Schuster Company
Englewood Cliffs, New Jersey 07632

Printed in the United States of America

INTRODUCTION

The ink was hardly dry on the original manuscript of the *Purchasing Manager's Desk Book Purchasing Law* when the need for an addition to it became evident. The publishing industry customarily meets the need of additions to a published text by producing a revised version of the original. Such an action makes the original edition outdated. It is to be consigned to the scrap heap, and the reader is encouraged to purchase the new revised edition.

We said last year when the need for an addition became evident, that our publisher, Prentice-Hall, Inc., thinks like a purchasing officer who searches for the most economical and cost-effective solution to a need. Instead of revising the original text, Prentice-Hall issued a supplement that made the original text continue to be updated, timely, and current.

There have been additional changes and modifications of the laws since last year to merit the publication of another current supplement. However, this time our publisher said, "Let's not burden our readers with an original text plus *two* supplements. Instead we will issue a new supplement that combines the original supplement with the new material, so there will continue to be only one separate publication in addition to the original text. We can produce the new supplement by reproducing what is to be repeated from the first supplement and add the new material." This is what has been done.

The major addition to this supplement is a section discussing the legal problems associated with the use of electronic data interchange (EDI) between buyers and suppliers. It is apparent that our law, as presently constituted, does not clearly indicate that EDI transactions would be enforceable in a court of law. The Business Law Section of the American Bar Association had a committee known as The Electronic Messaging Services Task Force study the situation. The Task Force submitted its report which was published in *The Business Lawyer,* June 1990 edition, Volume

45 No. s. Along with its report, the Task Force submitted a *Model Form of E D I Trading Partner Agreement and Commentary*, which can serve as a model contract to use with suppliers. A complete copy of that Trading Partner Agreement is included in the section on EDI.

The Convention for the International Sale of Goods continues to occupy a major portion of this second supplement. The reader will note that six more countries have adopted the Convention, including a major U.S. trading partner—Canada—and also the U.S.S.R. We have updated the names of the adopting states in the section on Article 2A—Leases. Included in this supplement is the full texts of both the C.I.S.G. and Article 2A, as well as the major amendment to Section 1-201(37) of the Uniform Commercial Code which was made effective at the time Article 2A was written.

Another modest section in the supplement deals with a recent trend in the law involving responsibility for violation of environmental regulations. This section is shown as a "Supplement to Chapter VI" of the original text that discusses personal liabilities of the purchasing officer. The current trend for enforcement of these environmental laws seems to be pointed toward individual responsibility rather than being solely placed on the corporate entity. Although there have been no recorded cases placing responsibility for pollution on a purchasing officer, the trend could possibly ensnare a purchasing officer in some type of liability at some future time.

Prentice-Hall and your author hope you find this second supplement both timely and cost-effective.

James J. Ritterskamp, Jr.

CONTENTS

	Page
Introduction	v

Supplement to Chapter VII
PERSONAL LIABILITIES OF THE AGENT 1

    RENTING AN AUTOMOBILE 1

    ENVIRONMENTAL LAWS 2

Supplement to Chapter X
ARTICLE 2A OF THE UNIFORM COMMERCIAL CODE—LEASES 5

    APPENDIX A: TEXT OF AMENDMENT TO SECTION 1-201(37) OF THE UNIFORM COMMERCIAL CODE .. 10

Supplement to Chapter XVI
ELECTRONIC DATA INTERCHANGE 57

    APPENDIX B: MODEL ELECTRONIC INTERCHANGE TRADING PARTNER AGREEMENT 68

Supplement to Chapter XXIII
PURCHASING FROM FOREIGN VENDORS 98

    APPENDIX C: UNITED NATIONS CONVENTION ON CONTRACTS FOR THE INTERNATIONAL SALE OF GOODS (1980) 177

Cumulative Index 210

Supplement to Chapter VII
PERSONAL LIABILITIES OF THE AGENT

RENTING AN AUTOMOBILE, PAGE 95 OF ORIGINAL TEXT

At the time the original text was written car rental companies were moving in the direction of having the person renting the car assume 100% of the responsibility for any damage to the rental car. Today this trend has continued to the point where it is normal practice.

The person renting the car, as previously, is given the option by the rental company to pay an additional charge per day for a "collision damage waiver." This so-called "CDW" customarily eliminates responsibility for all possible damage to the rented car. The problem with this is that the additional premium charged for such protection is fairly substantial.

There are now two other options available to most people who rent cars. The first option is one's own car liability insurance. Many automobile insurance companies now extend the liability protection in your policy to so-called "contractual liability" for the responsibility their insured's assume when renting an auto. The term "contracted liability" is applied because the person renting the car contracts with the rental company to assume any collision damage to the car. It is suggested the reader contact his or her private insurance carrier to determine whether this coverage is provided in your policy. It is also suggested you determine whether there is any deductible attached if this feature is included.

The other option available for covering this hazard is found in some types of credit cards. Those credit cards that extend this coverage require that you pay your rental bill with that credit card and then the coverage by the credit card company is automatic. However most of these cards providing this coverage will state that they will cover only what your regular auto liability insurance does not cover.

ENVIRONMENTAL LAWS, PAGE 99 OF ORIGINAL TEXT

Recent trends in court cases that involve violation of one or more of the plethora of environmental laws surrounding us show that the courts are becoming more willing to attach liability for violations on the shoulders of individual officers and directors of offending corporations. Part of this trend is occasioned by increased public awareness of the need for ecological control and protection of our planet. Part of the trend is also due to increased enforcement efforts by the various agencies involved, particularly against corporate offenders, and those who are responsible for the actions of such corporations.

It is singularly coincidental that the radio news report, on this morning that the final writing of this section was to occur, carried a story that four individuals were due to be sentenced today following their original conviction four years ago for operating an improperly ventilated factory. Thermometers were manufactured in this factory. Mercury is one of the ingredients of a thermometer and the handling of it requires proper ventilation. Without giving all of the minute details, it seems the factory had been warned several times by OSHA (the Occupational Safety and Health Administration), through their inspectors that it was operating under unsafe conditions. Fines had been levied against and paid by the company, but no improvements in ventilation had occurred, probably because of the heavy cost involved. In a subsequent inspection, the inspectors issued summonses to four of the operating officers of the company, including the plant superintendent, for the improper ventilation. One supposes the government agency grew tired of having the bad conditions persist after the fines had been paid and decided to "get the attention of" the operating officers by personally serving them with summonses. The threat of incarceration and/or heavy personal fines against the operators of the corporation is one approach to having a bad situation corrected.

Federal Environmental Laws.

There are many Federal environmental laws on our books. Here is a partial list:

1. Comprehensive Environmental Response, Compensation and Liability Act of 1980. This act is often referred to by its acronym of "CERCLA." The reader has probably heard references of "Superfund" which is the appropriation bill to fund CERCLA.
2. Resource Conservation and Recovery Act of 1982 which has a section

Supplement to Chap. 7 / Personal Liabilities of the Agent

termed "Imminent Hazard" that can be used to punish violators of our environment.
3. The Clean Water Act
4. The Refuse Act
5. The Safe Drinking Water Act
6. The 1980 Clear Air Act
7. The Toxic Substance Control Act
8. The Hazardous Materials Transportation Act

This is not a complete list. It does not include so-called "safety" acts such as the Federal Food, Drug and Cosmetics Act, the Occupational Safety and Health Administration Act, and the act that created the Environmental Protection Agency. It also does not include the various environmental control acts passed by the state legislatures. Many of the state acts are more strict than their counter-part Federal acts.

Who Is Liable and Responsible?

It has been fairly simple to make corporate America accountable under these various pieces of legislation. There are those who say it has been almost too simple because some corporations will pay their fine and proceed with "business as usual." Because our law has consistently held the corporate "entity" as being separate and distinct from the shareholders, directors, officers and employees, responsibility and liability for violations has been assessed against the corporation itself. And yet, many years ago, Chief Justice John Marshall of the Supreme Court of the United States told us a corporation is

> an artificial being, invisible, intangible, and existing only in contemplation of the law.

Those not well versed in corporate law will ask "How can a corporation be found guilty of a violation of the law if it is invisible and intangible?" The question is answered with the statement that the corporate "entity" is construed as the violator of the law by the law. But it is equally clear that the corporation must have "actors" or "agents" who actually commit these violations. And it is these individuals, these actors for the corporation, whom the government agencies and the courts are beginning to "ferret out" and hold liable for the acts they perform in the name of the corporation.

Recent Pertinent Litigation.

Two cases in the Federal courts have extended such liability to these corporate actors[1,2] In the Shore case an officer was held guilty of violating the law and in Northeastern Pharmaceutical, individual officers who had arranged for an illegal dumping and burial of hazardous waste were found guilty. These are the only two cases that went so far as to convict officers of a criminal act, but there are other instances where owners have been individually found guilty. Newspaper accounts continually refer to such actions.

Nota Bene to the Purchasing Officer.

The word to the purchasing officer who must arrange for disposal of hazardous waste for his or her organization is simple—follow the law. There are no known shortcuts to immunity. You must follow the law and act within its parameters. If you do not know what the law is, call one of the agencies and get a full explanation. Involve your legal counsel. The two of you should be able to plan a compliance program that will keep you and your corporation free from legal liability.

An additional note of caution. The Courts are attaching liability for environmental violations to executives of corporations who had no knowledge that their corporation was violating the law. Such executives are being convicted of a criminal action because "they had it within the power of their corporate office to prevent subordinates from violating the law." The lesson to a purchasing officer is clear—make certain your subordinates are living within the law. It is your legal duty to give them proper supervision so that such violations will not occur.

Finally, be a "buddy" of your corporate entity. If you know of, or observe, other divisions of the company violating the environmental laws, do what you can to correct the situation. Of course, be certain you are interpreting the law and the corporate procedures properly before you move. If you are convinced violations are occurring, "speak out and point out." Hopefully you will receive nothing but cooperation and gratitude. Should you run into backlash because of your intervention, you are working for the wrong type of corporation. Our people in this country and our government are "pro-environment" today. We must all get on this bandwagon.

---

[1] 759 F.2d 1032, *New York v. Shore Realty*

[2] 810 F.2d 726, *United States v. Northeastern Pharmaceutical*

Supplement to Chapter X, page 151

ARTICLE 2A OF THE UNIFORM COMMERCIAL CODE—LEASES

One of the fastest growing branches of business today is leasing. Over the past few years both businesses and consumers have discovered many advantages of leasing pieces of equipment rather than purchasing such items outright. For consumers, one of the most popular items to lease has been the automobile. Rather than using available cash or savings for the purchase of the auto, or for the required down payment, the buyer leases the automobile and pays a monthly rental fee. If the automobile is used partially for business purposes, that percentage of business use is applied to the total of the lease payments for the year. This figure then becomes a tax-deductible item. There is no need to calculate depreciation under the tax formulas provided, since the lease payments includes both interest and depreciation. Amendments to our tax laws have eliminated, as of this year (1991), 100% of the interest paid on a car loan as a tax deductible expense. Therefore the lease transaction should become even more popular, particularly for those who use their automobile for business purposes. The major disadvantage of the lease of an automobile is the fact that at the end of the lease period one has no equity in the car. But even that could be turned into an advantage, since the lessee can walk away from the car at the end of the lease. It is also possible to rent a new car at that time so that the lessee always has a bright and shiny car to drive about.

Businesses, too, find the lease arrangement to have advantages. For major plant assets there is no need to invest capital in the piece of equipment. The lease payments are fully deductible as an operating expense. There is no need to clutter one's financial statements with one of several types of depreciation methods that are allowed by tax regulations. Of course, here too, the disadvantage of the leasing process is that at the end of the lease term the lessee has no equity in the equipment. However many organizations do follow the lease program and find that because of the fact that they have no equity in the leased piece of equipment, their plants are equipped with more modern pieces of equipment.

Another disadvantage of the leasing procedure is that it has been difficult for some lessors and lessees to know what are their legal rights under a lease. There has been no body of law that addresses itself specifically to the rights and obligations of the parties to a lease. Under present conditions, leases are handled in one of four areas of the law:

1. under common law principles
2. under the law of bailments
3. under Article 2 (Sales) of the Uniform Commercial Code
4. under Article 9 (Secured Transactions) of the Uniform Commercial Code.

Having four alternatives as sources of available applicable law has left all parties, including the courts, scrambling for desperately needed assistance. Some courts have applied Article 2 to lease contracts since Article 2 applies to "transactions in goods" and they then follow with the reasoning that a lease of a piece of equipment is such a "transaction." But this approach has not been followed universally because there are too many inherent problems of applying Article 2 to every type of lease.

It is believed that assistance to the beleaguered lease participants is now at hand. The Commissioners who wrote the Uniform Commercial Code have written a new article—Article 2A—Leases—for adoption by the various states. If this article is adopted by all of the states, we will then have a uniform law pertaining exclusively to leases. Thus far (as of March 1991), the following states have adopted this article and made it the law in their jurisdiction:

California	Oklahoma
Florida	Oregon
Kentucky	South Dakota
Minnesota	Utah
Nevada	Wyoming

Let us hope this is just the beginning of the parade for the adoption of the article. Thus far, the rate of adoption by the states has not proceeded as smoothly and as quickly as had been hoped for. It should also be pointed out that the adoptions by states have not been on a completely uniform basis. The State of California found it necessary to amend a few sections of the article, particularly sections dealing with remedies upon default, to have the law conform to the needs of the state. Oregon used the California version when they adopted Article 2A. However, the Commissioners have stuck tenaciously to their original version of the law, even after considering the California amendments.

Article 2A has six major parts to it, five of which are within the Article itself:

1. general provisions
2. formation and construction of the lease contract
3. effect of the lease contract
4. performance of the lease contract
5. default by either lessor or lessee

The sixth section of the lease provisions presented by Article 2A really appears in Article 1 of the Code. It is an amendment of Section 1–201(37) which is dedicated to the definition of "Security interest." This definition is of importance not only to Article 2A, which deals with "true" leases, but also to Article 9 of the Code which is captioned "Secured Transactions." Leases covered by Article 9 are referred to as "security" leases—they are created by basically a sale of the piece of equipment, but it is designed as a lease for financing purposes. In other words, the seller is in a position if the goods were leased so that possession can be quickly re-acquired if the buyer fails to make payments as promised. At one time such security protection was given by a "chattel" mortgage but now Article 9 considers all such devices as a secured transaction. Article 2A deals with true leases and it is for such types of leases that the Article was written.

The amendment to Article 1–201(37) is shown at the beginning of Appendix B that follows this introduction. It is lengthy but hopefully it will do much to clear the air as to what is a true lease and what is a security lease. Many lawsuits have been tried to determine whether a given lease is one type or the other type. The law has leaned rather heavily on "what was the intent of the parties" when the leasing agreement was entered into. Obviously this can be difficult to determine at times. Then the law was forced to go to other tests. One test, often resorted to, was to go to a whole battery of possible factual situations to determine whether the transaction was a true lease or a security lease. Here is a partial list of some of the factors considered in one case.[1] An affirmative answer to a question implies the transaction was intended to be a security lease.

1. Does the lessee have the option to purchase the item at the end of the lease for a nominal value?
2. Does the lessee have an equity or property interest in the item?
3. Is lessor's business primarily financing?
4. Did the lessee pay a sales tax?
5. Is lessee responsible for insurance?
6. Is entire risk of loss on lessee?
7. Could lessor accelerate payments if lessee is in default?
8. Did lessee select the equipment?
9. Did lessee pay a substantial security deposit?
10. Was the default provision very favorable to the lessor?
11. Was there provision for liquidated damages?
12. Were aggregate rentals equal to purchase price?
13. Did lessor disclaim warranties of merchantability and/or fitness?
14. Did lessee have to join lessor in executing the UCC financing statement?
15. Did lessee have to pay license fees and maintain the equipment?

Obviously one could give affirmative answers to some of these questions even if the transaction was not a security lease. Thus the use of such a list still left the law in a confusing state.

The revised section 1–201(37) should assist in making more clear what is a secured lease and what is not a secured lease. The definition leans heavily on the common law's requirement that there must be a residual interest in the goods that reverts to the lessor when the term expires in a true lease. There are many other distinguishing features between the two as you will note when reading Section 1–201(37).

The purchasing officer should study this section carefully and understand the difference between the two types of leases. When purchasing a piece of equipment where a security interest is created, you will note the differences and the lack of protection given the lessee. Actually such a transaction is really a sale by the lessor to the purchasing officer's company with stringent

---

[1] 3 Bank 120 (1980), *In re* Brookside Drug.

penalties provided for default by the lessee. Most of the transaction, because it is a sale should be covered by Article 2. However there are provisions in Article 9 that will be applicable too, such as the registration of the lien by the seller or the financing agency. Corporate counsel should be able to guide the purchasing officer through these details. However it is up to the purchasing officer to negotiate the best possible deal for the purchase—including all of the terms and conditions of the purchase—except for payment. Counsel should handle the arrangements concerning this portion of the transaction. The purchasing officer should pay particular attention to warranties for the equipment. Many security leases try hard to do away with such assurances. Do not allow it to happen!

Article 2A applies to true leases. Section 2A–102, "Scope" reads this way:

> This Article applies to any transaction regardless of form, that creates a lease.

Then Article 2A-103(1)(j) defines a lease in this fashion:

> (j) "Lease" means a transfer of the right of possession and use of goods for a term in return for consideration, but a sale, including a sale on approval or a sale or return, or retention of creation of a security interest is not a lease. Unless the context clearly indicates otherwise, the term includes a sublease.

This definition makes it quite clear that only true leases are covered by Article 2A.

The complete text of Section 1–201(37) and Article 2A *in toto* follows in Appendix A. The reader will note that Article 2A closely resembles Article 2 with appropriate revisions to accommodate a lease transaction rather than a sale. You will also note that because 2A was patterned after Article 2, we continue to have the same problems we had with Article 2, such as how to deal with lease contracts that cover partly goods and partly services.

Appendix A
TEXT OF AMENDMENT TO SECTION 1–201(37) OF THE UNIFORM COMMERCIAL CODE

(37) "Security interest" means an interest in the personal property or fixtures which secures payment or performance of an obligation. The retention or reservation of title by a seller of goods notwithstanding shipment or delivery to the buyer (Section 2–401) is limited in effect to a reservation of a "security interest". The term also includes any interest of a buyer of accounts or chattel paper which is subject to Article 9. The special property interest of a buyer of goods on identification of those goods to a contract for sale under Section 2–401 is not a "security interest," but a buyer may also acquire a "security interest" by complying with Article 9. Unless a consignment is intended as a security, reservation of title thereunder is not a "security interest", but a consignment in any event is subject to the provisions on consignment sales (Section 2–326).

Whether a transaction creates a lease or security interest is determined by the facts of each case; however, a transaction creates a security interest if the consideration the lessee is to pay the lessor for the right to possession and use of the goods is an obligation for the term of the lease not subject to termination by the lessee, and
    (a) the original term of the lease is equal to or greater than the remaining economic life of the goods,
    (b) the lessee is bound to renew the lease for the remaining economic life of the goods or is bound to become the owner of the goods,
    (c) the lessee has an option to renew the lease for the remaining economic life of the goods for no additional consideration or nominal

additional consideration upon compliance with the lease agreement, or
- (d) the lessee has an option to become the owner of the goods for no additional consideration or nominal additional consideration upon compliance with the lease agreement.

A transaction does not create a security interest merely because it provides that
- (a) the present value of the consideration the lessee is obligated to pay the lessor for the right to possession and use of the goods is substantially equal to or is greater than the fair market value of the goods at the time the lease is entered into,
- (b) the lessee assumes risk of loss of the goods, or agrees to pay taxes, insurance, filing, recording, or registration fees, or service or maintenance costs with respect to the goods,
- (c) the lessee has an option to renew the lease or to become the owner of the goods,
- (d) the lessee has an option to renew the lease for a fixed rent that is equal to or greater than the reasonably predictable fair market rent for the use of the goods for the term of the renewal at the time the option is to be performed, or
- (e) the lessee has an option to become the owner of the goods for a fixed price that is equal to or greater than the reasonably predictable fair market value of the goods at the time the option is to be performed.

For purposes of this subsection (37):
- (x) Additional consideration is not nominal if (i) when the option to renew the lease is granted to the lessee the rent is stated to be the fair market rent for the use of the goods for the term of the renewal determined at the time the option is to be performed, or (ii) when the option to become the owner of the goods is granted to the lessee the price is stated to the fair market value of the goods determined at the time the option is to be performed. Additional consideration is nominal if it is less than the lessee's reasonably predictable cost of performing under the lease agreement if the option is not exercised;
- (y) "Reasonably predictable" and "remaining economic life of the goods" are to be determined with reference to the facts and circumstances at the time the transaction is entered into; and
- (z) "Present value" means the amount as of a date certain of one or more sums payable in the future, discounted to the date certain. The discount is determined by the interest rate specified by the

parties if the rate is not manifestly unreasonable at the time the transaction is entered into; otherwise, the discount is determined by a commercially reasonable rate that takes into account the facts and circumstances of each case at the time the transaction was entered into.

PART 1

GENERAL PROVISIONS

§ 2A–101. Short Title.

This Article shall be known and may be cited as the Uniform Commercial Code—Leases.

§ 2A–102. Scope.

This Article applies to any transaction, regardless of form, that creates a lease.

§ 2A–103. Definitions and Index of Definitions.

(1) In this article unless the context otherwise requires:
   (a) "Buyer in ordinary course of business" means a person who in good faith and without knowledge that the sale to him [or her] is in violation of the ownership rights or security interest or leasehold interest of a third party in the goods buys in ordinary course from a person in the business of selling goods of that kind but does not include a pawnbroker. "Buying" may be for cash or by exchange of other property or on secured or unsecured credit and includes receiving goods or documents of title under a pre-existing contract for sale but does not include a transfer in bulk or as security for or in total or partial satisfaction of a money debt.
   (b) "Cancellation" occurs when either party puts an end to the lease contract for default by the other party.
   (c) "Commercial unit" means such a unit of goods as by commercial usage is a single whole for purposes of lease and division of which materially impairs its character or value on the market or in use. A commercial unit may be a single article, as a machine, or a set of articles, as a suite of furniture or a line of machinery, or a quantity, as a gross or carload, or any other unit treated in use or in the relevant market as a single whole.
   (d) "Conforming" goods or performance under a lease contract means goods or performance that are in accordance with the obligations under the lease contract.
   (e) "Consumer lease" means a lease that a lessor regularly engaged in the business of leasing or selling makes to a lessee, except

an organization, who takes under the lease primarily for a personal, family, or household purpose, if the total payments to be made under the lease contract, excluding payments for options to renew or buy, do not exceed $25,000.

(f) "Fault" means wrongful act, omission, breach, or default.

(g) "Finance lease" means a lease in which (i) the lessor does not select, manufacture or supply the goods, (ii) the lessor acquires the goods or the right to possession and use of the goods in connection with the lease, and (iii) either the lessee receives a copy of the contract evidencing the lessor's purchase of the goods on or before signing the lease contract, or the lessee's approval of the contract evidencing the lessor's purchase of the goods is a condition to effectiveness of the lease contract.

(h) "Goods" means all things that are movable at the time of identification to the lease contract, or are fixtures (Section 2A–309), but the term does not include money, documents, instruments, accounts, chattel paper, general intangibles, or minerals or the like, including oil and gas, before extraction. The term also includes the unborn young of animals.

(i) "Installment lease contract" means a lease contract that authorizes or requires the delivery of goods in separate lots to be separately accepted, even though the lease contract contains a clause "each delivery is a separate lease" or its equivalent.

(j) "Lease" means a transfer of the right to possession and use of goods for a term in return for consideration, but a sale, including a sale on approval or a sale or return, or retention or creation of a security interest is not a lease. Unless the context clearly indicates otherwise, the term includes a sublease.

(k) "Lease agreement" means the bargain, with respect to the lease, of the lessor and the lessee in fact as found in their language or by implication from other circumstances including course of dealing or usage of trade or course of performance as provided in this Article. Unless the context clearly indicates otherwise, the term includes a sublease agreement.

(l) "Lease contract" means the total legal obligation that results from the lease agreement as affected by this Article and any other applicable rules of law. Unless the context clearly indicates otherwise, the term includes a sublease contract.

(m) "Leasehold interest" means the interest of the lessor or the lessee under a lease contract.

(n) "Lessee" means a person who acquires the right to possession and use of goods under a lease. Unless the context clearly indicates otherwise, the term includes a sublessee.

(o) "Lessee in ordinary course of business" means a person who in good faith and without knowledge that the lease to him [or her] is in violation of the ownership rights or security interest or leasehold interest of a third party in the goods, leases in ordinary course from a person in the business of selling or leasing goods of that kind but does not include a pawnbroker. "Leasing" may be for cash or by exchange of other property or on secured or unsecured credit and includes receiving goods or documents of title under a pre-existing lease contract but does not include a transfer in bulk or as security for or in total or partial satisfaction of a money debt.

(p) "Lessor" means a person who transfers the right to possession and use of goods under a lease. Unless the context clearly indicates otherwise, the term includes a sublessor.

(q) "Lessor's residual interest" means the lessor's interest in the goods after expiration, termination, or cancellation of the lease contract.

(r) "Lien" means a charge against or interest in goods to secure payment of a debt or performance of an obligation, but the term does not include a security interest.

(s) "Lot" means a parcel or a single article that is the subject matter of a separate lease or delivery, whether or not it is sufficient to perform the lease contract.

(t) "Merchant lessee" means a lessee that is a merchant with respect to goods of the kind subject to the lease.

(u) "Present value" means the amount as of a date certain of one or more sums payable in the future, discounted to the date certain. The discount is determined by the interest rate specified by the parties if the rate was not manifestly unreasonable at the time the transaction was entered into; otherwise, the discount is determined by a commercially reasonable rate that takes into account the facts and circumstances of each case at the time the transaction was entered into.

(v) "Purchase" includes taking by sale, lease, mortgage, security interest, pledge, gift, or any other voluntary transaction creating an interest in goods.

(w) "Sublease" means a lease of goods the right to possession and use of which was acquired by the lessor as a lessee under an existing lease.

(x) "Supplier" means a person from whom a lessor buys or leases goods to be leased under a finance lease.

(y) "Supply contract" means a contract under which a lessor buys or leases goods to be leased.

(z) "Termination" occurs when either party pursuant to a power created by agreement or law puts an end to the lease contract otherwise than for default.

(2) Other definitions applying to this Article and the sections in which they appear are:

"Accessions." Section 2A–310(1).
"Construction mortgage." Section 2A–309(1)(d).
"Encumbrance." Section 2A–309(1)(e).
"Fixtures." Section 2A–309(1)(a).
"Fixture filing." Section 2A–309(1)(b).
"Purchase money lease." Section 2A–309(1)(c).

(3) The following definitions in other Articles apply to this Article:

"Accounts." Section 9–106.
"Between merchants." Section 2–104(3).
"Buyer." Section 2–103(1)(a).
"Chattel paper." Section 9–105(1)(b).
"Consumer goods." Section 9–109(1).
"Documents." Section 9–105(1)(f).
"Entrusting." Section 2–403(3).
"General intangibles." Section 9–106.
"Good faith." Section 2–103(1)(b).
"Instruments." Section 9–105(1)(i).
"Merchant." Section 2–104(1).
"Mortgage." Section 9–105(1)(j).
"Pursuant to commitment." Section 9–105(1)(k).
"Receipt." Section 2–103(1)(c).
"Sale." Section 2–106(1).
"Sale on approval." Section 2–326.
"Sale or return." Section 2–326.
"Seller." Section 2–103(1)(d).

(4) In addition Article 1 contains general definitions and principles of construction and interpretation applicable throughout this Article.

§ 2A–104. Leases Subject to Other Statutes.

(1) A lease, although subject to this Article, is also subject to any applicable:

(a) statute of the United States;

(b) certificate of title statute of this State: (list any certificate of title statutes covering automobiles, trailers, mobile homes, boats, farm tractors, and the like);
(c) certificate of title statute or another jurisdiction (Section 2A–105); or
(d) consumer protection statute of this State.

(2) In case of conflict between the provisions of this Article, other than Sections 2A–105, 2A–304(3) and 2A–305(3), and any statute referred to in subsection (1), the provisions of that statute control.

(3) Failure to comply with any applicable statute has only the effect specified therein.

§ 2A–105. Territorial Application of Article to Goods Covered by Certificate of Title.

Subject to the provisions of Sections 2A–304(3) and 2A–305(3), with respect to goods covered by a certificate of title issued under a statute of this State or of another jurisdiction, compliance and the effect of compliance or noncompliance with a certificate of title statute are governed by the law (including the conflict of laws rules) of the jurisdiction issuing the certificate until the earlier of (a) surrender of the certificate, or (b) four months after the goods are removed from that jurisdiction and thereafter until a new certificate of title is issued by another jurisdiction.

§ 2A–106. Limitation on Power of Parties to Consumer Lease to Choose Applicable Law and Judicial Forum.

(1) If the law chosen by the parties to a consumer lease is that of a jurisdiction other than a jurisdiction in which the lessee resides at the time the lease agreement becomes enforceable or within 30 days thereafter or in which the goods are to be used, the choice is not enforceable.

(2) If the judicial forum chosen by the parties to a consumer lease is a forum that would not otherwise have jurisdiction over the lessee, the choice is not enforceable.

§ 2A–107. Waiver or Renunciation of Claim or Right After Default.

Any claim or right arising out of an alleged default or breach of warranty may be discharged in whole or in part without consideration by a written waiver or renunciation signed and delivered by the aggrieved party.

§ 2A–108. Unconscionability.

(1) If the court as a matter of law finds a lease contract or any clause of a lease contract to have been unconscionable at the time it was made the court may refuse to enforce the lease contract, or it may enforce the remainder of the lease contract without the unconscionable clause, or it may so limit the application of any unconscionable clause as to avoid any unconscionable result.

(2) With respect to a consumer lease, if the court as a matter of law finds that a lease contract or any clause of a lease contract has been induced by unconscionable conduct or that unconscionable conduct has occurred in the collection of a claim arising from a lease contract, the court may grant appropriate relief.

(3) Before making a finding of unconscionability under subsection (1) or (2), the court, on its own motion or that of a party, shall afford the parties a reasonable opportunity to present evidence as to the setting, purpose, and effect of the lease contract or clause thereof, or of the conduct.

(4) In an action in which the lessee claims unconscionability with respect to a consumer lease:

    (a) If the court finds unconscionability under subsection (1) or (2), the court shall award reasonable attorney's fees to the lessee.

    (b) If the court does not find unconscionability and the lessee claiming unconscionability has brought or maintained an action he [or she] knew to be groundless, the court shall award reasonable attorney's fees to the party against whom the claim is made.

    (c) In determining attorney's fees, the amount of the recovery on behalf of the claimant under subsections (1) and (2) is not controlling.

§ 2A–109. Option to Accelerate at Will.

(1) A term providing that one party or his [or her] successor in interest may accelerate payment or performance or require collateral or additional collateral "at will" or "when he [or she] deems himself [or herself] insecure" or in words of similar import must be construed to mean that he [or she] has power to do so only if he [or she] in good faith believes that the prospect of payment or performance is impaired.

(2) With respect to a consumer lease, the burden of establishing good faith under subsection (1) is on the party who exercised the power; otherwise the burden of establishing lack of good faith is on the party against whom the power has been exercised.

PART 2

FORMATION AND CONSTRUCTION OF LEASE CONTRACT

§ 2A–201. Statute of Frauds.

(1) A lease contract is not enforceable by way of action or defense unless:
    (a) the total payments to be made under the lease contract, excluding payments for options to renew or buy, are less than $1,000; or
    (b) there is a writing, signed by the party against whom enforcement is sought or by that party's authorized agent, sufficient to indicate that a lease contract has been made between the parties and to describe the goods leased and the lease term.

(2) Any description of leased goods or of the lease term is sufficient and satisfies subsection (1)(b), whether or not it is specific, if it reasonably identifies what is described.

(3) A writing is not insufficient because it omits or incorrectly states a term agreed upon, but the lease contract is not enforceable under subsection (1)(b) beyond the lease term and the quantity of goods shown in the writing.

(4) A lease contract that does not satisfy the requirements of subsection (1), but which is valid in other respects, is enforceable:
    (a) if the goods are to be specially manufactured or obtained for the lessee and are not suitable for lease or sale to others in the ordinary course of the lessor's business, and the lessor, before notice of repudiation is received and under circumstances that reasonably indicate that the goods are for the lessee, has made either a substantial beginning of their manufacture or commitments for their procurement;
    (b) if the party against whom enforcement is sought admits in that party's pleading, testimony or otherwise in court that a lease contract was made, but the lease contract is not enforceable under this provision beyond the quantity of goods admitted; or
    (c) with respect to goods that have been received and accepted by the lessee.

(5) The lease term under a lease contract referred to in subsection (4) is:
    (a) if there is a writing signed by the party against whom enforcement is sought or by that party's authorized agent specifying the lease term, the term so specified;

(b) if the party against whom enforcement is sought admits in that party's pleading, testimony, or otherwise in court a lease term, the term so admitted; or
(c) a reasonable lease term.

§ 2A–202. Final Written Expression: Parol or Extrinsic Evidence.

Terms with respect to which the confirmatory memoranda of the parties agree or which are otherwise set forth in a writing intended by the parties as a final expression of their agreement with respect to such terms as are included therein may not be contradicted by evidence of any prior agreement or of a contemporaneous oral agreement but may be explained or supplemented:

(a) by course of dealing or usage of trade or by course of performance; and
(b) by evidence of consistent additional terms unless the court finds the writing to have been intended also as a complete and exclusive statement of the terms of the agreement.

§ 2A–203. Seals Inoperative.

The affixing of a seal to a writing evidencing a lease contract or an offer to enter into a lease contract does not render the writing a sealed instrument and the law with respect to sealed instruments does not apply to the lease contract or offer.

§ 2A–204. Formation in General.

(1) A lease contract may be made in any manner sufficient to show agreement, including conduct by both parties which recognizes the existence of a lease contract.

(2) An agreement sufficient to constitute a lease contract may be found although the moment of its making is undetermined.

(3) Although one or more terms are left open, a lease contract does not fail for indefiniteness if the parties have intended to make a lease contract and there is a reasonably certain basis for giving an appropriate remedy.

§ 2A–205. Firm Offers.

An offer by a merchant to lease goods to or from another person in a signed writing that by its terms gives assurance it will be held open is not revocable, for lack of consideration, during the time stated or, if no time is stated, for a reasonable time, but in no event may the period of irrevocability exceed 3 months. Any such term of assurance on a form supplied by the offeree must be separately signed by the offeror.

§ 2A–206. Offer and Acceptance in Formation of Lease Contract.

(1) Unless otherwise unambiguously indicated by the language or circumstances, an offer to make a lease contract must be construed as inviting acceptance in any manner and by any medium reasonable in the circumstances.

(2) If the beginning of a requested performance is a reasonable mode of acceptance, an offeror who is not notified of acceptance within a reasonable time may treat the offer as having lapsed before acceptance.

§ 2A–207. Course of Performance or Practical Construction.

(1) If a lease contract involves repeated occasions for performance by either party with knowledge of the nature of the performance and opportunity for objection to it by the other, any course of performance accepted or acquiesced in without objection is relevant to determine the meaning of the lease agreement.

(2) The express terms of a lease agreement and any course of performance, as well as any course of dealing and usage of trade, must be construed whenever reasonable as consistent with each other; but if that construction is unreasonable, express terms control course of performance, course of performance controls both course of dealing and usage of trade, and course of dealing controls usage of trade.

(3) Subject to the provisions of Section 2A–208 on modification and waiver, course of performance is relevant to show a waiver or modification of any term inconsistent with the course of performance.

§ 2A–208. Modification, Rescission and Waiver.

(1) An agreement modifying a lease contract needs no consideration to be binding.

(2) A signed lease agreement that excludes modification or rescission except by a signed writing may not be otherwise modified or rescinded,

but, except as between merchants, such a requirement on a form supplied by a merchant must be separately signed by the other party.

(3) Although an attempt at modification or rescission does not satisfy the requirements of subsection (2), it may operate as a waiver.

(4) A party who has made a waiver affecting an executory portion of a lease contract may retract the waiver by reasonable notification received by the other party that strict performance will be required of any term waived, unless the retraction would be unjust in view of a material change of position in reliance on the waiver.

§ 2A–209. Lessee Under Finance Lease as Beneficiary of Supply Contract.

(1) The benefit of the supplier's promises to the lessor under the supply contract and of all warranties, whether express or implied, under the supply contract, extends to the lessee to the extent of the lessee's leasehold interest under a finance lease related to the supply contract, but subject to the terms of the supply contract and all of the supplier's defenses or claims arising therefrom.

(2) The extension of the benefit of the supplier's promises and warranties to the lessee (Section 2A–209(1))does not: (a) modify the rights and obligations of the parties to the supply contract, whether arising therefrom or otherwise, or (b) impose any duty or liability under the supply contract on the lessee.

(3) Any modification or rescission of the supply contract by the supplier and the lessor is effective against the lessee unless, prior to the modification or rescission, the supplier has received notice that the lessee has entered into a finance lease related to the supply contract. If the supply contract is modified or rescinded after the lessee enters the finance lease, the lessee has a cause of action against the lessor, and against the supplier if the supplier has notice of the lessee's entering the finance lease when the supply contract is modified or rescinded. The lessee's recovery from such action shall put the lessee in as good a position as if the modification or rescission had not occurred.

§ 2A–210. Express Warranties.

(1) Express warranties by the lessor are created as follows:
    (a) Any affirmation of fact or promise made by the lessor to the lessee which relates to the goods and becomes part of the basis of the bargain creates an express warranty that the goods

will conform to the affirmation or promise.
- (b) Any description of the goods which is made part of the basis of the bargain creates an express warranty that the goods will conform to the description.
- (c) Any sample or model that is made part of the basis of the bargain creates an express warranty that the whole of the goods will conform to the sample or model.

(2) It is not necessary to the creation of an express warranty that the lessor use formal words, such as "warrant" or "guarantee," or that the lessor have a specific intention to make a warranty, but an affirmation merely of the value of the goods or a statement purporting to be merely the lessor's opinion or commendation of the goods does not create a warranty.

§ 2A–211. Warranties Against Interference and Against Infringement; Lessee's Obligation Against Infringement.

(1) There is in a lease contract a warranty that for the lease term no person holds a claim to or interest in the goods that arose from an act or omission of the lessor, other than a claim by way of infringement or the like, which will interfere with the lessee's enjoyment of its leasehold interest.

(2) Except in a finance lease there is in a lease contract by a lessor who is a merchant regularly dealing in goods of the kind a warranty that the goods are delivered free of the rightful claim of any person by way of infringement or the like.

(3) A lessee who furnishes specifications to a lessor or a supplier shall hold the lessor and the supplier harmless against any claim by way of infringement or the like that arises out of compliance with the specifications.

§ 2A–212. Implied Warranty of Merchantability.

(1) Except in a finance lease, a warranty that the goods will be merchantable is implied in a lease contract if the lessor is a merchant with respect to goods of that kind.

(2) Goods to be merchantable must be at least such as
- (a) pass without objection in the trade under the description in the lease agreement;
- (b) in the case of fungible goods, are of fair average quality within the description;

(c) are fit for the ordinary purposes for which goods of that type are used;
(d) run, within the variation permitted by the lease agreement, of even kind, quality, and quantity within each unit and among all units involved;
(e) are adequately contained, packaged, and labeled as the lease agreement may require; and
(f) conform to any promises or affirmations of fact made on the container or label.

(3) Other implied warranties may arise from course of dealing or usage of trade.

§ 2A–213. Implied Warranty of Fitness for Particular Purpose.

Except in a finance lease, if the lessor at the time the lease contract is made has reason to know of any particular purpose for which the goods are required and that the lessee is relying on the lessor's skill or judgment to select or furnish suitable goods, there is in the lease contract an implied warranty that the goods will be fit for that purpose.

§ 2A–214. Exclusion or Modification of Warranties.

(1) Words or conduct relevant to the creation of an express warranty and words or conduct tending to negate or limit a warranty must be construed wherever reasonable as consistent with each other; but, subject to the provisions of Section 2A–202 on parol or extrinsic evidence, negation or limitation is inoperative to the extent that the construction is unreasonable.

(2) Subject to subsection (3), to exclude or modify the implied warranty of merchantability or any part of it the language must mention "merchantability", be by a writing, and be conspicuous. Subject to subsection (3), to exclude or modify any implied warranty of fitness the exclusion must be by a writing and be conspicuous. Language to exclude all implied warranties of fitness is sufficient if it is in writing, is conspicuous and states, for example, "There is no warranty that the goods will be fit for a particular purpose".

(3) Notwithstanding subsection (2), but subject to subsection (4),
(a) unless the circumstances indicate otherwise, all implied warranties are excluded by expressions like "as is," or "with all faults," or by other language that in common understanding calls the lessee's attention to the exclusion of warranties and makes

plain that there is no implied warranty, if in writing and conspicuous;

(b) if the lessee before entering into the lease contract has examined the goods or the sample or model as fully as desired or has refused to examine the goods, there is no implied warranty with regard to defects that an examination ought in the circumstances to have revealed; and

(c) an implied warranty may also be excluded or modified by course of dealing, course of performance, or usage of trade.

(4) To exclude or modify a warranty against interference or against infringement (Section 2A–211) or any part of it, the language must be specific, be by a writing, and be conspicuous, unless the circumstances, including course of performance, course of dealing, or usage of trade, give the lessee reason to know that the goods are being leased subject to a claim or interest of any person.

§ 2A–215. Cumulation and Conflict of Warranties Express or Implied.

Warranties, whether express or implied, must be construed as consistent with each other and as cumulative, but if that construction is unreasonable, the intention of the parties determines which warranty is dominant. In ascertaining that intention the following rules apply:

(a) Exact or technical specifications displace an inconsistent sample or model or general language of description.

(b) A sample from an existing bulk displaces inconsistent general language of description.

(c) Express warranties displace inconsistent implied warranties other than an implied warranty of fitness for a particular purpose.

§ 2A–216. Third-Party Beneficiaries of Express and Implied Warranties.

ALTERNATIVE A

A warranty to or for the benefit of a lessee under this Article, whether express or implied, extends to any natural person who is in the family or household of the lessee or who is a guest in the lessee's home if it is reasonable to expect that such person may use, consume, or be affected by the goods and who is injured in person by breach of the warranty. This section does not displace principles of law and equity that extend a warranty to or for the benefit of a lessee to other persons. The operation of this section may not be excluded, modified, or limited, but an exclusion, modification, or limitation of the warranty, including any with respect to rights and remedies, effective against the lessee is also effective against any beneficiary designated under this section.

ALTERNATIVE B

A warranty to or for the benefit of a lessee under this Article, whether express or implied, extends to any natural person who may reasonably be expected to use, consume, or be affected by the goods and who is injured in person by breach of the warranty. This section does not displace principles of law and equity that extend a warranty to or for the benefit of a lessee to other persons. The operation of this section may not be excluded, modified, or limited, but an exclusion, modification, or limitation of the warranty, including any with respect to rights and remedies, effective against the lessee is also effective against the beneficiary designated under this section.

ALTERNATIVE C

A warranty to or for the benefit of a lessee under this Article, whether express or implied, extends to any person who may reasonably be expected to use, consume, or be affected by the goods and who is injured by breach of the warranty. The operation of this section may not be excluded, modified, or limited with respect to injury to the person of an individual to whom the warranty extends, but an exclusion, modification, or limitation of the warranty, including any with respect to rights and remedies, effective against the lessee is also effective against the beneficiary designated under this section.

§ 2A–217. Identification.

Identification of goods as goods to which a lease contract refers may be made at any time and in any manner explicitly agreed to by the parties. In the absence of explicit agreement, identification occurs:
- (a) when the lease contract is made if the lease contract is for a lease of goods that are existing and identified;
- (b) when the goods are shipped, marked, or otherwise designated by the lessor as goods to which the lease contract refers, if the lease contract is for a lease of goods that are not existing and identified; or
- (c) when the young are conceived, if the lease contract is for a lease of unborn young of animals.

§ 2A–218. Insurance and Proceeds.

(1) A lessee obtains an insurable interest when existing goods are identified to the lease contract even though the goods identified are nonconforming and the lessee has an option to reject them.

(2) If a lessee has an insurable interest only by reason of the lessor's identification of the goods, the lessor, until default or insolvency or notification to the lessee that identification is final, may substitute other goods for those identified.

(3) Notwithstanding a lessee's insurable interest under subsections (1) and (2), the lessor retains an insurable interest until an option to buy has been exercised by the lessee and risk of loss has passed to the lessee.

(4) Nothing in this section impairs any insurable interest recognized under any other statute or rule of law.

(5) The parties by agreement may determine that one or more parties have an obligation to obtain and pay for insurance covering the goods and by agreement may determine the beneficiary of the proceeds of the insurance.

§ 2A–219. Risk of Loss.

(1) Except in the case of a finance lease, risk of loss is retained by the lessor and does not pass to the lessee. In the case of a finance lease, risk of loss passes to the lessee.

(2) Subject to the provisions of this Article on the effect of default on risk of loss (Section 2A–220), if risk of loss is to pass to the lessee and the time of passage is not stated, the following rules apply:
    (a) If the lease contract requires or authorizes the goods to be shipped by carrier
        (i) and it does not require delivery at a particular destination, the risk of loss passes to the lessee when the goods are duly delivered to the carrier; but
        (ii) if it does require delivery at a particular destination and the goods are there duly tendered while in the possession of the carrier, the risk of loss passes to the lessee when the goods are there duly so tendered as to enable the lessee to take delivery.
    (b) If the goods are held by a bailee to be delivered without being moved, the risk of loss passes to the lessee on acknowledgment by the bailee of the lessee's right to possession of the goods.

(c) In any case not within subsection (a) or (b), the risk of loss passes to the lessee on the lessee's receipt of the goods if the lessor, or, in the case of a finance lease, the supplier, is a merchant; otherwise the risk passes to the lessee on tender of delivery.

§ 2A–220. Effect of Default on Risk of Loss.

(1) Where risk of loss is to pass to the lessee and the time of passage is not stated:
- (a) If the tender or delivery of goods so fails to conform to the lease contract as to give a right of rejection, the risk of their loss remains with the lessor, or, in the case of a finance lease, the supplier, until cure or acceptance.
- (b) If the lessee rightfully revokes acceptance, he [or she], to the extent of any deficiency in his [or her] effective insurance coverage, may treat the risk of loss as having remained with the lessor from the beginning.

(2) Whether or not risk of loss is to pass to the lessee, if the lessee as to conforming goods already identified to a lease contract repudiates or is otherwise in default under the lease contract, the lessor, or, in the case of a finance lease, the supplier, to the extent of any deficiency in his [or her] effective insurance coverage may treat the risk of loss as resting on the lessee for a commercial reasonable time.

§ 2A–221. Casualty to Identified Goods.

If a lease contract requires goods identified when the lease contract is made, and the goods suffer casualty without fault of the lessee, the lessor or the supplier before delivery, or the goods suffer casualty before risk of loss passes to the lessee pursuant to the lease agreement or Section 2A–219, then:
- (a) if the loss is total, the lease contract is avoided; and
- (b) if the loss is partial or the goods have so deteriorated as to no longer conform to the lease contract, the lessee may nevertheless demand inspection and at his [or her] option either treat the lease contract as avoided or, except in a finance lease that is not a consumer lease, accept the goods with due allowance from the rent payable for the balance of the lease term for the deterioration or the deficiency in quantity but without further right against the lessor.

PART 3

EFFECT OF LEASE CONTRACT

§ 2A–301. Enforceability of Lease Contract.

Except as otherwise provided in this Article, a lease contract is effective and enforceable according to its terms between the parties, against purchasers of the goods and against creditors of the parties.

§ 2A–302. Title to and Possession of Goods.

Except as otherwise provided in this Article, each provision of this Article applies whether the lessor or a third party has title to the goods, and whether the lessor, the lessee, or a third party has possession of the goods, notwithstanding any statute or rule of law that possession or the absence of possession is fraudulent.

§ 2A–303. Alienability of Party's Interest Under Lease Contract or of Lessor's Residual Interest in Goods; Delegation of Performance; Assignment of Rights.

(1) Any interest of a party under a lease contract and the lessor's residual interest in the goods may be transferred unless
    (a) the transfer is voluntary and the lease contract prohibits the transfer; or
    (b) the transfer materially changes the duty of or materially increases the burden or risk imposed on the other party to the lease contract, and within a reasonable time after notice of the transfer the other party demands that the transferee comply with subsection (2) and the transferee fails to comply.

(2) Within a reasonable time after demand pursuant to subsection (1)(b), the transferee shall:
    (a) cure or provide adequate assurance that he [or she] will promptly cure any default other than one arising from the transfer;
    (b) compensate or provide adequate assurance that he [or she] will promptly compensate the other party to the lease contract and any other person holding an interest in the lease contract, except the party whose interest is being transferred, for any loss to that party resulting from the transfer;

(c) provide adequate assurance of future due performance under the lease contract; and

(d) assume the lease contract.

(3) Demand pursuant to subsection (1)(b) is without prejudice to the other party's rights against the transferee and the party whose interest is transferred.

(4) An assignment of "the lease" or of "all my rights under the lease" or an assignment in similar general terms is a transfer of rights, and unless the language or the circumstances, as in an assignment for security, indicate the contrary, the assignment is a delegation of duties by the assignor to the assignee and acceptance by the assignee constitutes a promise by him [or her] to perform those duties. This promise is enforceable by either the assignor or the other party to the lease contract.

(5) Unless otherwise agreed by the lessor and the lessee, no delegation of performance relieves the assignor as against the other party of any duty to perform or any liability for default.

(6) A right to damages for default with respect to the whole lease contract or a right arising out of the assignor's due performance of his [or her] entire obligation can be assigned despite agreement otherwise.

(7) To prohibit the transfer of an interest of a party under a lease contract, the language of prohibition must be specific, by a writing, and conspicuous.

§ 2A–304. Subsequent Lease of Goods by Lessor.

(1) Subject to the provisions of Section 2A–303, a subsequent lessee from a lessor of goods under an existing lease contract obtains, to the extent of the leasehold interest transferred, the leasehold interest in the goods that the lessor had or had power to transfer, and except as provided in subsection (2) and Section 2A–527(4), takes subject to the existing lease contract. A lessor with voidable title has power to transfer a good leasehold interest to a good faith subsequent lessee for value, but only to the extent set forth in the preceding sentence. When goods have been delivered under a transaction of purchase the lessor has that power even though:

(a) the lessor's transferor was deceived as to the identity of the lessor;

(b) the delivery was in exchange for a check which is later dishonored;

(c) it was agreed that the transaction was to be a "cash sale"; or

(d) the delivery was procured through fraud punishable as larcenous under the criminal law.

(2) A subsequent lessee in the ordinary course of business from a lessor who is a merchant dealing in goods of that kind to whom the goods were entrusted by the existing lessee before the interest of the subsequent lessee became enforceable against the lessor obtains, to the extent of the leasehold interest transferred, all of the lessor's and the existing lessee's rights to the goods, and takes free of the existing lease contract.

(3) A subsequent lessee from the lessor of goods that are subject to an existing lease contract and are covered by a certificate of title issued under a statute of this State or of another jurisdiction takes no greater rights than those provided both by this section and by the certificate of title statute.

§ 2A–305. Sale or Sublease of Goods by Lessee.

(1) Subject to the provisions of Section 2A–303, a buyer or sublessee from the lessee of goods under an existing lease contract obtains, to the extent of the interest transferred, the leasehold interest in the goods that the lessee had or had power to transfer, and except as provided in subsection (2) and Section 2A–511(4), takes subject to the existing lease contract. A lessee with a voidable leasehold interest has power to transfer a good leasehold interest to a good faith buyer for value or a good faith sublessee for value, but only to the extent set forth in the preceding sentence. When goods have been delivered under a transaction of lease the lessee has that power even though:
   (a) the lessor was deceived as to the identity of the lessee;
   (b) the delivery was in exchange for a check which is later dishonored; or
   (c) the delivery was procured through fraud punishable as larcenous under the criminal law.

(2) A buyer in the ordinary course of business or a sublessee in the ordinary course of business from a lessee who is a merchant dealing in goods of that kind to whom the goods were entrusted by the lessor obtains, to the extent of the interest transferred, all of the lessor's and lessee's rights to the goods, and takes free of the existing lease contract.

(3) A buyer or sublessee from the lessee of goods that are subject to an existing lease contract and are covered by a certificate of title issued under a statute of this State or of another jurisdiction takes no greater rights than those provided both by this section and by the certificate of title statute.

§ 2A–306. Priority of Certain Liens Arising by Operation of Law.

If a person in the ordinary course of his [or her] business furnishes services or materials with respect to goods subject to a lease contract, a lien upon those goods in the possession of that person given by statute or rule of law for those materials or services takes priority over any interest of the lessor or lessee under the lease contract or this Article unless the lien is created by statute and the statute provides otherwise or unless the lien is created by rule of law and the rule of law provides otherwise.

§ 2A–307. Priority of Liens Arising by Attachment or Levy on, Security Interests in, and Other Claims to Goods.

(1) Except as otherwise provided in Section 2A–306, a creditor of a lessee takes subject to the lease contract.

(2) Except as otherwise provided in subsections (3) and (4) of this section and in Sections 2A–306 and 2A–308, a creditor of a lessor takes subject to the lease contract:
> (a) unless the creditor holds a lien that attached to the goods before the lease contract became enforceable, or
> (b) unless the creditor holds a security interest in the goods that under the Article on Secured Transactions (Article 9) would have priority over any other security interest in the goods perfected by a filing covering the goods and made at the time the lease contract became enforceable, whether or not any other security interest existed.

(3) A lessee in the ordinary course of business takes the leasehold interest free of a security interest in the goods created by the lessor even though the security interest is perfected and the lessee knows of its existence.

(4) A lessee other than a lessee in the ordinary course of business takes the leasehold interest free of a security interest to the extent that it secures future advances made after the secured party acquires knowledge of the lease or more than 45 days after the lease contract becomes enforceable, whichever first occurs, unless the future advances are made pursuant to a commitment entered into without knowledge of the lease and before the expiration of the 45-day period.

§ 2A–308. Special Rights of Creditors.

(1) A creditor of a lessor in possession of goods subject to a lease contract may treat the lease contract as void if as against the creditor retention of possession by the lessor is fraudulent under any statute or rule of law, but retention of possession in good faith and current course of trade by the lessor for a commercially reasonable time after the lease contract becomes enforceable is not fraudulent.

(2) Nothing in this Article impairs the rights of creditors of a lessor if the lease contract (a) becomes enforceable, not in current course of trade but in satisfaction of or as security for a pre-existing claim for money, security, or the like, and (b) is made under circumstances which under any statute or rule of law apart from this Article would constitute the transaction a fraudulent transfer or voidable preference.

(3) A creditor of a seller may treat a sale or an identification of goods to a contract for sale as void if as against the creditor retention of possession by the seller is fraudulent under any statute or rule of law, but retention of possession of the goods pursuant to a lease contract entered into by the seller as lessee and the buyer as lessor in connection with the sale or identification of the goods is not fraudulent if the buyer bought for value and in good faith.

§ 2A–309. Lessor's and Lessee's Rights When Goods Become Fixtures.

(1) In this section:
   (a) goods are "fixtures" when they become so related to particular real estate that an interest in them arises under real estate law;
   (b) a "fixture filing" is the filing, in the office where a mortgage on the real estate would be recorded or registered, of a financing statement concerning goods that are or are to become fixtures and conforming to the requirements of subsection (5) of Section 9–402;
   (c) a lease is a "purchase money lease" unless the lessee has possession or use of the goods or the right to possession or use of the goods before the lease agreement is enforceable;
   (d) a mortgage is a "construction mortgage" to the extent it secures an obligation incurred for the construction of an improvement on land including the acquisition cost of the land, if the recorded writing so indicates; and

(e) "encumbrance" includes real estate mortgages and other liens on real estate and all other rights in real estate that are not ownership interests.

(2) Under this Article a lease may be of goods that are fixtures or may continue in goods that become fixtures, but no lease exists under this Article of ordinary building materials incorporated into an improvement on land.

(3) This Article does not prevent creation of a lease of fixtures pursuant to real estate law.

(4) The perfected interest of a lessor of fixtures has priority over a conflicting interest of an encumbrancer or owner of the real estate if:

   (a) the lease is a purchase money lease, the conflicting interest of the encumbrancer or owner arises before the goods become fixtures, the interest of the lessor is perfected by a fixture filing before the goods become fixtures or within ten days thereafter, and the lessee has an interest of record in the real estate or is in possession of the real estate; or

   (b) the interest of the lessor is perfected by a fixture filing before the interest of the encumbrancer or owner is of record, the lessor's interest has priority over any conflicting interest of a predecessor in title of the encumbrancer or owner, and the lessee has an interest of record in the real estate or is in possession of the real estate.

(5) The interest of a lessor of fixtures, whether or not perfected, has priority over the conflicting interest of an encumbrancer or owner of the real estate if:

   (a) the fixtures are readily removable factory or office machines, readily removable equipment that is not primarily used or leased for use in the operation of the real estate, or readily removable replacements of domestic appliances that are goods subject to a consumer lease, and before the goods become fixtures the lease contract is enforceable; or

   (b) the conflicting interest is a lien on the real estate obtained by legal or equitable proceedings after the lease contract is enforceable; or

   (c) the encumbrancer or owner has consented in writing to the lease or has disclaimed an interest in the goods as fixtures; or

   (d) the lessee has a right to remove the goods as against the encumbrancer or owner. If the lessee's right to remove terminates, the priority of the interest of the lessor continues for a reasonable time.

(6) Notwithstanding paragraph (a) of subsection (4) but otherwise subject to subsections (4) and (5), the interest of a lessor of fixtures is subordinate to the conflicting interest of an encumbrancer of the real estate under a construction mortgage recorded before the goods become fixtures if the goods become fixtures before the completion of the construction. To the extent given to refinance a construction mortgage, the conflicting interest of an encumbrancer of the real estate under a mortgage has this priority to the same extent as the encumbrancer of the real estate under the construction mortgage.

(7) In cases not within the preceding subsections, priority between the interest of a lessor of fixtures and the conflicting interest of an encumbrancer or owner of the real estate who is not the lessee is determined by the priority rules governing conflicting interests in real estate.

(8) If the interest of a lessor has priority over all conflicitng interests of all owners and encumbrancers of the real estate, the lessor or the lessee may (a) on default, expiration, termination, or cancellation of the lease agreement by the other party but subject to the provisions of the lease agreement and this Article, or (b) if necessary to enforce his [or her] other rights and remedies under this Article, remove the goods from the real estate, free and clear of all conflicting interests of all owners and encumbrancers of the real estate, but he [or she] must reimburse any encumbrancer or owner of the real estate who is not the lessee and who has not otherwise agreed for the cost of repair of any physical injury, but not for any diminution in value of the real estate caused by the absence of the goods removed or by any necessity of replacing them. A person entitled to reimbursement may refuse permission to remove until the party seeking removal gives adequate security for the performance of this obligation.

(9) Even though the lease agreement does not create a security interest, the interest of a lessor of fixtures is perfected by filing a financing statement as a fixture filing for leased goods that are or are to become fixtures in accordance with the relevant provisions of the Article on Secured Transactions (Article 9).

§ 2A–310. Lessor's and Lessee's Rights When Goods Become Accessions.

(1) Goods are "accessions" when they are installed in or affixed to other goods.

(2) The interest of a lessor or a lessee under a lease contract entered into before the goods become accessions is superior to all interests in the whole except as stated in subsection (4).

(3) The interest of a lessor or a lessee under a lease contract entered into at the time or after the goods became accessions is superior to all subsequently acquired interests in the whole except as stated in subsection (4) but is subordinate to interests in the whole existing at the time the lease contract was made unless the holders of such interests in the whole have in writing consented to the lease or disclaimed an interest in the goods as part of the whole.

(4) The interest of a lessor or a lessee under a lease contract described in subsection (2) or (3) is subordinate to the interest of
- (a) a buyer in the ordinary course of business or a lessee in the ordinary course of business of any interest in the whole acquired after the goods became accessions; or
- (b) a creditor with a security interest in the whole perfected before the lease contract was made to the extent that the creditor makes subsequent advances without knowledge of the lease contract.

(5) When under subsections (2) or (3) and (4) a lessor or a lessee of accessions holds an interest that is superior to all interests in the whole, the lessor or the lessee may (a) on default, expiration, termination, or cancellation of the lease contract by the other party but subject to the provisions of the lease contract and this Article, or (b) if necessary to enforce his [or her] other rights and remedies under this Article, remove the goods from the whole, free and clear of all interests in the whole, but he [or she] must reimburse any holder of an interest in the whole who is not the lessee and who has not otherwise agreed for the cost of repair of any physical injury but not for any diminution in value of the whole caused by the absence of the goods removed or by any necessity for replacing them. A person entitled to reimbursement may refuse permission to remove until the party seeking removal gives adequate security for the performance of this obligation.

PART 4

PERFORMANCE OF LEASE CONTRACT: REPUDIATED, SUBSTITUTED AND EXCUSED

§ 2A–401. Insecurity: Adequate Assurance of Performance.

(1) A lease contract imposes an obligation on each party that the other's expectation of receiving due performance will not be impaired.

(2) If reasonable grounds for insecurity arise with respect to the performance of either party, the insecure party may demand in writing adequate

assurance of due performance. Until the insecure party receives that assurance, if commercially reasonable the insecure party may suspend any performance for which he [or she] has not already received the agreed return.

(3) A repudiation of the lease contract occurs if assurance of due performance adequate under the circumstances of the particular case is not provided to the insecure party within a reasonable time, not to exceed 30 days after receipt of a demand by the other party.

(4) Between merchants, the reasonableness of grounds for insecurity and the adequacy of any assurance offered must be determined according to commercial standards.

(5) Acceptance of any nonconforming delivery or payment does not prejudice the aggrieved party's right to demand adequate assurance of future performance.

§ 2A–402. Anticipatory Repudiation.

If either party repudiates a lease contract with respect to a performance not yet due under the lease contract, the loss of which performance will substantially impair the value of the lease contract to the other, the aggrieved party may:
  (a) for a commercially reasonable time, await retraction of repudiation and performance by the repudiating party;
  (b) make demand pursuant to Section 2A–401 and await assurance of future performance adequate under the circumstances of the particular case; or
  (c) resort to any right or remedy upon default under the lease contract or this Article, even though the aggrieved party has notified the repudiating party that the aggrieved party would await the repudiating party's performance and assurance and has urged retraction. In addition, whether or not the aggrieved party is pursuing one of the foregoing remedies, the aggrieved party may suspend performance or, if the aggrieved party is the lessor, proceed in accordance with the provisions of this Article on the lessor's right to identify goods to the lease contract notwithstanding default or to salvage unfinished goods (Section 2A–524).

§ 2A–403. Retraction of Anticipatory Repudiation.

(1) Until the repudiating party's next performance is due, the repudiating party can retract the repudiation unless, since the repudiation, the aggrieved

party has cancelled the lease contract or materially changed the aggrieved party's position or otherwise indicated that the aggrieved party considers the repudiation final.

(2) Retraction may be by any method that clearly indicates to the aggrieved party that the repudiating party intends to perform under the lease contract and includes any assurance demanded under Section 2A–401.

(3) Retraction reinstates a repudiating party's rights under a lease contract with due excuse and allowance to the aggrieved party for any delay occasioned by the repudiation.

§ 2A–404. Substituted Performance.

(1) If without fault of the lessee, the lessor and the supplier, the agreed berthing, loading, or unloading facilities fail or the agreed type of carrier becomes unavailable or the agreed manner of delivery otherwise becomes commercially impracticable, but a commercially reasonable substitute is available, the substitute performance must be tendered and accepted.

(2) If the agreed means or manner of payment fails because of domestic or foreign governmental regulation:
- (a) the lessor may withhold or stop delivery or cause the supplier to withhold or stop delivery unless the lessee provides a means or manner of payment that is commercially a substantial equivalent; and
- (b) if delivery has already been taken, payment by the means or in the manner provided by the regulation discharges the lessee's obligation unless the regulation is discriminatory, oppressive, or predatory.

§ 2A–405. Excused Performance.

Subject to Section 2A–404 on substituted performance, the following rules apply:
- (a) Delay in delivery or nondelivery in whole or in part by a lessor or a supplier who complies with paragraphs (b) and (c) is not a default under the lease contract if performance as agreed has been made impracticable by the occurrence of a contingency the nonoccurrence of which was a basic assumption on which the lease contract was made or by compliance in good faith

with any applicable foreign or domestic governmental regulation or order, whether or not the regulation or order later proves to be invalid.
- (b) If the causes mentioned in paragraph (a) affect only part of the lessor's or the supplier's capacity to perform, he [or she] shall allocate production and deliveries among his [or her] customers but at his [or her] option may include regular customers not then under contract for sale or lease as well as his [or her] own requirements for further manufacture. He [or she] may so allocate in any manner that is fair and reasonable.
- (c) The lessor seasonably shall notify the lessee and in the case of a finance lease the supplier seasonably shall notify the lessor and the lessee, if known, that there will be delay or nondelivery and, if allocation is required under paragraph (b), of the estimated quota thus made available for the lessee.

§ 2A–406. Procedure on Excused Performance.

(1) If the lessee receives notification of a material or indefinite delay or an allocation justified under Section 2A–405, the lessee may by written notification to the lessor as to any goods involved, and with respect to all of the goods if under an installment lease contract the value of the whole lease contract is substantially impaired (Section 2A–510):
- (a) terminate the lease contract (Section 2A–505(2)); or
- (b) except in a finance lease that is not a consumer lease, modify the lease contract by accepting the available quota in substitution, with due allowance from the rent payable for the balance of the lease term for the deficiency but without further right against the lessor.

(2) If, after receipt of a notification from the lessor under Section 2A–405, the lessee fails so to modify the lease agreement within a reasonable time not exceeding 30 days, the lease contract lapses with respect to any deliveries affected.

§ 2A–407. Irrevocable Promises: Finance Leases.

(1) In the case of a finance lease that is not a consumer lease the lessee's promises under the lease contract become irrevocable and independent upon the lessee's acceptance of the goods.

(2) A promise that has become irrevocable and independent under subsection (1):
> (a) is effective and enforceable between the parties, and by or against third parties including assignees of the parties, and
> (b) is not subject to cancellation, termination, modification, repudiation, excuse, or substitution without the consent of the party to whom the promise runs.

PART 5

DEFAULT

A. IN GENERAL

§ 2A–501. Default: Procedure.

(1) Whether the lessor or the lessee is in default under a lease contract is determined by the lease agreement and this Article.

(2) If the lessor or the lessee is in default under the lease contract, the party seeking enforcement has rights and remedies as provided in this Article and, except as limited by this Article, as provided in the lease agreement.

(3) If the lessor or the lessee is in default under the lease contract, the party seeking enforcement may reduce the party's claim to judgment, or otherwise enforce the lease contract by self-help or any available judicial procedure or nonjudicial procedure, including administrative proceeding, arbitration, or the like, in accordance with this Article.

(4) Except as otherwise provided in this Article or the lease agreement, the rights and remedies referred to in subsections (2) and (3) are cumulative.

(5) If the lease agreement covers both real property and goods, the party seeking enforcement may proceed under this Part as to the goods, or under other applicable law as to both the real property and the goods in accordance with his [or her] rights and remedies in respect of the real property, in which case this Part does not apply.

§ 2A–502. Notice After Default.

Except as otherwise provided in this Article or the lease agreement, the lessor or lessee in default under the lease contract is not entitled to notice of default or notice of enforcement from the other party to the lease agreement.

§ 2A–503. Modification or Impairment of Rights and Remedies.

(1) Except as otherwise provided in this article, the lease agreement may include rights and remedies for default in addition to or in substitution for those provided in this Article and may limit or alter the measure of damages recoverable under this Article.

(2) Resort to a remedy provided under this Article or in the lease agreement is optional unless the remedy is expressly agreed to be exclusive. If circumstances cause an exclusive or limited remedy to fail of its essential purpose, or provision for an exclusive remedy is unconscionable, remedy may be had as provided in this Article.

(3) Consequential damages may be liquidated under Section 2A–504, or may otherwise be limited, altered, or excluded unless the limitation, alteration, or exclusion is unconscionable. Limitation of consequential damages for injury to the person in the case of consumer goods is prima facie unconscionable but limitation of damages where the loss is commercial is not.

(4) Rights and remedies on default by the lessor or the lessee with respect to any obligation or promise collateral or ancillary to the lease contract are not impaired by this Article.

§ 2A–504. Liquidation of Damages.

(1) Damages payable by either party for default, or any other act or omission, including indemnity for loss or diminution of anticipated tax benefits or loss or damage to lessor's residual interest, may be liquidated in the lease agreement but only at an amount or by a formula that is reasonable in light of the then anticipated harm caused by the default or other act or omission.

(2) If the lease agreement provides for liquidation of damages, and such provision does not comply with subsection (1), or such provision is an exclusive or limited remedy that circumstances cause to fail of its essential purpose, remedy may be had as provided in this Article.

(3) If the lessor justifiably withholds or stops delivery of goods because of the lessee's default or insolvency (Section 2A–525 or 2A–526), the lessee is entitled to restitution of any amount by which the sum of his [or her] payments exceeds:

    (a) the amount to which the lessor is entitled by virtue of terms liquidating the lessor's damages in accordance with subsection (1); or

(b) in the absence of those terms, 20 percent of the then present value of the total rent the lessee was obligated to pay for the balance of the lease term, or, in the case of a consumer lease, the lesser of such amount or $500.

(4) A lessee's right to restitution under subsection (3) is subject to offset to the extent the lessor establishes:
    (a) a right to recover damages under the provisions of this Article other than subsection (1); and
    (b) the amount or value of any benefits received by the lessee directly or indirectly by reason of the lease contract.

§ 2A–505. Cancellation and Termination and Effect of Cancellation, Termination, Rescission, or Fraud on Rights and Remedies.

(1) On cancellation of the lease contract, all obligations that are still executory on both sides are discharged, but any right based on prior default or performance survives, and the cancelling party also retains any remedy for default of the whole lease contract or any unperformed balance.

(2) On termination of the lease contract, all obligations that are still executory on both sides are discharged but any right based on prior default or performance survives.

(3) Unless the contrary intention clearly appears, expressions of "cancellation," "rescission," or the like of the lease contract may not be construed as a renunciation or discharge of any claim in damages for an antecedent default.

(4) Rights and remedies for material misrepresentation or fraud include all rights and remedies available under this Article for default.

(5) Neither rescission nor a claim for rescission of the lease contract nor rejection or return of the goods may bar or be deemed inconsistent with a claim for damages or other right or remedy.

§ 2A–506. Statute of Limitations.

(1) An action for default under a lease contract, including breach of warranty or indemnity, must be commenced within 4 years after the cause of action accrued. By the original lease contract the parties may reduce the period of limitation to not less than one year.

(2) A cause of action for default accrues when the act or omission on which the default or breach of warranty is based is or should have been discovered by the aggrieved party, or when the default occurs, whichever

is later. A cause of action for indemnity accrues when the act or omission on which the claim for indemnity is based is or should have been discovered by the indemnified party, whichever is later.

(3) If an action commenced within the time limited by subsection (1) is so terminated as to leave available a remedy by another action for the same default or breach of warranty or indemnity, the other action may be commenced after the expiration of the time limited and within 6 months after the termination of the first action unless the termination resulted from voluntary discontinuance or from dismissal for failure or neglect to prosecute.

(4) This section does not alter the law on tolling of the statute of limitations nor does it apply to causes of action that have accrued before this Article becomes effective.

§ 2A–507. Proof of Market Rent: Time and Place.

(1) Damages based on market rent (Section 2A–519 or 2A–528) are determined according to the rent for the use of the goods concerned for a lease term identical to the remaining lease term of the original lease agreement and prevailing at the time of the default.

(2) If evidence of rent for the use of the goods concerned for a lease term identical to the remaining lease term of the original lease agreement and prevailing at the times or places described in this Article is not readily available, the rent prevailing within any reasonable time before or after the time described or at any other place or for a different lease term which in commercial judgment or under usage of trade would serve as a reasonable substitute for the one described may be used, making any proper allowance for the difference, including the cost of transporting the goods to or from the other place.

(3) Evidence of a relevant rent prevailing at a time or place or for a lease term other than the one described in this Article offered by one party is not admissible unless and until he [or she] has given the other party notice the court finds sufficient to prevent unfair surprise.

(4) If the prevailing rent or value of any goods regularly leased in any established market is in issue, reports in official publications or trade journals or in newspapers or periodicals of general circulation published as the reports of that market are admissible in evidence. The circumstances of the preparation of the report may be shown to affect its weight but not its admissibility.

B. DEFAULT BY LESSOR

§ 2A–508. Lessee's Remedies.

(1) If a lessor fails to deliver the goods in conformity to the lease

contract (Section 2A–509) or repudiates the lease contract (Section 2A–402), or a lessee rightfully rejects the goods (Section 2A–509) or justifiably revokes acceptance of the goods (Section 2A–517), then with respect to any goods involved, and with respect to all of the goods if under an installment lease contract the value of the whole lease contract is substantially impaired (Section 2A–510), the lessor is in default under the lease contract and the lessee may:

    (a) cancel the lease contract (Section 2A–505(1));

    (b) recover so much of the rent and security as has been paid, but in the case of an installment lease contract the recovery is that which is just under the circumstances;

    (c) cover and recover damages as to all goods affected whether or not they have been identified to the lease contract (Sections 2A–518 and 2A–520), or recover damages for nondelivery (Sections 2A–519 and 2A–520).

(2) If a lessor fails to deliver the goods in conformity to the lease contract or repudiates the lease contract, the lessee may also:

    (a) if the goods have been identified, recover them (Section 2A–522); or

    (b) in a proper case, obtain specific performance or replevy the goods (Section 2A–521).

(3) If a lessor is otherwise in default under a lease contract, the lessee may exercise the rights and remedies provided in the lease contract and this Article.

(4) If a lessor has breached a warranty, whether express or implied, the lessee may recover damages (Section 2A–519(4)).

(5) On rightful rejection or justifiable revocation of acceptance, a lessee has a security interest in goods in the lessee's possession or control for any rent and security that has been paid and any expenses reasonably incurred in their inspection, receipt, transportation, and care and custody and may hold those goods and dispose of them in good faith and in a commercially reasonable manner, subject to the provisions of Section 2A–527(5).

(6) Subject to the provisions of Section 2A–407, a lessee, on notifying the lessor of the lessee's intention to do so, may deduct all or any part of the damages resulting from any default under the lease contract from any part of the rent still due under the same lease contract.

§ 2A–509. Lessee's Rights on Improper Delivery; Rightful Rejection.

(1) Subject to the provisions of Section 2A–510 on default in installment lease contracts, if the goods or the tender or delivery fail in any respect

to conform to the lease contract, the lessee may reject or accept the goods or accept any commercial unit or units and reject the rest of the goods.

(2) Rejection of goods is ineffective unless it is within a reasonable time after tender or delivery of the goods and the lessee seasonably notifies the lessor.

§ 2A–510. Installment Lease Contracts: Rejection and Default.

(1) Under an installment lease contract a lessee may reject any delivery that is nonconforming if the nonconformity substantially impairs the value of that delivery and cannot be cured or the nonconformity is a defect in the required documents; but if the nonconformity does not fall within subsection (2) and the lessor or the supplier gives adequate assurance of its cure, the lessee must accept that delivery.

(2) Whenever nonconformity or default with respect to one or more deliveries substantially impairs the value of the installment lease contract as a whole there is a default with respect to the whole. But, the aggrieved party reinstates the installment lease contract as a whole if the aggrieved party accepts a nonconforming delivery without seasonably notifying of cancellation or brings an action with respect only to past deliveries or demands performance as to future deliveries.

§ 2A–511. Merchant Lessee's Duties as to Rightfully Rejected Goods.

(1) Subject to any security interest of a lessee (Section 2A–508(5)), if a lessor or a supplier has no agent or place of business at the market of rejection, a merchant lessee, after rejection of goods in his [or her] possession or control, shall follow any reasonable instructions received from the lessor or the supplier with respect to the goods. In the absence of those instructions, a merchant lessee shall make reasonable efforts to sell, lease, or otherwise dispose of the goods for the lessor's account if they threaten to decline in value speedily. Instructions are not reasonable if on demand indemnity for expenses is not forthcoming.

(2) If a merchant lessee (subsection (1)) or any other lessee (Section 2A–512) disposes of goods, he [or she] is entitled to reimbursement either from the lessor or the supplier or out of the proceeds for reasonable expenses of caring for and disposing of the goods and, if the expenses include no disposition commission, to such commission as is usual in the trade, or if there is none, to a reasonable sum not exceeding 10 percent of the gross proceeds.

(3) In complying with this section or Section 2A–512, the lessee is held only to good faith. Good faith conduct hereunder is neither acceptance or conversion nor the basis of an action for damages.

(4) A purchaser who purchases in good faith from a lessee pursuant to this section or Section 2A–512 takes the goods free of any rights of the lessor and the supplier even though the lessee fails to comply with one or more of the requirements of this Article.

§ 2A–512. Lessee's Duties as to Rightfully Rejected Goods.

(1) Except as otherwise provided with respect to goods that threaten to decline in value speedily (Section 2A–511) and subject to any security interest of a lessee (Section 2A–508(5)):

- (a) the lessee, after rejection of goods in the lessee's possession, shall hold them with reasonable care at the lessor's or the supplier's disposition for a reasonable time after the lessee's seasonable notification of rejection;
- (b) if the lessor or the supplier gives no instructions within a reasonable time after notification of rejection, the lessee may store the rejected goods for the lessor's or the supplier's account or ship them to the lessor or the supplier or dispose of them for the lessor's or the supplier's account with reimbursement in the manner provided in Section 2A–511; but
- (c) the lessee has no further obligations with regard to goods rightfully rejected.

(2) Action by the lessee pursuant to subsection (1) is not acceptance or conversion.

§ 2A–513. Cure by Lessor of Improper Tender or Delivery; Replacement.

(1) If any tender or delivery by the lessor or the supplier is rejected because nonconforming and the time for performance has not yet expired, the lessor or the supplier may seasonably notify the lessee of the lessor's or the supplier's intention to cure and may then make a conforming delivery within the time provided in the lease contract.

(2) If the lessee rejects a nonconforming tender that the lessor or the supplier had reasonable grounds to believe would be acceptable with or without money allowance, the lessor or the supplier may have a further reasonable time to substitute a conforming tender if he [or she] seasonably notifies the lessee.

§ 2A–514. Waiver of Lessee's Objections.

(1) In rejecting goods, a lessee's failure to state a particular defect that is ascertainable by reasonable inspection precludes the lessee from relying on the defect to justify rejection or to establish default:
>   (a) if, stated seasonably, the lessor or the supplier could have cured it (Section 2A–513); or
>   (b) between merchants if the lessor or the supplier after rejection has made a request in writing for a full and final written statement of all defects on which the lessee proposes to rely.

(2) A lessee's failure to reserve rights when paying rent or other consideration against documents precludes recovery of the payment for defects apparent on the face of the documents.

§ 2A–515. Acceptance of Goods.

(1) Acceptance of goods occurs after the lessee has had a reasonable opportunity to inspect the goods and
>   (a) the lessee signifies or acts with respect to the goods in a manner that signifies to the lessor or the supplier that the goods are conforming or that the lessee will take or retain them in spite of their nonconformity; or
>   (b) the lessee fails to make an effective rejection of the goods (Section 2A–509(2)).

(2) Acceptance of a part of any commercial unit is acceptance of that entire unit.

§ 2A–516. Effect of Acceptance of Goods; Notice of Default; Burden of Establishing Default After Acceptance; Notice of Claim or Litigation to Person Answerable Over.

(1) A lessee must pay rent for any goods accepted in accordance with the lease contract, with due allowance for goods rightfully rejected or not delivered.

(2) A lessee's acceptance of goods precludes rejection of the goods accepted. In the case of a finance lease, if made with knowledge of a nonconformity, acceptance cannot be revoked because of it. In any other case, if made with knowledge of a nonconformity, acceptance cannot be revoked because of it unless the acceptance was on the reasonable assumption that the nonconformity would be seasonably cured. Acceptance does not of itself

impair any other remedy provided by this Article or the lease agreement for nonconformity.

 (3) If a tender has been accepted:
  (a) within a reasonable time after the lessee discovers or should have discovered any default, the lessee shall notify the lessor and the supplier, or be barred from any remedy;
  (b) except in the case of a consumer lease, within a reasonable time after the lessee receives notice of litigation for infringement or the like (Section 2A–211) the lessee shall notify the lessor or be barred from any remedy over for liability established by the litigation; and
  (c) the burden is on the lessee to establish any default.

 (4) If a lessee is sued for breach of a warranty or other obligation for which a lessor or a supplier is answerable over:
  (a) The lessee may give the lessor or the supplier written notice of the litigation. If the notice states that the lessor or the supplier may come in and defend and that if the lessor or the supplier does not do so he [or she] will be bound in any action against him [or her] by the lessee by any determination of fact common to the two litigations, then unless the lessor or the supplier after seasonable receipt of the notice does come in and defend he [or she] is so bound.
  (b) The lessor or the supplier may demand in writing that the lessee turn over control of the litigation including settlement if the claim is one for infringement or the like (Section 2A–211) or else be barred from any remedy over. If the demand states that the lessor or the supplier agrees to bear all expense and to satisfy any adverse judgment, then unless the lessee after seasonable receipt of the demand does turn over control the lessee is so barred.

 (5) The provisions of subsections (3) and (4) apply to any obligation of a lessee to hold the lessor or the supplier harmless against infringement or the like (Section 2A–211).

§ 2A–517. Revocation of Acceptance of Goods.

 (1) A lessee may revoke acceptance of a lot or commercial unit whose nonconformity substantially impairs its value to the lessee if he [or she] has accepted it:
  (a) except in the case of a finance lease, on the reasonable assumption that its nonconformity would be cured and it has not been seasonably cured; or

(b) without discovery of the nonconformity if the lessee's acceptance was reasonably induced either by the lessor's assurances or, except in the case of a finance lease, by the difficulty of discovery before acceptance.

(2) Revocation of acceptance must occur within a reasonable time after the lessee discovers or should have discovered the ground for it and before any substantial change in condition of the goods which is not caused by the nonconformity. Revocation is not effective until the lessee notifies the lessor.

(3) A lessee who so revokes has the same rights and duties with regard to the goods involved as if the lessee had rejected them.

§ 2A–518. Cover; Substitute Goods.

(1) After default by a lessor under the lease contract (Section 2A–508(1)), the lessee may cover by making any purchase or lease of or contract to purchase or lease goods in substitution for those due from the lessor.

(2) Except as otherwise provided with respect to damages liquidated in the lease agreement (Section 2A–504) or determined by agreement of the parties (Section 1–102(3)), if a lessee's cover is by lease agreement substantially similar to the original lease agreement and the lease agreement is made in good faith and in a commercially reasonable manner, the lessee may recover from the lessor as damages (a) the present value, as of the date of default, of the difference between the total rent for the lease term of the new lease agreement and the total rent for the remaining lease term of the original lease agreement and (b) any incidental or consequential damages less expenses saved in consequence of the lessor's default.

(3) If a lessee's cover is by lease agreement that for any reason does not qualify for treatment under subsection (2), or is by purchase or otherwise, the lessee may recover from the lessor as if the lessee had elected not to cover and Section 2A–519 governs.

§ 2A–519. Lessee's Damages for Non-delivery, Repudiation, Default and Breach of Warranty in Regard to Accepted Goods.

(1) Except as otherwise provided with respect to damages liquidated in the lease agreement (Section 2A–504) or determined by agreement of the parties (Section 1–102(3)), if a lessee elects not to cover or a lessee electes to cover and the cover is by lease agreement that for any reason

does not qualify for treatment under Section 2A–518(2), or is by purchase or otherwise, the measure of damages for non-delivery or repudiation by the lessor or for rejection or revocation of acceptance by the lessee is the present value as of the date of the default of the difference between the then market rent and the original rent, computed for the remaining lease term of the original lease agreement together with incidental and consequential damages, less expenses saved in consequence of the lessor's default.

(2) Market rent is to be determined as of the place for tender or, in cases of rejection after arrival or revocation of acceptance, as of the place of arrival.

(3) If the lessee has accepted goods and given notification (Section 2A–516(3)), the measure of damages for non-conforming tender or delivery by a lessor is the loss resulting in the ordinary course of events from the lessor's default as determined in any manner that is reasonable together with incidental and consequential damages, less expenses saved in consequence of the lessor's default.

(4) The measure of damages for breach of warranty is the present value at the time and place of acceptance of the difference between the value of the use of the goods accepted and the value if they had been as warranted for the lease term, unless special circumstances show proximate damages of a different amount, together with incidental and consequential damages, less expenses saved in consequence of the lessor's default or breach of warranty.

§ 2A–520. Lessee's Incidental and Consequential Damages.

(1) Incidental damages resulting from a lessor's default include expenses reasonably incurred in inspection, receipt, transportation, and care and custody of goods rightfully rejected or goods the acceptance of which is justifiably revoked, any commercially reasonable charges, expenses or commissions in connection with effecting cover, and any other reasonable expense incident to the default.

(2) Consequential damages resulting from a lessor's default include:
- (a) any loss resulting from general or particular requirements and needs of which the lessor at the time of contracting had reason to know and which could not reasonably be prevented by cover or otherwise; and
- (b) injury to person or property proximately resulting from any breach of warranty.

§ 2A–521. Lessee's Right to Specific Performance or Replevin.

(1) Specific performance may be decreed if the goods are unique or in other proper circumstances.

(2) A decree for specific performance may include any terms and conditions as to payment of the rent, damages, or other relief that the court deems just.

(3) A lessee has a right of replevin, detinue, sequestration, claim and delivery, or the like for goods identified to the lease contract if after reasonable effort the lessee is unable to effect cover for those goods or the circumstances reasonably indicate that the effort will be unavailing.

§ 2A–522. Lessee's Right to Goods on Lessor's Insolvency.

(1) Subject to subsection (2) and even though the goods have not been shipped, a lessee who has paid a part or all of the rent and security for goods identified to a lease contract (Section 2A–217) on making and keeping good a tender of any unpaid portion of the rent and security due under the lease contract may recover the goods identified from the lessor if the lessor becomes insolvent within 10 days after receipt of the first installment of rent and security.

(2) A lessee acquires the right to recover goods identified to a lease contract only if they conform to the lease contract.

C. *DEFAULT BY LESSEE*

§ 2A–523. Lessor's Remedies.

(1) If a lessee wrongfully rejects or revokes acceptance of goods or fails to make a payment when due or repudiates with respect to a part or the whole, then, with respect to any goods involved, and with respect to all of the goods if under an installment lease contract the value of the whole lease contract is substantially impaired (Section 2A–510), the lessee is in default under the lease contract and the lessor may:

    (a) cancel the lease contract (Section 2A–505(1));
    (b) proceed respecting goods not identified to the lease contract (Section 2A–524);
    (c) withhold delivery of the goods and take possession of goods previously delivered (Section 2A–525);
    (d) stop delivery of the goods by any bailee (Section 2A–526);

(e) dispose of the goods and recover damages (Section 2A–527), or retain the goods and recover damages (Section 2A–528), or in a proper case recover rent (Section 2A–529).

(2) If a lessee is otherwise in default under a lease contract, the lessor may exercise the rights and remedies provided in the lease contract and this Article.

§ 2A–524. Lessor's Right to Identify Goods to Lease Contract.

(1) A lessor aggrieved under Section 2A–523(1) may:
   (a) identify to the lease contract conforming goods not already identified if at the time the lessor learned of the default they were in the lessor's or the supplier's possession or control; and
   (b) dispose of goods (Section 2A–527(1)) that demonstrably have been intended for the particular lease contract even though those goods are unfinished.

(2) If the goods are unfinished, in the exercise of reasonable commercial judgment for the purposes of avoiding loss and of effective realization, an aggrieved lessor or the supplier may either complete manufacture and wholly identify the goods to the lease contract or cease manufacture and lease, sell, or otherwise dispose of the goods for scrap or salvage value or proceed in any other reasonable manner.

§ 2A–525. Lessor's Right to Possession of Goods.

(1) If a lessor discovers the lessee to be insolvent, the lessor may refuse to deliver the goods.

(2) The lessor has on default by the lessee under the lease contract the right to take possession of the goods. If the lease contract so provides, the lessor may require the lessee to assemble the goods and make them available to the lessor at a place to be designated by the lessor which is reasonably convenient to both parties. Without removal, the lessor may render unusable any goods employed in trade or business, and may dispose of goods on the lessee's premises (Section 2A–527).

(3) The lessor may proceed under subsection (2) without judicial process if that can be done without breach of the peace or the lessor may proceed by action.

Article 2A—Leases

§ 2A–526. Lessor's Stoppage of Delivery in Transit or Otherwise.

(1) A lessor may stop delivery of goods in the possession of a carrier or other bailee if the lessor discovers the lessee to be insolvent and may stop delivery of carload, truckload, planeload, or larger shipments of express or freight if the lessee repudiates or fails to make a payment due before delivery, whether for rent, security or otherwise under the lease contract, or for any other reason the lessor has a right to withhold or take possession of the goods.

(2) In pursuing its remedies under subsection (1), the lessor may stop delivery until

    (a) receipt of the goods by the lessee;

    (b) acknowledgement to the lessee by any bailee of the goods, except a carrier, that the bailee holds the goods for the lessee; or

    (c) such an acknowledgment to the lessee by a carrier via reshipment or as warehouseman.

(3) (a) To stop delivery, a lessor shall so notify as to enable the bailee by reasonable diligence to prevent delivery of the goods.

    (b) After notification, the bailee shall hold and deliver the goods according to the directions of the lessor, but the lessor is liable to the bailee for any ensuing charges or damages.

    (c) A carrier who has issued a nonnegotiable bill of lading is not obliged to obey a notification to stop received from a person other than the consignor.

§ 2A–527. Lessor's Rights to Dispose of Goods.

(1) After a default by a lessee under the lease contract (Section 2A–523(1)) or after the lessor refuses to deliver or takes possession of goods (Section 2A–525 or 2A–526), the lessor may dispose of the goods concerned or the undelivered balance thereof by lease, sale or otherwise.

(2) Except as otherwise provided with respect to damages liquidated in the lease agreement (Section 2A–504) or determined by agreement of the parties (Section 1–102(3)), if the disposition is by lease agreement substantially similar to the original lease agreement and the lease agreement is made in good faith and in a commercially reasonable manner, the lessor may recover from the lessee as damages (a) accrued and unpaid rent as of

the date of default, (b) the present value as of the date of default of the difference between the total rent for the remaining lease term of the original lease agreement and the total rent for the lease term of the new lease agreement, and (c) any incidental damages allowed under Section 2A–530, less expenses saved in consequence of the lessee's default.

(3) If the lessor's disposition is by lease agreement that for any reason does not qualify for treatment under subsection (2), or is by sale or otherwise, the lessor may recover from the lessee as if the lessor had elected not to dispose of the goods and Section 2A–528 governs.

(4) A subsequent buyer or lessee who buys or leases from the lessor in good faith for value as a result of a dispositon under this section takes the goods free of the original lease contract and any rights of the original lessee even though the lessor fails to comply with one or more of the requirements of this Article.

(5) The lessor is not accountable to the lessee for any profit made on any disposition. A lessee who has rightfully rejected or justifiably revoked acceptance shall account to the lessor for any excess over the amount of the lessee's security interest (Section 2A–508(5)).

§ 2A–528. Lessor's Damages for Non-acceptance or Repudiation.

(1) Except as otherwise provided with respect to damages liquidated in the lease agreement (Section 2A–504) or determined by agreement of the parties (Section 1–102(3)), if a lessor elects to retain the goods or a lessor elects to dispose of the goods and disposition is by lease agreement that for any reason does not qualify for treatment under Section 2A–527(2), or is by sale or otherwise, the lessor may recover from the lessee as damages for non-acceptance or repudiation by the lessee (a) accrued and unpaid rent as of the date of default, (b) the present value as of the date of default of the difference between the total rent for the remaining lease term of the original lease agreement and the market rent at the time and place for tender computed for the same lease term, and (c) any incidental damages allowed under Section 2A–530, less expenses saved in consequence of the lessee's default.

(2) If the measure of damages provided in subsection (1) is inadequate to put a lessor in as good a position as performance would have, the measure of damages is the profit, including reasonable overhead, the lessor would have made from full performance by the lessee, together with any incidental damages allowed under Section 2A–530, due allowance for costs reasonably incurred and due credit for payments or proceeds of disposition.

§ 2A–529. Lessor's Action for the Rent.

(1) After default by the lessee under the lease contract (Section 2A–523(1)), if the lessor complies with subsection (2), the lessor may recover from the lessee as damages:

    (a) for goods accepted by the lessee and for conforming goods lost or damaged within a commercially reasonable time after risk of loss passes to the lessee (Section 2A–219), (i) accrued and unpaid rent as of the date of default, (ii) the present value as of the date of default of the rent for the remaining lease term of the lease agreement, and (iii) any incidental damages allowed under Section 2A–530, less expenses saved in consequence of the lessee's default; and

    (b) for goods identified to the lease contract if the lessor is unable after reasonable effort to dispose of them at a reasonable price or the circumstances reasonably indicate that effort will be unavailing, (i) accrued and unpaid rent as of the date of default, (ii) the present value as of the date of default of the rent for the remaining lease term of the lease agreement, and (iii) any incidental damages allowed under Section 2A–530, less expenses saved in consequence of the lessee's default.

(2) Except as provided in subsection (3), the lessor shall hold for the lessee for the remaining lease term of the lease agreement any goods that have been identified to the lease contract and are in the lessor's control.

(3) The lessor may dispose of the goods at any time before collection of the judgment for damages obtained pursuant to subsection (1). If the disposition is before the end of the remaining lease term of the lease agreement, the lessor's recovery against the lessee for damages will be governed by Section 2A–527 or Section 2A–528.

(4) Payment of the judgment for damages obtained pursuant to subsection (1) entitles the lessee to use and possession of the goods not then disposed of for the remaining lease term of the lease agreement.

(5) After a lessee has wrongfully rejected or revoked acceptance of goods, has failed to pay rent then due, or has repudiated (Section 2A–402), a lessor who is held not entitled to rent under this section must nevertheless be awarded damages for non-acceptance under Sections 2A–527 and 2A–528.

§ 2A–530. Lessor's Incidental Damages.

Incidental damages to an aggrieved lessor include any commercially reasonable charges, expenses, or commissions incurred in stopping delivery, in the transportation, care and custody of goods after the lessee's default, in connection with return or disposition of the goods, or otherwise resulting from the default.

§ 2A–531. Standing to Sue Third Parties for Injury to Goods.

(1) If a third party so deals with goods that have been identified to a lease contract as to cause actionable injury to a party to the lease contract (a) the lessor has a right of action against the third party, and (b) the lessee also has a right of action against the third party if the lessee:
    (i) has a security interest in the goods;
    (ii) has an insurable interest in the goods; or
    (iii) bears the risk of loss under the lease contract or has since the injury assumed that risk as against the lessor and the goods have been converted or destroyed.

(2) If at the time of the injury the party plaintiff did not bear the risk of loss as against the other party to the lease contract and there is no arrangement between them for disposition of the recovery, his [or her] suit or settlement, subject to his [or her] own interest, is as a fiduciary for the other party to the lease contract.

(3) Either party with the consent of the other may sue for the benefit of whom it may concern.

Supplement to Chapter XVI, page 277
ELECTRONIC DATA INTERCHANGE

The electronic transmission and receipt of essential purchasing data is beginning to replace the long-standing practice of using paper-based documents to accomplish the same communication between purchaser and supplier. The use of computers by both buyer and seller to communicate with each other is leading the parade to establish a "paperless purchasing" operation and a sales office bereft of paper too.

The process of talking to each other with a computer is known as electronic data interchange (EDI). It is remarkably successful in accelerating the speed by which a purchase may be accomplished. The rapidity of communication makes the procurement process more efficient and enables it to meet the needs of the organization promptly. Because of the speed of the procurement process under EDI companies do not require inventories as large as previously. The process also eliminates much paper preparation and handling which enables the purchasing organization to take on an added volume of work or to handle the same volume with less personnel. It is a modern age answer to the search for efficiency and economy in today's business world.

There are some legal considerations that must be reckoned with before all of these accolades can be comfortably laid on the EDI process. Since almost all purchasing officers live in a paper-oriented society and under a body of business laws that place heavy emphasis on a "paper trail," it should come as no surprise that there are legal problems that are occasioned by our quest for the "paperless" purchasing operation. However, it is believed that most of the legal concerns can be satisfactorily dealt with under the existing bodies of contract and sales law that are now with us. It must be admitted that amending the Uniform Commercial Code would be a more feasible manner to achieve complete legal compliance for EDI processes.

That will probably come in time but our need is now and we must use the law we have available on the subject.

The Electronic Messaging Services Task Force.

The Electronic Messaging Task Force of the American Bar Association's Business Law Section has prepared and published a careful and extensive analysis of the legal considerations involved in the use of electronic data interchange for procurement and other related business activities. Their report is printed in *The Business Lawyer*, June 1990 edition, Volume 45 No. S, pages 1645 to 1749. In these pages the Committee gives us a careful analysis of the potential legal involvement arising from the use of EDI in purchasing, and their opinion of how these problems can be overcome. At the conclusion of this article, the Committee presents a Model Agreement that is suggested as a pattern for trading partners (buyer and supplier) to execute. This agreement is suggested by the Committee as a model for attorneys to follow when writing a contract for their clients who are engaging in EDI procurement and sales. The purpose is to give their clients the fullest opportunity to have their transactions hold to the fullest legal effect possible. This Model Agreement, together with the Comments of the Committee and their suggestions of how the agreement should be used as a draft model, is reproduced in full in this supplement with the permission of the Business Law Section of the American Bar Association.[1]

The Major Legal Hurdle.

When one contemplates what legal problems could arise if a purchasing officer allows a computer to do the talking, the most obvious question would be whether the transaction would be enforceable in a court of law. That question arises because Section 2–201(1) of the Uniform Commercial Code requires that every contract for the sale of goods amounting to $500 or more be evidenced by a signed writing if the contract is to be enforceable in litigation. Both a "writing" and a "signature" are required by this Code Section. This leads us to the question of whether a computer printout of a purchase order or a supplier's computer acceptance of an offer to buy meets the needs of Section 2–201(1).

Applicable Provisions of the Uniform Commercial Code.

Nowhere can there be found any reported law cases that answer the question of the need of a signed writing when a computer printout is used. There

---

[1] 45 *Business Lawyer*, June 1990. No. S. Page 1690

are some indications that this computer set-up is "almost the same" or "seems similar" to other situations, but no precise answer can be found in litigated cases. When we turn to the Uniform Commercial Code itself we can again find many sections that indicate transactions accomplished by EDI should be legally proper and legally sound, but the exact words are not there to give such transactions proper credence. As a result of this absence of specificity the Electronic Messaging Services Task Force of the American Bar Association recommends that trading partners—buyers and suppliers—enter into an agreement similar to the one they have proposed and which is included at the end of this chapter. Their proposed Model Agreement takes advantage of all of the positive expressions of "probable" legality contained in various Code sections as well as providing for waivers to prevent either party from taking advantage of possible lapses of "all out" Code approval of EDI transactions. You will have a better understanding of these comments if you read some of the relevant sections of the Code that we quote here, with the thought in your mind that the Commissioners who wrote the Code were making room in the law to accommodate electronic data interchange. Your author believes such thoughts were there!

We can begin at the beginning of the Code to get the Commissioners' first instructions that are in the direction of our inquiry. Section 1–102(1) tells us "this Act shall be liberally construed and applied to promote its underlying purposes and policies." With these words the Commissioners tell us not to interpret the Code with the idea that EDI does not fall within it. Rather, we should think positively and find how to bring it within its folds. The next subsection, 1–102(2), when it states "the underlying purposes and policies of this Act are "(b) to permit the continued expansion of commercial practices through custom, usage and agreement of the parties," plays right into our hands. EDI is an expansion of commercial practices of vast importance to modern business methods. It will become more and more widely used and we should make every effort to make this expansion possible under the protective fields of the Uniform Commercial Code.

You will also note that 1–102(2)(b) suggests "agreement of the parties" is one suggested avenue of expanding the role of the Uniform Commercial Code in commercial practices. The next subsection (3) invites us to vary the effect of provisions of the Uniform Commercial Code by agreement. Subsection (3) reads as follows:

> (3) The effect of provisions of this Act may be varied by agreement, except as otherwise provided in this Act and except that the obligations of good faith, diligence, reasonableness and care prescribed by this Act may not be disclaimed by agreement but the parties may by agreement

determine the standards by which the performance of such obligations is to be measured if such standards are not manifestly unreasonable.

This subsection invites the buyer and the supplier to enter into a type of agreement such as the trading partner agreement we are showing at the end of this chapter. If that agreement perchance affects some of the provisions of the Code, subsection (3) says "so be it." As long as the fundamentals of good faith, diligence, reasonableness and care are not disturbed, subsection (3) gives us carte blanche to change any other non-restricted provisions. (A restricted provision that is not changeable by agreement of the parties is one such as is in Section 2-725 the Statute of Limitations provision, which establishes a four year period to bring actions for breach. That section concludes with this ". . . the parties may reduce the period of limitation to not less than one year but may not extend it." The four year period cannot be extended by agreement of the parties, no matter how desirable such a change might be to the both of them.) The Official Comment to Section 1-102 begins with this statement:[1]

> This Act is drawn to provide flexibility so that, since it is intended to be a semi-permanent piece of legislation, it will provide its own machinery for expansion of commercial practices. It is intended to make it possible for the law embodied in this Act to be developed by the courts in the light of unforeseen and new circumstances and practices.

This Comment seems to suggest the writers of the Code had the uncanny feeling and belief that something akin to EDI was on the horizon. So much so that they made provision for it at the time the Code was being written in the 1950s.

The Electronic Messaging Task Force of the American Bar Association received encouragement for many of the provisions in their Model Agreement for Trading Partners from Subsection (3) of Section 1-102 (repeated above) and from Official Comment 2 which refers to that subsection.[1] The Comment states in part:

> (2) Subsection 3 states affirmatively at the outset that freedom of contract is a principle of the Code: "the effect" of its provisions may be varied by "agreement" . . .
>
> This principle of freedom of contract is subject to specific exceptions

---

[1] Copyright 1989 by The American Law Institute and the National Conference of Commissioners on Uniform State Laws. Reprinted with the permission of the Permanent Editorial Board for the Uniform Commercial Code.

found elsewhere in the Act and to the general exception stated here. The specific exceptions vary in explicitness: the statute of frauds found in Section 2–201, for example, does not explicitly preclude oral waiver of the requirement of a writing, but a fair reading denies enforcement to such a waiver as part of the "contract" made unenforceable, . . .

The above quote could be interpreted to mean that a written agreement to waive the Statute of Frauds probably would be enforceable. You will note later that this approach is made part of the Model Agreement.

The Official Comment continues by calling attention to Section 1–205 which defines a "course of dealing" between parties. Section 1–205(1) reads:

(1) A course of dealing is a sequence of previous conduct between the parties to a particular transaction which is fairly to be regarded as establishing a common basis of understanding for interpreting their expressions and other conduct.

You will note Section 3.3.3 of the Model Agreement takes advantage of this suggestion contained in the Code.

Another section of the Code—2–208(1)—is also taken advantage of in the Model Agreement in the same Section 3.3.3. This Code section reads:

(1) Where the contract for sale involves repeated occasions for performance by either party with knowledge of the nature of the performance and opportunity for objection to it by the other, any course of performance accepted or acquiesced in without objection shall be relevant to determine the meaning of the agreement.

Since EDI transactions normally occur between the same parties with some degree of regularity, the buyer and the supplier can readily establish a course of performance for doing business. When this course of performance is established there should be no concern about the validity and enforceability of each purchase and sale. You will see shortly how the Model Agreement takes advantage of these provisions.

We should also take note of the definitions of the two troublesome words—"signed" and "writing"—that appear in the Code. Section 1–201(46) defines a writing in this manner:

(46) "Written" or "writing" includes printing, typewriting or any other intentional reduction to tangible form.

One must ask if this definition is broad enough to include a computer print-out of a purchase order sent via the buyer's computer and received by either the "mailbox" or the seller's computer. We believe it is. Furthermore could the same print-out be signed according to the Uniform Commercial Code's definition of the word "signed"? Here is 1–201(39) which defines the word:

> (39) "Signed" includes any symbol executed or adopted by a party with present intention to authenticate a writing.

You will note Section 1.5 of the Model Agreement which is captioned "Signatures," requires each party to adopt an electronic identification as its official signature. Such official signature is to be affixed to any document that is transmitted by either party so that the other party will know that it is an authorized transmittal. This requirement conforms to the requirement of Section 1–201(39) that any official symbol be "adopted" by the party using it. When it is adopted by that party, it expresses the intention of that party that it be his or her official signature.

Federal Rules of Evidence.

Further evidence that the law is ready to receive advanced methods of modern communication such as EDI can be found in the Federal Rules of Evidence (FRE). FRE 1002 specifies that the original of a record of a transaction be used as evidence in a federal trial. In defining an original, Section 1001(1) of the FRE includes this among other sources:

> . . . letters, words, or numbers or their equivalents set down by . . . magnetic impulse, mechanical or electronic recording or other forms of data compilation.

Computer storage of data seems to satisfy this definition of an original. Section 1001(3) confirms this by including ". . . any print out or other output readable by sight . . ."[2]

There is an additional suggestion in the Federal Rules of Evidence that computer data is acceptable for establishing document authenticity. In what is known as the "Business Records Exception" to the hearsay rule, certain types of business records qualify as acceptable evidence. FRE 803(6) states, *inter alia*, "A data compilation . . . made . . . from information transmitted by a person with knowledge, if kept in the course of regularly

---

[2] Federal Rules of Evidence 1001(3).

conducted buisness activity . . . is regular." Thus it would seem the person who programs the computer would be the reliable witness to testify to the validity of business records transmitted and maintained in a computer. There is much more involved in this legal documentation which your author is certain should be left to the legal counsel representing the purchasing officer's organization.

In summation the purchasing officer should recognize that although the computer and its output is probably within the folds of present legal boundaries, there always will remain some lingering doubts as to its full enforceability until there are some amendments made to existing laws. Therefore, the Model Agreement prepared by the American Bar Association's Task Force Committee appears to be just what we need to make certain our transaction accomplished by EDI complies with the existing law and will be enforceable in a court of law, if need be. It is suggested that you consult with your legal counsel with the Model Agreement in hand to plan what your operations will require to enable you to conduct your business transactions when feasible, via EDI and continue to remain legally proper. Remember that EDI is not for all seasons! Only certain repetitive transactions can be handled in this manner.

The Strategy Employed by the Task Force Committee.

When you consult with your legal counsel, he or she will readily recognize that the Task Force Committee of the American Bar Association employed manifold legal strategies in making its Model Agreement responsive to the legal involvements of EDI transactions. This is particularly true where it concerns meeting the needs of the Statute of Frauds Section 2–201.[3] The first strategy employed is what the Task Force refers to as the "definition strategy."[4] You will note that Section 3.3.2. of the Model Agreement specifies that any document properly transmitted shall be considered to be a "writing" and if there is a signature attached, it shall be considered a "signed writing." Thus, if both parties agree via the Model Agreement that such documents are "signed writings," the Uniform Commercial Code will probably say "So be it!" Further, Section 3.3.2. of the Model Agreement also states the agreement of the parties is that such signed documents will constitute an "original" when printed from computer files.

The second strategy employed by the Task Force has the Model Agreement providing that the conduct of the parties shall evidence a course of

---

[3] 45 *Business Lawyer*, June 1990 No. S. Section of Business Law, American Bar Association. Page 1690.

[4] Ibid. Page 1690.

dealing and a course of performance as provided in Section 3.3.3.[5] In this manner there will be a prior history of contract performance that can be referred to if some problem arises in a current transaction.

The third strategy adopted by the Task Force is found in Section 3.3.4.[6] In this section the parties agree not to contest the enforceability of the signed documents used by the other party under provisions of Section 2–201 of the Uniform Commercial Code. By agreeing to this provision the Model Agreement, a party is estopped (see pages 208–10 in the original text for an understanding of the doctrine of estoppel) or prevented from bringing up the question of the adequacy of the print-out as a signed writing. Each party has made this promise to the other party and the other party has acted in reliance of that promise. You will also note that the same section in the Model Agreement goes on to have each party not contest the admissibility of the signed documents under either the business records exception to the hearsay rule or to the best evidence rule. You can see from this strategy that the Task Force is implying that if strategies #1 or #2 do not work, there is always number 3 to fall back on. This model agreement is carefully drawn! But hold on! The Task Force has one more ace in the hole. They have provided for one last "fall back" provision. It is Section 4.2 of the Model Agreement.[7] That section is captioned "Severability" and provides that if any section of the entire agreement is found to be invalid or unenforceable, all of the remaining sections are to continue in full force and effect. Thus, the odds are all in favor of the agreement holding the parties to its terms. There remains little doubt after the parties sign the agreement and begin to perform under it, it should hold firm for a good period of time. It should cover all transactions between the parties.

Nota Bene to the Purchasing Officer.

There are some provisions of the Model Agreement your author wishes to emphasize. First on this list, is Section 3 captioned "Transaction Terms." The Task Force has given three options to handle the difficult topic of terms and conditions of a contract for the purchase and sale of goods. Your author encourages each purchasing officer entering into a trading partner agreement to opt for "Option A." When a purchasing officer and a supplier sit down together to work out their Trading Partner Agreement, they should "go all the way" in reaching agreement. Any differences between their respec-

---

[5] 45 *Business Lawyer*, op. cit. Page 1693.
[6] Ibid. Page 1194.
[7] The *Business Lawyer*, op. cit. Page 1194.

Supplement to Chap. 16 / Electronic Data Interchange

tive terms and conditions should be resolved and agreed to as is every other provision of the agreement. They should reach agreement on all of the terms and conditions as they will apply to each and every transaction between them. This is an ideal opportunity to avoid the ugly consequences of Section 2–207! The parties are encouraged to take advantage of this feature.

Rule of "Acceptance" under the Model Agreement.

You will note that Sections 2.2 and 2.3 deal with "verification and acceptance." It should be pointed out that the Model Agreement is written to have two messages go from the supplier-receiver to the purchasing officer. First the original purchase (offer to buy) should be verified by the supplier-receiver. Then a second message need be sent accepting that offer to buy. You will note that the Task Force's comment for this section suggests the supplier may either send an acceptance of the purchase order or a shipping notice. Either form of acceptance is permitted under the Code and the Task Force makes the suggestion the trading partners agree on the use of one or the other.

You will also note that the acceptance rules under the agreement dictates that an acceptance is not effective until received by the offeror. This is the same rule that is followed under the Convention for the International Sale of Goods. Under the common law rule, which is followed in the United States, acceptance is effective when the acceptance document is "dispatched" from the offeree. (See pages 232 and 233 of the original text for an explanation of the "Dispatch" rule of acceptance of an offer.)

Applicability of the Model Agreement.

The reader should note that the Model Agreement is prepared to make EDI transactions conform to the Uniform Commercial Code. You will recall in the original text on page 151 we remind you that the Uniform Commercial Code deals only with transactions in goods. Therefore you must realize that the Model Agreement is to be used only for transactions in goods with your supplier. You will also note the Task Force suggests the agreement not be used for sourcing with foreign suppliers.

Service Contracts.

It is certain that the question "How about service contracts?" will arise. You are reminded that service contracts that are to be performed within one year from the date of the agreement do not have to be in writing to be enforceable in a court of law. (See page 266 of the original text.) Therefore all of the first part of Sections 3.3.2. and 3.3.4. of the Model Agreement would be unnecessary in a contract for services that may be performed within one year. The balance of the proposed agreement should be acceptable but your author counsels you to check this suggestion with your own legal counsel.

Foreign Sourcing.

The Convention for the International Sale of Goods does not require contracts for the sale of goods to be in writing. (See Article 11.) Therefore, if you are trading with a supplier and using the C.I.S.G., the same exceptions to the Model Agreement as spelled out above will apply. However the purchasing officer is advised to read the last page of this supplement that applies to the C.I.S.G. and note that there it is suggested the purchasing officer attempt to have the foreign supplier do business under the Uniform Commercial Code of your own state. Then the Model Agreement, as presented in Appendix B, would be applicable but your legal counsel should review the Agreement for other necessary alterations made essential by dealing with a foreign supplier.

Utilization of the Trading Agreement.

The Task Force, in their report, suggested the Model Trading Agreement could be used either for withdrawals under a requirements contract previously negotiated or as a repetitive transaction type of purchase and sale.[8] It is written carefully enough to "cover" both types of transactions. In either instance, the trading partners can be assured they are operating under a legal arrangement that should prove to be enforceable in a court of law, if it proves essential.

Note: Your author is deeply indebted to the Section of Business Law of the American Bar Association for its permission to reproduce the following Model Trading Partner Agreement and the applicable commentary thereto. The agreement and the commentary were prepared by the Subcommittee on Electronic Commercial Practices of the Uniform Commercial Code Committee.

The model agreement appeared in the June 1990 *Business Lawyer*. It was prefaced by a detailed analysis of the present law applicable to electronic data interchange. This report is recommended reading for anyone interested in the present state of the law pertaining to EDI as well as for anyone

---

[8] *Business Lawyer*, op. cit. Page 1657.

wishing to use the Trading Partner Agreement. To order *The Commercial Use of Electronic Data Interchange—A Report,* send your letterhead with check/money order payable to The American Bar Association or include credit card information·(MasterCard or Visa) for $40 plus $2.95 for handling/shipping. Product Code #507-0233-B9; ABA Order Fulfillment, 750 North Lake Shore Dr., Chicago, IL 60611 (312/988-5555).

CREDIT AND COPYRIGHT NOTICE

This Model Agreement and Commentary was prepared by the Electronic Messaging Services Task Force under the auspices of the Subcommittee on Electronic Commercial Practices of the Uniform Commercial Code Committee, Section of Business Law, American Bar Association. The Agreement and Commentary is the subject of an extensive Report that is available from the ABA Section of Business Law. Before using the Model Agreement, the Report should be consulted. © 1990 American Bar Association. All rights reserved.

Appendix B
ELECTRONIC DATA INTERCHANGE TRADING PARTNER AGREEMENT

USE OF THE MODEL AGREEMENT AND COMMENTARY

The following should be considered by counsel in reviewing and implementing the Model Agreement and Commentary:

1. Provisions of the Model Agreement contained in brackets ([ ]) identify options for counsel to consider; in several cases, the bracketed language represents alternatives presented within the Model Agreement, while in other instances the provisions are themselves presented as optional.
2. The Commentary has the following purposes:

   To explain how the Model Agreement works, the purposes of each section and the intended effect of certain provisions in the context of existing commercial law.

   To provide background technical information relating to certain aspects of EDI and prevailing general industry practices.

   To provide specific drafting considerations on the manner in which provisions of the Model Agreement may be utilized or modified in preparing a definitive agreement.
3. The Appendix is an essential component of the Model Agreement. The parties should use the Appendix to set forth information essential to the proposed trading relationship as well as additional terms and conditions. Counsel should not consider the Appendix merely a "technical" item; rather, it is the field upon which mutual business decisions which affect the substance of the relationship of the parties, as well as the validity and enforceability of the underlying transactions, are to be specified. For that reason, the format of the Appendix is a suggested format, but does not represent a

required structure. Counsel is encouraged to adapt the form and content of the Appendix to meet the requirements of any particular business relationship.

MODEL
ELECTRONIC DATA INTERCHANGE
TRADING PARTNER AGREEMENT

THIS ELECTRONIC DATA INTERCHANGE TRADING PARTNER AGREEMENT (the "Agreement") is made as of _____, 19__, by and between _____ ("ABC"), a _____ corporation, with offices at _____ and _____ ("XYZ"), a _____ corporation, with offices at _____.

RECITALS

ABC and XYZ desire to facilitate purchase and sale transactions ("Transactions") by electronically transmitting and receiving data in agreed formats in substitution for conventional paper-based documents and to assure that such Transactions are not legally invalid or unenforceable as a result of the use of available electronic technologies for the mutual benefit of the parties.

NOW THEREFORE, the parties, intending to be legally bound, agree as follows:

Comment

1. The scope and purposes of the Agreement are as follows:

   The Agreement is to be used between commercial trading partners; the Agreement is not intended for use in consumer transactions.

   The Agreement is to be used only in connection with domestic purchase and sale transactions involving goods, as contemplated by Article 2 of the Uniform Commercial Code (the "Code"). Counsel may wish to consider the Agreement in developing suitable provisions for use in other types of EDI relationships, such as those which are international in scope, or which involve the performance of services (including transportation and shipping activities).

   The Agreement is intended to facilitate the commercial relationship of the trading parties. The Agreement does not generally advocate particular solutions to what are essentially business issues; freedom of contract is encouraged.

   The Agreement does not attempt to resolve all aspects of commercial trading relationships which are within the scope of Article 2 of the Code.

Counsel is cautioned to consider the additional issues which arise from the underlying Transactions (issues which are not unique to the use of EDI) and to develop appropriate responses.

2. Certain provisions of the Agreement have the effect of varying the application of provisions of Article 2. In this respect, the Agreement implements two of the fundamental purposes of the Code, namely (a) to simplify, clarify and modernize the law governing commercial transactions, and (b) to permit the continued expansion of commercial practices through custom, usage and agreement of the parties. *See* UCC § 1–102(2). In order to accomplish these purposes, the Code is to be liberally construed and applied. *See* UCC § 1–102(1). This flexibility is intended to allow the underlying principles to be developed in light of unforeseen and new circumstances and practices. *See* UCC § 1–102, comment 1. Freedom of contract is also an important principle of the Code. *See* UCC § 1–102(3) and § 1–102, comment 2. Thus, parties are free to vary by agreement the effect of all provisions of the Code, except to the extent the general obligations of good faith, diligence, reasonableness and care may not be displaced. *See* UCC § 1–102(3) and § 1–102, comment 3.

3. The Recitals set forth the mutual intention of the parties for valid and enforceable obligations to result from the electronic communication of data in substitution for conventional paper-based documents. *See also* Sections 1.1, 2.1 and 3.3, and the Comments thereto. The execution and delivery of the Agreement and the performance of Transactions, together with the conduct of the parties in accordance with its terms, should be considered sufficient to show the existence of contracts for the sale of goods. *See* UCC § 2–204.

Drafting Considerations

1. The Agreement does not designate either party as buyer or seller. Either party may, therefore, purchase or sell goods in accordance with its provisions, unless appropriate modifications are made. For example, counsel may wish to add to the Appendix, as to each Document (as defined in Section 1.1), which party may be the "Sender" of that Document. *See* Sections 1.1 and 3.1, and the Comments and Drafting Considerations thereto.

2. Consider whether either or both of the parties are merchants, and the implications under the Code of that classification on the underlying commercial relationship and the rules of conduct which are defined by the Agreement. *See* UCC §§ 2–104(1) and 2–104(3). Note that if the parties are not corporations, appropriate changes should be made.

Model EDI Trading Partner Agreement

§ 1. PREREQUISITES

1.1 Documents: Standards.

Each party may electronically transmit to or receive from the other party any of the transaction sets listed in the Appendix, [transaction sets which the parties regularly transmit] and transaction sets which the parties by written agreement add to the Appendix (collectively "Documents"). Any transmission of data which is not a Document shall have no force or effect between the parties unless justifiably relied upon by the receiving party. All Documents shall be transmitted in accordance with the standards [and the published industry guidelines] set forth in the Appendix.

Comment

General:

1. Establishing an EDI trading relationship, by necessity, involves a series of decisions, primarily technical in nature, by both parties regarding: (a) the formats in which the data will be transmitted, and the standards and possible implementation guidelines to be adopted in connection with such formats; (b) the possible selection of third-party service providers (as well as the various business decisions required in connection with establishing such relationship); and (c) the development and maintenance of appropriate computer and communication systems and security procedures. Section 1 and the Appendix provide a framework for the parties to mutually structure these decisions. Compliance with the provisions of Section 1 will confirm their intent to give legal significance to the transmissions. *See* Sections 2.1, 2.3 and 3.3.3, and the Comments thereto.
2. Implementing EDI should also involve careful evaluation of existing internal business procedures and controls of the parties relating to paper-based commercial practices, and consideration of the extent to which such procedures and controls should be strengthened and/or modified in connection with the establishment of an electronic communication and trading environment. For example, authorizations to release purchase orders or approve payments, as well as rules regarding security and confidentiality, should be reviewed. *See also* Sections 2.1 and 3, and the Comments thereto.
3. This Section contains the first use of "by written agreement" or "in writing" in the Agreement. The Agreement provides the flexibility to allow notices, modifications, amendments or other communications required or permitted by the Agreement to be "in writing" to consist of electronic transmissions,

but only if the transmissions satisfy the criteria of the Agreement for "Signed Documents" (as defined in Section 3.3.2). Alternatively, the Agreement could specify paper-based writings are required, if the parties consider it appropriate.

Documents:

4. "Transaction sets" define the types of data which the specified transmission must contain and the format in which the data must appear. Transaction sets function like conventional paper document forms, and include purchase orders, requests for quotation, purchase order acknowledgements, invoices, remittance advices and purchase order change requests. In addition, transaction sets exist in which "free text" may be communicated as a segment; this type of transaction set would be appropriate for notices, modifications or amendments (such as those described in Comment 3 above).

5. The Agreement generally applies only to those transmissions of data classified as "Documents" under Section 1.1. At a minimum, transaction sets listed in the Appendix (including subsequent additions) are Documents.

6. The Agreement provides, as an option, for transaction sets which are not listed in the Appendix but which are regularly transmitted to be considered as Documents. No attempt to define "regularly transmit" has been made. However, *see* Section 3.3.3 (and UCC § 2–208).

7. The "regularly transmit" option should be considered when both parties wish to give effect to new transaction sets without express prior agreement. Parties who wish to retain tight control over which transmissions qualify as documents under Section 1.1 will eliminate the "regularly transmit" option from the Agreement. Note that, if the "regularly transmit" option is not included, regularly transmitted transaction sets may still be given effect, though inconsistent with the terms of this Agreement. *See* UCC §§ 1–103, 2–208 and 2–209. In addition, such parties may wish to eliminate from the second sentence of Section 1.1 the phrase ". . . unless justifiably relied upon by the receiving party" or make other modifications to, or entirely delete, that sentence. Note, however, that such changes may not effectively prevent a transmission which is not a Document from having legal effect, where the receiving party has under the circumstances, including the language in the Agreement, justifiably relied on that transmission. *See* Comment 6 above and Comment 8 below.

8. The second sentence of Section 1.1 is not intended to alter the law of reliance; the provision simply prevents a party which has transmitted data from avoiding the legal effect of the receiving party's justifiable reliance merely because the format had not been previously classified as a Document. However, note that the remaining provisions of the Agreement

relating to Documents are not applicable in those circumstances. *See,* for example, Sections 1.2.3, 2.1, 3.3, and 4.6.

Standards:

9. "Standards" are the uniform specifications for the electronic interchange of business data and include provisions of the structure and format of data as well as the transmission of the formatted data. There are also standards, among other things, for certain security and communication procedures.

10. The selection of applicable standards is a matter of some flexibility. The parties may mutually select and utilize one or more sets of recognized standards, or, within certain technical limits, customize those standards to their mutual benefit. Existing technology also permits each party to adopt a different standard for transmission of a Document, with Providers (as defined in Section 1.2.1) subsequently conforming the different formats to each party's adopted standard.

11. Virtually all standards for EDI include detailed technical requirements to facilitate EDI, including transaction sets, data dictionaries, segment dictionaries and other uniform controls. Pursuant to the provisions of the Appendix, the selection by the parties of applicable standards acts to incorporate by reference these additional requirements. Should the parties desire to exclude or modify any of such requirements, such changes may be made in the Appendix.

Guidelines:

12. "Published industry guidelines" contain recommended procedures and implementation guidelines for the use of EDI within particular industry groups (recent examples include guidelines of the automotive, chemical and pharmaceutical industries). In contrast to standards, which require compliance for the effective interchange of data, guidelines generally are intended to aid implementation among trading partners. The Agreement, as an option, provides the parties the ability to require compliance with any guidelines which they mutually adopt and specify.

13. Counsel should carefully evaluate any available guidelines to assure that any conflicts between the guidelines and the standards, or between different guidelines, are understood and resolved. The adoption of certain guidelines, for example, may affect the process of contract formation in an unintended manner, since several current guidelines suggest certain procedures (e.g., which Documents are acceptable responses to other specified Documents) which may be in conflict with what the parties mutually negotiate and specify in the Appendix. Language in the Appendix has been included to avoid this result by subordinating the content of any selected guidelines to the provisions of the Agreement.

14. Counsel should evaluate whether any existing guidelines, whether or not

adopted, may be considered, in any interpretation of the Agreement, as a usage of trade to be considered with respect to any Transaction. *See* UCC § 1–205(2).

Drafting Considerations

1. The parties should identify and list the transaction sets which may be transmitted between them as Documents. The Appendix is structured in accordance with most common methods of identifying Documents. However, proprietary Documents, not based upon any particular standard, may also be utilized and listed.

2. In specifying Documents in the Appendix, it is recommended that the parties agree that any selected Document be communicated only in the then current release version or the release version immediately preceding the then current release version. Consistent with the provisions of Section 1.3, this will require the parties to periodically install new release versions of software corresponding to new revisions of the applicable standards. *See* Section 1.3, and the Comments thereto. Counsel may wish to consider establishing a time frame in which any such releases must be installed.

3. In completing the Appendix, any transaction set listed as an Acceptance Document (pursuant to Section 2.3) should also be listed as a Document. *See* Section 2.3, and the Comments thereto.

4. The Agreement permits any Document specified in the Appendix to be transmitted by either party. If this result is not desired, appropriate restrictions should be specified in the Appendix. *See* Recitals, Drafting Consideration 1.

5. If the parties do not wish transmissions which are not Documents to be given any force or effect, appropriate changes may be made. *See* Comments 7 and 8 above.

1.2. Third Party Service Providers.

1.2.1. Documents will be transmitted electronically to each party either, as specified in the Appendix, directly or through any third party service provider ("Provider") with which either party may contract. Either party may modify its election to use, not use or change a Provider upon 30 days prior written notice.

Comment

1. Section 1.2 provides the structure to specify the channel(s) of communication to be used in transmitting Documents between the parties. Transmissions may be made directly between the parties or through Providers. To the extent Providers are selected, Section 1.2 provides a framework for consid-

ering those aspects of the trading partners' relationship under the Agreement which are related to the use of Providers.

2. Among other things, Providers function as electronic mail processing systems and may (a) maintain electronic "mailboxes" into which communications can be placed for trading partners and (b) interconnect with other Providers to permit communication between their respective customers. Providers have become an important aspect of general industry practice relating to EDI.

3. Section 1.2.1 provides maximum flexibility for each party to choose and maintain the desired channel of communication. Decisions to communicate directly or through Providers will be affected by factors such as cost, the nature of available services, the volume of transmissions, the bargaining power of the respective parties and continued evolutions in technology.

4. Counsel should note that Section 1.2.1 requires the parties to have contracted with any Provider specified for them in the Appendix. This assures that each party has obtained the availability of each such Provider.

5. Notice of any modification of a party's election provides a reasonable opportunity for the other party to make corresponding adjustments in operations. Generally, 30 days is considered, consistent with general industry practice, as a reasonable notice period; however, that period may be adjusted, based on what may be reasonable for a particular relationship.

Drafting Considerations

1. If the parties elect to communicate directly, counsel may wish to consider specifying in the Appendix appropriate technical information.

2. If either party uses one or more Providers, the names and related information of such Providers are to be set forth in the Appendix. If Providers are to be used for particular services or transactions, such indications would be appropriate in the Appendix.

1.2.2. Each party shall be responsible for the costs of any Provider with which it contracts, unless otherwise set forth in the Appendix.

Comment

1. Section 1.2.2 permits the parties to allocate between them the various expenses incurred in the use of Providers. Such expenses relate to the basic services of transmission, receipt, data storage, and data translation as well as additional services which may be offered. Counsel should consider the effect of this Section 1.2.2 when Providers offer a service permitting the parties to automatically agree on-line as to the allocation of these types of expenses.

2. The Agreement is consistent with the general industry practice within a paper-based environment that each party absorb its respective communication costs (i.e., postage, courier costs, and printing expenses).

Drafting Considerations

To the extent the parties allocate costs in a manner other than as provided in Section 1.2.2, such allocation may be added in the Appendix; no change in the Agreement is required.

[**1.2.3.** Each party shall be liable for the acts or omissions of its Provider while transmitting, receiving, storing or handling Documents, or performing related activities, for such party; provided, that if both the parties use the same Provider to effect the transmission and receipt of a Document, the originating party shall be liable for the acts or omissions of such Provider as to such Document.]

Comment

1. This optional Section permits the parties to establish contractual responsibility between them for the conduct of their respective Providers. This Section, if used, has the effect of providing a clear rule within the Agreement for allocating the risk of loss between the parties arising from the Provider's conduct. If this Section is omitted, the parties will have no contractual liability to each other under the Agreement for the conduct of their respective Providers, except where such conduct is attributable to either party and causes such party to breach the provisions of the Agreement.
2. The originating party is responsible for the acts of a shared Provider on the basis that such party initiates the final action, with respect to any Document, to use the Provider.
3. The Agreement does not address the respective right of either party to assert claims against any Provider under any applicable service contract, nor does the Agreement alter the liability of the parties to each other, if any, pursuant to any applicable legal principles.

Drafting Considerations

1. Liability arising under Section 1.2.3 is subject to the exclusion of damages contained in Section 4.6; counsel should consider whether this result is appropriate. The possible effect of Section 4.5 (*Force Majeure*) to relieve a party of liability under Section 1.2.3 should also be evaluated.
2. Note that Section 1.2.3 does not act to allocate liability between the parties where a Provider is not used. *See* Section 1.2.1.

3. This Section, if used, may be modified to allocate liability in any other manner upon which the parties agree.

1.3. System Operations.

Each party, at its own expense, shall provide and maintain the equipment, software, services and testing necessary to effectively and reliably transmit and receive Documents.

Comment

1. This Section imposes a reciprocal obligation upon the parties to support effective and reliable communications, and allocates the related costs.
2. Consistent with general industry practice, the obligation to "maintain" is intended to require the parties to update the specified items as necessary to assure that effective and reliable communications are maintained in accordance with prevailing commercial practices and technology. *See* Section 1.1, and the Comments thereto. Section 1.3 may require, therefore, additional hardware or software acquisitions by the parties as well as the possible adoption of new security procedures satisfying the requirements of Section 1.4.
3. The conduct of the parties in establishing and maintaining effective and reliable communication enhances the reliability of Documents (including their content). *See* Sections 2.1, 3.3, and the Comments thereto.

Drafting Considerations

To the extent the parties agree upon a different allocation of expenses, appropriate changes may be made.

1.4. Security Procedures.

Each party shall properly use those security procedures, including those specified in the Appendix, if any, which are reasonably sufficient to ensure that all transmissions of Documents are authorized and to protect its business records and data from improper access.

Comment

1. Adequate security procedures are recognized by general industry practice as critical to the efficacy of electronic communication. This Section imposes affirmative duties to use security procedures to ensure the reliability of the communication systems and resulting business records. The use of adequate security enhances the reliability of those records and enhances

the ability to prove the substantive terms of any underlying commercial transaction. *See* Section 3.3.4, and the Comments thereto.

2. This Section imposes two obligations. First, each party must use security procedures sufficient to "reasonably" ensure proper authorization of transmissions. If a party fails to adequately secure its transmission activities, it may be liable for any unauthorized transmissions, and the consequences thereof. Second, each party must use security procedures sufficient to "reasonably" protect business records and data from improper access. In this case a failure to comply may again result in liability. This second obligation, when properly performed, also gives one party some measure of assurance that its own operations will not be subject to improper access through the systems and operations of the other party. A party failing to meet this second duty would, in addition, likely be estopped from submitting its records as superior to those of the other party, where the other party has properly met its own duty under Section 1.4.

3. Security procedures may be far-ranging in both sophistication and detail. Examples include the confidential exchange of Signatures (*see* Section 1.5) to authenticate the parties and the content of Documents which are transmitted or received, the exchange of encryption keys (by which the content of communications may be scrambled and unscrambled only pursuant to the exchanged keys), physical control of access to equipment and facilities, and the exchange of identifying information regarding the terminals from which authorized EDI transmissions may originate (which identifying information may be contained as part of the electronic "envelope" in which transmissions are exchanged).

4. Whether in any circumstance procedures which have been adopted or implemented will be considered as "reasonable" will vary based on the size and relative sophistication of the parties, the complexity of the operations of the parties, the nature of the communications and the underlying commercial transactions and additional factors. This Section provides an objective but flexible test by which to measure the conduct of the parties. *See* UCC § 1–204(2).

5. Under this Section, the parties may specify in the Appendix additional security procedures in connection with either or both of the requirements described in the above comments. This provision provides flexibility; as EDI and related technologies continue to advance, increasingly sophisticated security procedures will likely emerge which may be appropriate for one or both parties to implement. Parties should consider specifying in the Appendix any existing, generally accepted security procedures, special industry standards and any proprietary or unique security procedures required by the underlying commercial relationship.

6. This Section encourages the parties to negotiate the level of security required to induce them to enter Transactions. *See* Section 3.3, Comment

Model EDI Trading Partner Agreement

5. However, to the extent any duty of care may exist between the parties, liability may also arise at common law. *See* UCC § 1–103.

7. This Section relates to obtaining access to business records and data; the use of such records and data is covered by Section 3.2. Counsel should consider the relationship between security procedures required by Section 1.4 and the treatment of confidentiality in Section 3.2.

Drafting Considerations

Counsel should note that the provisions of Section 4.6 (*Exclusion of Damages*) do not apply to any breach of the obligations arising under Section 1.4.

1.5 Signatures.

Each party shall adopt as its signature an electronic identification consisting of symbol(s) or code(s) which are to be affixed to or contained in each Document transmitted by such party ("Signatures"). Each party agrees that any Signature of such party affixed to or contained in any transmitted Document shall be sufficient to verify such party originated such Document. Neither party shall disclose to any unauthorized person the Signatures of the other party.

Comment

1. This Section establishes a mechanism for the adoption by each party of an electronic signature by which each Document may be signed. UCC § 1–201(39) defines "signed" to include ". . . any *symbol* executed or *adopted* by a *party* with present intention to authenticate a writing (emphasis added)." Use of a Signature is important to establishing the validity of any EDI communication. *See* Section 3.3, and the Comments thereto.

2. This Section requires each party to adopt a Signature, but retains considerable flexibility as to what symbols or codes shall be adopted. The decision of each party will be made in light of existing technology, the relative sophistication of the parties, the requirements of applicable standards and any security procedures which are in use. A party may select as its Signature the use of its name on a Document (similar to a form of purchase order imprinted with the buyer's name and containing no other authorized signature). What is important is that the use of the adopted symbol or code reflect the intent to authenticate required by the Code. Regulating the use of any Signature may also be part of security procedures required by the Agreement; counsel should evaluate any such procedures to assure that the required intent to authenticate is preserved.

3. The electronic signature of any party may change from time to time, in

order to protect its confidential character. Accordingly, the Appendix does not provide for disclosure of any Signature, but relies on general industry practice for the exchange of Signatures by other means of communication. If any Signature is used by a party as part of adopted security procedures the practice of periodically changing the Signature could be considered as consistent with the obligations of such party under Section 1.4 to use reasonable security procedures.

4. The last sentence of Section 1.5 prohibits only disclosure of the Signatures of the other party. If security procedures required by the Agreement relate to non-disclosure of Signatures, a party which discloses its own Signature to an unauthorized person may breach the provisions of Section 1.4.

§ 2. TRANSMISSIONS.

2.1. Proper Receipt.

Documents shall not be deemed to have been properly received, and no Document shall give rise to any obligation, until accessible to the receiving party at such party's Receipt Computer designated in the Appendix.

Comment

1. The increased speed and accuracy of electronic commerce fundamentally differ when compared to contract formation practices in a paper-based environment. Parties engaging in electronic commerce have the ability to efficiently determine whether a particular transmission has been received by the other party, whether any transmission is inconsistent with prior business arrangements, or whether any transmission may be outside negotiated contractual limits. Consequently, the procedures of electronic commerce, when effectively implemented, offer the opportunity to achieve greater certainty in the contracting process. Section 2 provides a framework for the effective implementation of those procedures for the mutual benefit of both parties. The provisions set forth rules pertaining to the timing of receipt (Section 2.1), the obligation of the receiving party to verify receipt (Section 2.2), the manner in which acceptance occurs within an EDI environment (Section 2.3), and the disposition of unintelligible or garbled transmissions (Section 2.4).

2. Section 2.1 provides that no Document may create any legal obligation until properly received. This Section, therefore, represents a departure from the "mailbox rule" and parallel legal doctrines. Since the technology exists by which the party originating the transmission of any Document

can effectively confirm receipt has occurred, it is inappropriate that the mere dispatch of any Document should be sufficient for any legal purpose.

3. "Properly received" requires that the transmitted Document be accessible at a computer designated by the receiving party. This permits each party to determine the appropriate system location. A Receipt Computer may be the computer of the third party service provider, the computer of either party or a specific terminal within a party's internal network (for example, a billing supervisor's desk). The Receipt Computer should be situated to enable the receiving party to promptly and properly transmit a functional acknowledgement upon proper receipt of any Document, as required by Section 2.2. Such acknowledgement may be sent by the Receipt Computer or by a computer with which the Receipt Computer communicates. Counsel should review the applicable operations to ensure that a functional acknowledgement cannot be transmitted before a Document reaches the Receipt Computer. Counsel should carefully consider the effects under remaining provisions of the Agreement of selecting as the Receipt Computer a computer which is not under the respective control of each party. Note that receipt does not require that any Document actually be examined, only that the Document be accessible. In a paper-based environment, this is similar to when a letter is delivered, but the envelope remains unopened. Each party thereby defers "receipt" until the "right" person or machine has an opportunity to have access to the transmitted data.

4. Note that Section 2.1 operates to relieve both parties from any obligation until the Document has been properly received.

5. Except as described in Comment 2 above, the provisions of Section 2 are not intended to displace other applicable laws relating to contract formation or the underlying commercial relationship of the parties.

6. Several examples which illustrate the operation of the provisions of Section 2 appear at Section 2.4, Comment 6.

Drafting Considerations

1. In identifying the proper Receipt Computer, counsel may wish to consider, by example, current internal practices of the parties for giving notice under existing agreements and identify the person designated for such purposes (*see* Section 1.1, Comment 2). Since virtually any Document may be sent without direct human involvement, care should be taken that adequate controls have been established regulating the level of approval (and human authorization) required to properly receive any Document.

2. Counsel should consider whether any modification by either party under Section 1.2.1 will require conforming changes in the designation of the Receipt Computer for such party.

2.2. Verification.

Upon proper receipt of any Document, the receiving party shall promptly and properly transmit a functional acknowledgement in return, unless otherwise specified in the Appendix. A functional acknowledgement shall constitute conclusive evidence a Document has been properly received.

Comments

1. In light of the capability of technology to facilitate nearly immediate verification of receipt, and also to verify that no defect in receipt has occurred, Section 2.2 imposes an affirmative obligation to provide verification of receipt. Effective verification practices increase the opportunity for the early detection and resolution of transmission errors, thereby reducing the exposure of both parties to possibly significant damages.
2. A "functional acknowledgement" is a transaction set which confirms that receipt of a Document (in the format specified by such functional acknowledgement) has occurred and that all required portions of the Document have been received and are syntactically correct, but otherwise does not confirm the substantive content of the related Document. A functional acknowledgement can verify receipt, but is also designed to identify whether, in fact, omissions or errors in format or syntax have occurred. To the extent a party transmitting a functional acknowledgement identifies any errors or omissions, such notice would satisfy the notice requirements of Section 2.4. *See* Section 2.4, and the Comments thereto.
3. A party will "properly transmit" a functional acknowledgement or Document if it has been transmitted in a manner which complies with the provisions of Section 1.
4. Whether or not verification is provided will not alter the legal significance of the initial Document; Section 2.1 controls in that respect.
5. Counsel may wish to evaluate whether any circumstances exist where the affirmative obligation to verify receipt should not be imposed and make appropriate exceptions in the Appendix. For example, a party's system may not include functional acknowledgements or the parties may elect to verify in another manner, such as transaction sequence checking.
6. A party initially transmitting a Document may have an obligation to make reasonable inquiries or take other actions to discharge any duty which may exist to mitigate damages arising from a breach of the provisions of Section 2.2 by the receiving party.
7. The conclusive quality of a functional acknowledgement established by this Section assures that subsequent reliance thereon is reasonable.

Model EDI Trading Partner Agreement

2.3. Acceptance.

If acceptance of a Document is required by the Appendix, any such Document which has been properly received shall not give rise to any obligation unless and until the party initially transmitting such Document has properly received in return an Acceptance Document (as specified in the Appendix).

Comment

1. Section 2.3 unambiguously indicates, with respect to the offer and acceptance of any contract, that no obligation will arise except upon satisfaction of the provisions of the Agreement. *See* UCC § 2-206(1). The parties, by designating appropriate Acceptance Documents, have the opportunity to define what will constitute acceptance and can assure that no contract arises from any Document until there has been mutual and certain agreement upon the terms contained in such Document.
2. This Section permits the parties to designate Acceptance Documents for Documents not specifically included in the contract formation process.
3. An Acceptance Document might be a computer generated response or a more significant communication, possibly requiring human evaluation at the receiving end. Selection of the appropriate Acceptance Document in a particular context may also be influenced by the manner in which either party interacts with its Provider and by the commercial relationship of the parties. Note that Section 2.3 operates to relieve both parties from any obligation until an Acceptance Document has been properly received in return.
4. Note that the party receiving a Document also controls whether the Acceptance Document is to be sent. If the proposed terms or content of an initial Document is objectionable, neither party has any obligation if the Acceptance Document is not properly received in return.

Drafting Considerations

1. In identifying possible Acceptance Documents, counsel may wish to consider, by example, current internal practices of the parties for giving notice under existing agreements and identify the person designated for such purposes (*see* Section 1.1, Comment 2). Since virtually any Document may be sent without direct human involvement, care should be taken that adequate controls have been established regulating the level of approval (and human authorization) required to transmit any Document.
2. Counsel is strongly encouraged to review the substantive content of possible Acceptance Documents in selecting the appropriate confirmation of any Document. For example, in response to a purchase order, the Acceptance Document may be:

- a purchase order acknowledgement (which substantively confirms the terms of the purchase order); or
- a shipping notice (specifying that the goods have been or will be shipped; *see* UCC § 2–206(1)(b)).

3. For certain Documents (for example, a notice of rejection of goods from the buyer), no Acceptance Document will be appropriate. Note, however, if the buyer, having sent such notice does not receive a functional acknowledgement in return, the buyer is on notice that its notice of rejection may not have been received, and should consider either re-sending the notice, or providing such notice by means other than EDI. *See* UCC § 1–201(26).
4. Counsel may wish to consider applicable industry implementation guidelines in selecting appropriate Acceptance Documents. *See* Section 1.1, Comments 2 and 13.
5. Counsel should also consider what effects, if any, the selection and use of Acceptance Documents may have upon the additional terms and conditions of the underlying commercial relationship, which may more specifically address contract formation issues (such as the time period in which offers must be accepted or rejected, and the manner of communicating rejection, if at all), rights of rejection and other matters. In addition, notwithstanding the last sentence of Section 3.1, counsel should endeavor to assure that the contract formation practices develop under the Agreement are consistent with any commercial relationship established by any other agreement described in Section 3.1. *See* Section 3.1, and the Comments thereto.

2.4. Garbled Transmissions.

If any transmitted Document is received in an unintelligible or garbled form, the receiving party shall promptly notify the originating party (if identifiable from the received Document) in a reasonable manner. In the absence of such a notice, the originating party's records of the contents of such Document shall control.

Comment

1. Section 2.4 is intended to apply only to unintelligible or garbled messages, incapable of having effective meaning or missing material data components, for which the originating party may be identified within the context of the relevant Document. In those cases, the originating party's records control unless the receiving party gives prompt notification in a reasonable manner. *See* UCC § 1–204. Such notice may be given by other than electronic means. The obligation to provide notice under this Section is not burdensome in an electronic environment, and has the advantage of assisting the transmitting party to correct promptly a miscommunication.

Model EDI Trading Partner Agreement

2. The phrase "unintelligible or garbled" is not intended to include Documents which are, in human readable form, capable of being read but which contain information which the receiving party knows, or has reason to know, may be incorrrect. For example, if ABC has always ordered no more than 200 pencils, its purchase order for 200,000 pencils should not be considered unintelligible or garbled, since pursuant to Section 2.1, the parties can adopt a procedure where XYZ can always review, confirm or reject the substantive terms contained in any Document.

3. Section 2.4 is not intended to displace the applicable principles of the law of mistake. *See* UCC § 1–103.

4. If, pursuant to Section 2.3, no obligation arises with respect to a Document otherwise subject to this Section because the required Acceptance Document has not been properly received in return, then the fact that such Document is unintelligible or garbled should have no consequences under this Section.

5. Section 4.6 (*Exclusion of Damages*) clearly applies to liabilities which may arise in connection with any unintelligible or garbled transmission; if the parties wish a different result, appropriate changes may be made.

6. The following examples illustrate the operation of the provisions of Section 2, taken as a whole:

   Example 1. XYZ has specified its mainframe computer as its Receipt Computer. ABC sends a Document to XYZ's Provider, but the Document is never made accessible to XYZ's Receipt Computer. ABC's transmission of the Document has no legal effect.

   Example 2. XYZ properly receives a purchase order from ABC but never transmits in return either a functional acknowledgement or an Acceptance Document. No contract has been formed but XYZ is liable for any damages suffered by ABC, if any, from XYZ's failure to provide verification as required.

   Example 3. XYZ properly receives a purchase order from ABC which by its terms is open for 10 days. XYZ properly transmits an Acceptance Document within the 10 day period, but the Acceptance Document is not "properly received" until the 11th day. No contract is formed.

   Example 4. The Appendix requires, as to a purchase order, that a purchase order acknowledgement be sent as an Acceptance Document. ABC, as buyer, sends a purchase order, receipt of which is verified by XYZ, as seller, by sending a functional acknowledgement. However, XYZ never sends an Acceptance Document. No contract for sale has been formed.

   Example 5. XYZ properly transmits an Acceptance Document, which is received by XYZ's Provider and stored. Meanwhile, ABC properly transmits a revocation of its offer, which revocation is properly received by XYZ's Receipt Computer before the Acceptance Document is forwarded to ABC's Receipt Computer by XYZ's Provider. No contract is formed; the revocation is effective.

Example 6. The Appendix requires, as to a purchase order, that a purchase order acknowledgement be sent as an Acceptance Document. XYZ, as seller, properly receives a purchase order from ABC, as buyer, but the price data is missing. XYZ sends a functional acknowledgement which identifies the omitted data. Under Section 2.4, XYZ has met its obligations. If XYZ, without the price data, then sends an Acceptance Document, a contract is formed, with the price to be determined pursuant to applicable law. *See* UCC § 2–305.

§ 3. TRANSACTION TERMS.

3.1. Terms and Conditions.

This Agreement is to be considered part of any other written agreement referencing it or referenced in the Appendix. In the absence of any other written agreement applicable to any Transaction made pursuant to this Agreement, such Transaction (and any related communication) also shall be subject to [CHOOSE ONE]:

[A] those terms and conditions, including any terms for payment, included in the Appendix.

[B] the terms and conditions included on each party's standard printed applicable forms attached to or identified in the Appendix [as the same may be amended from time to time by either party upon written notice to the other]. The parties acknowledge that the terms and conditions set forth on such forms may be inconsistent, or in conflict, but agree that any conflict or dispute that arises between the parties in connection with any such Transaction will be resolved as if such Transaction had been effected through the use of such forms.

[C] such additional terms and conditions as may be determined in accordance with applicable law.

The terms of this Agreement shall prevail in the event of any conflict with any other terms and conditions applicable to any Transaction.

Comment

1. Section 3 recognizes that the exchange of Documents furthers the commercial relationship of the parties, and that the use of available technology pursuant to its terms should not create any conflict with other written agreements between the parties, or fail to properly accommodate the terms and conditions which define the dimensions of the commercial transactions.

2. Section 3.1 responds to three situations:
   - The parties have previously or concurrently executed a separate contract for the sale of goods, which may, by example, be in the form of a master purchase, requirements or outputs agreement. *See* UCC § 2–306.
   - The parties execute such an agreement after the Agreement is signed.
   - The parties conduct business in the absence of, or outside the scope of, any such agreements, relying solely upon the Documents and the conduct of the parties pursuant to the Agreement to establish any contract.

   In either the first or second case, the other agreement is assumed to be the instrument by which the parties have had the opportunity to negotiate and agree upon terms and conditions applicable to any Transaction which are not defined by the content of any Document. However, in the final case, Section 3.1 requires the parties to elect from among three alternatives the manner for providing the additional terms and conditions not anticipated by the standard formats of applicable transaction sets.

3. Option [A] requires negotiation and agreement upon the additional terms and conditions. Such option, as compared to the remaining options, achieves the highest level of certainty in establishing the terms of any contract of sale. Essential terms and conditions to be negotiated, by way of example, may include warranty, delivery, rejection, liability for non-conforming goods and attorney's fees. The negotiated terms would be included in the Appendix.

4. Option [B] permits incorporation into the electronic environment of existing paper-based methods of conducting business. Option [B] has the objective of clearly defining, for each party, the terms and conditions upon which it wishes to conduct business, and, to the extent amendments may be accommodated, the terms and conditions applicable at any time during the commercial relationship. If selected, however, Option [B], in anticipating, but not resolving, inconsistencies or conflicts in the respective forms of the parties, will not achieve the highest level of certainty as to the terms of any contract of sale.

5. Option [B] requires each party's standard printed forms to be incorporated as a part of the Agreement. The parties may attach such forms to the Appendix or may identify the appropriate forms which are to be incorporated by reference. Any identification provided should be sufficiently specific to identify only one form. However, selecting the option of attaching such forms to the Appendix assures that the terms and conditions of such forms are explicitly known and disclosed.

6. In response to general industry practice, Option [B] includes, as a further option, language permitting the terms and conditions of any form attached to or identified in the Appendix to be amended by subsequent written

notice (which notice must be sufficient to adequately identify the new form or changes). If this option is elected, either party may incorporate into EDI trading the changes in terms and conditions which may occur in its paper-based trading practices. Parties wishing to retain greater control over subsequent amendments would not elect the optional language. In that case, subsequent forms would require mutual agreement for subsequent attachment or identification.

7. In the event of any inconsistency or conflict between the respective forms of the parties, Option [B] incorporates the method of resolution set forth in UCC § 2–207 and other applicable law. Since the attached or identified forms will correspond to Documents which have been transmitted, the terms and conditions contained in such forms should be considered in the same sequence in which the related Documents are transmitted and received between the parties.

8. Option [C], if elected, incorporates into each contract for sale of goods the manner by which applicable law determines additional terms and conditions (other than quantity) which have not been agreed upon by the parties. *See, e.g.*, UCC § 2–305 (Open Price Term), § 2–307 (Delivery and Single Lot), § 2–308 (Place for Delivery) and § 2–309 (Time for Shipment or Delivery). Under the circumstances contemplated by the Agreement, any contract for sale should not fail for indefiniteness. *See* UCC § 2–204(3).

9. The last sentence of Section 3.1 confirms that the intent of the parties to give effect to the provisions of the Agreement is not contradicted by other terms and conditions applicable to any Transaction, whether set forth in any agreement described in Section 3.1 or by applicable law. For example, a separate contract for the sale of goods may provide for acceptance, in a paper-based environment, to occur upon the receipt of a signed purchase order acknowledgement at the offices of buyer by certified mail. The last sentence of Section 3.1 provides for the acceptance mechanism established pursuant to the Agreement to control with respect to EDI transmissions. Thus, the commercial intent of the parties, taken as a whole, is given effect.

Drafting Considerations

1. If the parties clearly intend that the Agreement is to be used solely and exclusively in connection with other written agreements, and that no other EDI transactions should be authorized, the second sentence of this Section may be deleted. However, such sentence serves as a "safety basket" for future transactions not otherwise contemplated and should be deleted only after careful analysis.

2. If the parties elect Option [A], counsel is encouraged to carefully consider whether additional terms and conditions should be included to fully implement

the commercial intentions of the parties expressed in other provisions of the Agreement. *See* Section 1.1, Comment 2, and Section 2.3, Drafting Consideration 5.

3. If the parties elect Option [B], counsel may wish to consider specifying the method of providing notice of any amendments to the printed forms adopted by either party, as well as any minimum period before such notices take effect.

3.2. Confidentiality.

No information contained in any Document or otherwise exchanged between the parties shall be considered confidential, except to the extent provided in Section 1.5, by written agreement between the parties, or by applicable law.

Comment

1. Section 3.2 focuses on whether the information transmitted in any Document requires confidential treatment by the parties. This Section provides for no confidential treatment except for Signatures (as provided in Section 1.5), and as required by other written agreements (*see* Section 1.1, Comment 3) or by applicable law. Examples of applicable law would include common law relating to trade secrets, any court order imposing confidentiality obligations as to any relevant information or 47 USC 605.

2. If confidential treatment is to be provided, counsel, in substitution for the provisions of Section 3.2, should prepare appropriate provisions as to the scope and duration of any obligations, as well as appropriate remedies. Counsel may wish to give special emphasis, if only certain information is to be considered as confidential, on the manner in which, in an electronic environment, information is to be designated as confidential by the parties. Information may be designated as confidential on a transaction-by-transaction basis by including an appropriate designation (by the use of special codes) within the related electronic transmissions. Such a technique would satisfy the requirement of this Section 3.2 for "written agreement" if the parties intend for that effect. *See* Section 1.1, Comment 3.

3.3. Validity; Enforceability.

3.3.1. This Agreement has been executed by the parties to evidence their mutual intent to create binding purchase and sale obligations pursuant to the electronic transmission and receipt of Documents specifying certain of the applicable terms.

3.2.2. Any Document properly transmitted pursuant to this Agreement shall be considered, in connection with any Transaction, any other written agreement described in Section 3.1, or this Agreement, to be a "writing" or "in writing"; and any such Document when containing, or to which there is affixed, a Signature ("Signed Documents") shall be deemed for all purposes (a) to have been "signed" and (b) to constitute an "original" when printed from electronic files or records established and maintained in the normal course of business.

3.3.3. The conduct of the parties pursuant to this Agreement, including the use of Signed Documents properly transmitted pursuant to this Agreement, shall, for all legal purposes, evidence a course of dealing and a course of performance accepted by the parties in furtherance of this Agreement, any Transaction and any other written agreement described in Section 3.1.

3.3.4. The parties agree not to contest the validity or enforceability of Signed Documents under the provisions of any applicable law relating to whether certain agreements are to be in writing or signed by the party to be bound thereby. Signed Documents, if introduced as evidence on paper in any judicial, arbitration, mediation or administrative proceedings, will be admissible as between the parties to the same extent and under the same conditions as other business records originated and maintained in documentary form. Neither party shall contest the admissibility of copies of Signed Documents under either the business records exception to the hearsay rule or the best evidence rule on the basis that the Signed Documents were not originated or maintained in documentary form.

Comment

1. This Section confirms the validity and enforceability of the underlying contracts formed by the electronic transmission and receipt of Documents. *See* Recitals, Comment 3.
2. The intent of any party to a contract that the contract be legally binding is an essential predicate for the underlying transaction. The Recitals of the Agreement initially stated the parties' intentions that Transactions arising under the Agreement be legally valid and enforceable; Section 3.3.1 implements such intent.
3. Section 3.3.2 establishes any properly transmitted Document as a "writing". This provision expands upon the existing definition contained in UCC § 1–201(46) (defining "writing" to include "printing, typewriting or any other intentional reduction to tangible form."). This modification is of the type contemplated by the Code. *See* UCC § 1–102(3) and Recitals, Comment 2.

4. Section 3.3.2 (taken with the provisions of Section 1.5) also establishes Signed Documents as sufficient to satisfy the formal requirements of UCC § 2–201 (the Statute of Frauds) when the Documents relate to the formation of any contract for the sale of goods for the price of $500 or more. *See* UCC § 2–201 and comments thereto. Finally, Section 3.3.2 also establishes that Signed Documents shall be deemed to constitute "original" business records under certain circumstances. *See* Comment 7 below; *see also* Section 1.4, Comment 1.

5. Under Section 3.3.3, the conduct of the parties pursuant to the Agreement constitutes a course of dealing and a course of performance upon which they may rely in structuring their business relationship. This conduct includes the identification of the Documents to be transmitted, the establishment of channels of communication and the adoption of mutually acceptable security procedures, all pursuant to the provisions of Section 1. UCC § 2–208 contemplates that such conduct be considered in determining the meaning of this Agreement and any underlying contract for the sale of goods. *See* UCC §§ 1–205 and 2–208. This conduct, either as a course of dealing or as a course of performance, should be given effect with respect to both the Agreement and other applicable purchase contracts, independent of the status of Signed Documents as signed writings under applicable law. *See also* UCC §§ 2–202(a) and 2–207(3).

6. Nothing in the Agreement, other than the prohibition on oral waivers contained in Section 4.3, operates to prevent either party from contending that the terms and conditions applicable to any Transaction, or those set forth in the Agreement, may be modified or waived as contemplated by UCC § 2–209.

7. Section 3.3.4 establishes rules of conduct for the parties in connection with the use of Signed Documents as evidence in any proceeding between the parties. By way of example, *see* Federal Rules of Evidence 802, 803(6) and 1002. However, Section 3.3.4 (together with Section 3.3.2) does not waive the need for a proper foundation to be established for the admissibility of the evidence. In this regard, the effectiveness and reliability of each party's security procedures, record retention policies, confidentiality obligations and their conduct under the provisions of the Agreement may be relevant in individual cases to the ultimate admissibility of any Signed Documents.

§ 4. MISCELLANEOUS.

4.1. Termination.

This Agreement shall remain in effect until terminated by either party with not less than 30 days prior written notice, which notice shall specify the effective date of termination; provided, however, that any termination shall not affect the respective obligations or rights of the parties arising under any Documents or otherwise under this Agreement prior to the effective date of termination.

Comment

1. The provisions of Section 4 include provisions often found in many types of agreements. These provisions are not exclusive, and counsel may wish to consider other similar customary provisions which, for the most part, are not effected by the use of electronic communications. However, as discussed in these Comments, these provisions focus upon some significant legal factors relating to the use of electronic communication under the Agreement.
2. Section 4.1 assures freedom of contract, but also assures the non-terminating party an appropriate opportunity to establish (or re-institute) alternative procedures of communication.
3. A 30-day notice period is considered reasonable by general industry practice. However, *see* Section 1.2.1, Comment 5.
4. Any notice of termination under Section 4.1 does not affect obligations under the underlying commercial relationship; any notices relating to such obligations would be separately required.
5. With respect to the requirement that notice under this Section be "written", *see* Section 1.1, Comment 3.

4.2. Severability.

Any provision of this Agreement which is determined to be invalid or unenforceable will be ineffective to the extent of such determination without invalidating the remaining provisions of this Agreement or affecting the validity or enforceability of such remaining provisions.

Comment

The Agreement has been prepared for implementation in a variety of situations; Section 4.2 has been included to assure that the entire contract does not fail in the event any specific provision is determined to be unenforceable under any particular circumstances.

4.3. Entire Agreement.

This Agreement and the Appendix constitute the complete agreement of the parties relating to the matters specified in this Agreement and supersede all prior representations or agreements, whether oral or written, with respect to such matters. No oral modification or waiver of any of the provisions of this Agreement shall be binding on either party. No obligation to enter into any Transaction is to be implied from the execution or delivery of this Agreement. This Agreement is for the benefit of, and shall be binding upon, the parties and their respective successors and assigns.

Comment

1. Section 4.3 integrates the Appendix with the Agreement into a complete agreement. The provisions of Section 3.1 are effective to integrate the Agreement (with the Appendix) into any other specified purchasing contract.
2. Section 4.3 permits modifications and waivers of the Agreement by Signed Documents (but the parties must include "freetext" Documents to have this result). *See* Section 1.1, Comments 3 and 4. If the parties wish to require paper-based writing for modifications or waivers, appropriate changes should be made.
3. This Section confirms that the Agreement itself creates no obligations relating to the purchase and sale of goods; such obligations arise only from the Documents and the conduct of the parties.

4.4. Governing Law.

This Agreement shall be governed by and interpreted in accordance with the laws of the State of _____.

Comment

In addition to customary factors considered in selecting applicable law, counsel may wish to evaluate various state laws which may be in effect relating to criminal use of computers, computer privacy and similar issues relating to technology.

4.5. Force Majeure.

No party shall be liable for any failure to perform its obligations in connection with any Transaction or any Document, where such failure results from any act of God or other cause beyond such party's reasonable control (including, without limitation, any mechanical, electronic or communications failure) which prevents such party from transmitting or receiving any Documents.

Comment

1. The scope of this Section is limited to events which prevent the transmission or receipt of Documents and does not extend to the impact of those events on any other obligations of the parties, whether under the Agreement or in connection with any underlying Transaction.
2. Among other things, this Section is specifically intended to excuse performance resulting from such events as a general power outage in the community or unscheduled "down-time" events outside the reasonable control of one of the parties.
3. Counsel should carefully consider the effect of this Section upon the obligations arising under Section 1.2.3, if such Section is included. To the extent Section 1.2.3 imposes liability, counsel should evaluate whether Section 4.5 reduces or eliminates liability to the extent the actions of a Provider may be considered beyond the reasonable control of either party.

4.6. Limitation of Damages.

Neither party shall be liable to the other for any special, incidental, exemplary or consequential damages arising from or as a result of any delay, omission or error in the electronic transmission or receipt of any Documents pursuant to this Agreement, even if either party has been advised of the possibility of such damages.

Comment

Since the benefits of conducting electronic commerce are substantial and far-reaching, an exclusion of damages is appropriate and consistent with general industry practice to encourage recognition of those benefits. However, the scope of this Section is also limited, as provided in Section 4.5, solely to damages arising from or as a result of any delay, omission or error in the transmission or receipt of Documents pursuant to the Agreement. *See* Section 2.4, Comment 5. Section 4.6 does not limit any damages resulting from a breach of Section 1.4 (*Security Procedures*) or Section 1.5 (*Confidentiality*) and does not apply to damages resulting from a breach of any related Transaction. If different results are desired, appropriate changes should be made.

[4.7. Arbitration.

Any controversy or claim arising out of or relating to this Agreement, or the breach thereof, shall be settled in accordance with the Commercial Arbitration Rules of the American Arbitration Association, and judgment on the award rendered by the arbitrator(s) may be entered in any court having jurisdiction thereof.]

Comment

1. Section 4.7 sets forth, as an option, the recommended arbitration clause of the American Arbitration Association.
2. Counsel is encouraged to consider the advisability of arbitration and other forms of alternative dispute resolution in connection with the Agreement and Transactions conducted pursuant to the Agreement. Of course, to the extent arbitration or other similar methods are considered appropriate, the parties may modify or amend the suggested language.

Each party has caused this Agreement to be properly executed on its behalf as of the date first above written.

ABC

By _____

Name: _____

Title: _____

XYZ

By _____

Name: _____

Title: _____

APPENDIX

Standards

Specify *ALL* applicable standards (and the issuing organizations)

Selected standards include, as applicable, all data dictionaries, segment dictionaries and transmission controls referenced in those standards, but include only the Transaction Sets listed in the DOCUMENTS section of this Appendix below.

Documents

Transaction Set No.	Document Name or Description	Version Release	Verification Required (Yes or No)	Acceptance Required (Yes or No)	Transaction Set No.	Acceptance Document Document Name or Description
		Then current and one prior version				

Guidelines

Specify *ALL* applicable published industry guidelines: _____

The provisions of the Agreement (including this Appendix) shall control in the event of any conflict with any listed guidelines.

Third Party Service Providers

(If the parties will be transmitting Documents directly, insert "NONE")

	Name	Address	Telephone Number

ABC -

XYZ -

Receipt Computer

ABC -

XYZ -

Allocation of Provider Costs

(If no special allocation has been agreed upon, enter "NONE"): _____

Security Procedures

(If no security procedures have been agreed upon, enter "NONE"): _____

Existing Agreements

(If the Agreement is not to be considered a part of any existing written agreement, enter "NONE"): _____

[Terms and Conditions

If the parties select Section 3.1[A], specify terms and conditions: _____

If the parties select Section 3.1[B], attach applicable forms or provide sufficient identification of each form being incorporated:] _____

Supplement to Chapter XXIII,
pages 395 to 406

PURCHASING FROM FOREIGN VENDORS

The first part of Chapter XXIII in the original text is devoted to the general theme of purchasing from foreign vendors. One article in that chapter is captioned "Applicable Law" (page 405). It is directed to the question of what body of law will govern the purchase contract between an American buyer and a foreign supplier. The article suggests to the American purchasing officer that a clause be inserted in the contract to make the law of the buyer's home state the applicable law to cover the legal questions pertaining to the contract. The alternative to this, of course, is to make applicable the law of the country from which the foreign supplier hails.

To the American buyer and to his or her legal counsel, this latter choice is not always palatable. Many of us have a fear that justice will be difficult to obtain against a foreign supplier in his own country. Most of this fear is born of ignorance of the foreign law, to be sure, but it is nonetheless a belief that many of us possess. And, of course, the foreign supplier probably feels the same about our American system of justice if his case is to be tried in an American court. Add to this fact the realization that the foreign supplier and his legal counsel will find trying a case in an American court very expensive, and one can readily understand that the American purchasing officer might have some difficulty in getting the foreign supplier to agree to the choice of law clause on page 405.

At the time the original text was written these were the two choices of applicable law available to the foreign supplier and the American purchasing officer when they were contracting with each other. "Your law or my law" remained one of the negotiable items in a foreign contract. Most of the time the final answer was determined by the party with the stronger negotiating power. Of course the parties could agree to use a neutral third country's laws too. And then again—perhaps the two parties simply did not think of choosing an applicable law for their contract. If a legal question arose in the formation or performance of the contract, the law where the question arose would be applied by the courts.

Since January 1, 1988 there is a third alternative body of law that has become available for American purchasing officers and some foreign suppliers. It is known as the "United Nations Convention for the International Sale of Goods." "The Convention" or "C.I.S.G." are shorter titles for this new body of law. No matter what it is called, it has become a third alternative; perhaps, a compromise of independent stature between American law and the law of the land of the foreign supplier.

Genesis of the Convention. Member states of the United Nations made strenuous efforts for more than 50 years to develop a uniform law governing the formation and performance of contracts for the international sale (and purchase) of goods.[1] Success of the project was finally realized in Vienna on April 11, 1980 when 42 states unanimously approved what is now known as the Convention for the International Sale of Goods. There were no dissenting votes but several states abstained from voting. It is suggested that perhaps many of the abstainers were in favor of the Convention but had not received formal approval from the "home government" to vote for it when the roll was called.

President Reagan submitted the Convention to the United States Senate for ratification in 1983. The Senate finally approved it in October 1986 and the United Nations Treaty Section recorded our formal ratification on December 11, 1986. This was the same day that the ratifications by China and Italy were also recorded. December 11, 1986 thus became the "trigger" date for the Convention to become effective. Article 99(1) of the Convention provides "This Convention enters into force . . . on the first day of the month following expiration of 12 months after the date of the deposit of the tenth instrument of ratification . . ." The following 8 countries had ratified the Convention prior to December 11, 1986:

---

[1] For an excellent discussion of the history of the various attempts to get consensus on a body of international law, see John Honnold *Uniform Law for International Sales*, Kluwer Law and Taxation Publishers, 101 Philip Drive, Norwell Mass 02061. The same text provides an excellent discussion of the various articles of the present Convention.

Argentina	Lesotho
Egypt	Syrian Arab Republic
France	Yugoslavia
Hungary	Zambia

Then when China, Italy and the U.S.A. ratified on December 11, 1986 the Article 99(1) formula made January 1, 1988 the date the Convention entered into force in these eleven countries. The following countries have since ratified:

Australia	Guinea
Austria	Iraq
Bulgaria	Mexico
Byelorussian Soviet Socialist Republic	Netherlands
Canada	Norway
Chile	Spain
Czechoslavakia	Sweden
Denmark	Switzerland
Federal Republic of Germany	Ukranian Soviet Socialist Republic
Finland	United Soviet Socialist Republic (U.S.S.R.)
German Democratic Republic	

Thus a total of 32 countries, including the United States of America, have the Convention for the International Sale of Goods as part of the law of their land.

An Unusual Source of Law for Us. This law came on the books of the United States in an unusual manner. It was submitted to the Senate of the United States for approval as a treaty and was ratified as such! There is nothing wrong in this procedure except for the fact that the Convention covers the international sale of goods. This then is a law that affects business activities, and business activities are the province of the individual states to legislate. The 10th Amendment of our Constitution, which is the last amendment under the Bill of Rights, states:

> The powers not delegated to the United States by the Constitution, nor prohibited by it to the states, are reserved to the States respectively, or to the people.

The power then to regulate and control business activity was not delegated to the Federal Government by the Constitution, and it is only a prerogative of the States to legislate it. However, in one fell swoop, the Senate by exercising their Constitutionally granted prerogative of approving treaties, approved this treaty and applied this Convention for the International Sale of Goods to all of our 50 states, including the State of Louisiana which has not even adopted the Uniform Commercial Code. There may be repercussions about this sometime in the future, but at the present, most states seem to acquiesce in this action of the Federal Government.

Just What Is the C.I.S.G.? The C.I.S.G. (the Convention) is a body of law dealing with contracts involving the international sale of goods. It was written by a representative group of members of the United Nations. In many respects it is a composite body of law that includes the civil law of Continental Europe, the common law of the United States and England, and the law of Third World countries. The C.I.S.G. covers much of the same subject matter as Article II (Sales) of the Uniform Commercial Code. There are some major differences however between the Code and the Convention. We will point out many of these variances as we proceed in the discussion of the C.I.S.G.

The C.I.S.G. has been written in six languages so that presumably everyone subject to the law will find it written in a language they can read. It is hoped the various judges who will be called upon to interpret and apply the law will interpret each part of it in the same manner. But one may never know whether that uniformity will come to pass because there is no known reporting service that will give us the text of the court decisions where the C.I.S.G. has been applied. Of course, if the law is applied in a United States court, the case will be reported in the usual services. But what of the cases decided in the courts of the other 31 countries that have adopted the C.I.S.G.? It will be interesting to see if some reporting service will be developed so that everyone will have the opportunity to know how a particular section of C.I.S.G. is applied in a foreign country where "I do business."

The C.I.S.G. Is American Law. Purchasing officers and legal counsel must recognize that the Convention is a body of law we must live with when we are dealing with vendors from other ratifying countries. Suppose an American purchasing officer concludes a contract with a supplier whose place of business is located in one of the other 31 countries who have adopted the Convention. The C.I.S.G. is immediately applicable to that contract! The two parties might agree to apply the law of the state where the buyer is located. That would be the C.I.S.G.! Or the parties might agree to apply the law of the country where the supplier's business is located. Again, that would be the C.I.S.G.

Should the parties want to eliminate the C.I.S.G. from their contract, they must be very specific about it. They must state positively that "the C.I.S.G. does not apply to this contract." Then they can specify which law they wish to apply. If no choice of law is selected for the contract by the parties, the contract in our example above automatically will have the C.I.S.G. applied by the American court if it has jurisdiction, or the court of the foreign country will apply it when it has jurisdiction.

Nota Bene to the Purchasing Officer Doing Foreign Sourcing. The C.I.S.G. is with us and we need to learn its details. The succeeding sections in this chapter will discuss this law and compare some of its provisions with the Uniform Commercial Code. When you are doing business with a supplier from one of the countries that has adopted the C.I.S.G. you will be called upon to decide whether you and your company will be better off with the C.I.S.G. applying to your contracts. The alternatives for applicable law to a foreign contract are now these three:

1. The Convention (C.I.S.G.)
2. The law of your home state—the U.C.C. or the sales law if your home state is Louisiana.
3. The law of the land where the foreign supplier is located.

(You and your supplier would also have the opportunity of selecting the law of some other foreign country that has not adopted the C.I.S.G. if the two of you are really searching for an independent law to apply.) As you read through these sections discussing the C.I.S.G., keep asking yourself the question "Am I better off with the U.C.C.?". There is a section at the end of this chapter that summarizes the areas in which the C.I.S.G. differs from the U.C.C. and where C.I.S.G. seems to favor the supplier. Review this section before making your final decision.

One more point to keep in mind. At the time of the writing of this supplement 32 countries have embraced the C.I.S.G. There is the possibility more countries will also get on the band wagon. For those who desire an up-to-date summary of the countries who have ratified this Convention, the place to write is:

>Treaty Section
>United Nations
>New York, N.Y. 10017

The Text of the Convention. The complete text of the Convention for the International Sale of Goods—herein referred to as "The Convention" or "C.I.S.G."—occupies Appendix G of this supplement. Here we will begin our discussion of the law by commenting upon its provisions and noting any major variations from the common law and the Uniform Commercial Code as we discussed them in the original text. The provisions of the C.I.S.G. will be discussed in the numerical sequence of the Articles that make up the law. (The C.I.S.G.'s numerical sequence of "Articles" compares with the numerical sequence of "Sections" in the Uniform Commercial Code.) The Articles of the Convention follow this general outline:

Part I. Sphere of Application and General Provisions. (Articles 1–13).

    Chapter I. Sphere of Application. (Articles 1–6).

    Chapter II. General Provisions. (Articles 7–13).

Part II. Formation of the Contract. (Articles 14–24).

Part III. Sales of Goods. (Articles 25–88).

    Chapter I. General Provisions. (Articles 25–29).

    Chapter II. Obligations of the Seller. (Articles 30–52).
        Section *I*. Delivery of the Goods and Handing over the Documents. (Articles 31–34).
        Section *II*. Conformity of Goods and Third Party Claims. (Articles 35–44).
        Section *III*. Remedies for Breach of Contract by the Seller. (Articles 45–52).

    Chapter III. Obligations of the Buyer. (Articles 53–65).
        Section *I*. Payment of the Price. (Articles 54–59).
        Section *II*. Taking Delivery. (Article 60).
        Section *III*. Remedies for Breach of Contract by Buyer. (Articles 61–65).

    Chapter IV. Passing of Risk. (Articles 66–70).

    Chapter V. Provisions Common to the Obligation of The Seller and the Buyer. (Articles 71–88).
        Section *I*. Anticipatory Breach and Installment Contracts. (Articles 71–73).
        Section *II*. Damages. (Articles 74–77).
        Section *III*. Interest (Article 78).
        Section *IV*. Exemptions. (Articles 79–80).

Section V. Effects of Avoidance. (Articles 81–84).
Section VI. Preservation of the Goods. (Articles 85–88).

Part IV. Final Provisions. (Articles 89–101).

Our discussion of each article will follow the above general structure of the Convention.

PART I.
SPHERE OF APPLICATION AND GENERAL PROVISIONS. (ARTICLES 1–13).

Chapter I. Sphere of Application. Articles 1–6.

Applicability of the Convention and Where Inapplicable. Article 1(1)(a) specifies that the Convention applies to contracts for the sale of goods between parties whose places of business are in different contracting states. (A contracting state would be one who has adopted the Convention.) Article 1(1)(b) expands the coverage of the Convention by providing it is applicable if only one of the contracting parties has their place of business in a contracting state. (Article 10 specifies that if a party does not have a place of business, reference is made to his habitual residence.) However, the United States rejected Article 1(1)(b) when it ratified the balance of the Convention. The ability of a contracting state to make this rejection is found in Article 95.

Article 2 lists six categories of sales of goods that are not covered by the Convention. Chief among these exceptions are sales to consumers. Also exempted are auction sales, sales of ships and vessels, electricity, investment securities, and forced sales by Court order.

The Convention makes it quite clear in Article 3(2) that sales of services also are not covered by the Convention. Where there is a mixture of goods and services in the contract, Article 3(2) specifies that the preponderant part of the contract governs the applicability or inapplicability of the Convention. If the preponderant part of the sale is goods, the Convention is applicable; if the preponderant part of the contract is the furnishing of services, the Convention is not applicable and local law will be utilized. Most courts in the United States follow the rule in Article 3(2) although the Uniform Commercial Code is not specific on that point. Section 2–102 of the Code states affirmatively that the Code applies to "transactions in goods," but no mention is made of mixed contracts for goods and services. It is the interpretations of the courts that make the U.C.C. applicable to mixed contracts where the supplying of services is not the major portion of the contract.

Specific Legal Issues in and Outside the Convention. Article 4 asserts positively that the issues governed by the Convention include "the formation of the contract of sale and the rights and obligations of the seller and the buyer arising from such a contract." The Article goes on to specify that the Convention is not concerned with the validity of the contract (Article 4(a)) and the effect of the property in the goods sold (Article 4 (b)).

Thus Article 4(a) of the Convention tells us it is not concerned with the legality of the subject matter of the contract nor whether the parties possess the necessary authority to obligate their respective corporate organizations. This means that two of the generally accepted essentials of a valid contract—a legal subject matter and capable parties—are not covered by the Convention. (The other two essentials of a valid contract are mutual consideration and agreement of the parties. See page 158 et ff in the original text.) The Convention allows these topics to be controlled by the law of the forum where the case is being tried. That means the controlling law could vary from one country to another.

Strange as it may seem, subject matter and capacity of the parties is not covered by the Uniform Commercial Code either, except by an indirect reference to them in Section 1–103. That section reminds the reader that unless replaced by provisions of the U.C.C., the "principles of law and equity, capacity to contract . . ." etc. shall supplement its provisions. That again means that the law of the forum in a contract between citizens of the United States will be governed by the laws of the state which is holding the trial.

In the United States local law would also control any products liability cases. That is because we basically bring products liability cases as actions in tort and avoid using the breach of contract or warranty approach. This is done for many reasons including a longer period of time in which to file suit, better legal theorems for the plaintiffs, and many other similar justifications. And the Convention follows this same lead. Article 5 states "This Convention does not apply to the liability of the seller for death or personal injury caused by the goods to any person."

"Unless Otherwise Agreed." These words are used in many sections of the Uniform Commercial Code to invite the contracting parties to write the contract in any manner they see fit. There is no need to make the contract conform to the general rules of the Uniform Commercial Code. Most of these rules can be changed by agreement of the parties. A few

U.C.C. rules cannot be changed such as the manner in which a supplier may disclaim an implied warranty or the three months limit on firm offers in Section 2–205 or extending the Code's Statute of Limitations in Section 2–725 beyond the prescribed four years.

Article 6 of the Convention extends a similar invitation to the contracting parties to "make their own law." First off, the Article suggests the entire Convention may be excluded if the parties so desire. Then there is the provision that the parties may "derogate from or vary the effect of any of its provisions." (The Convention brought to your author's attention a new use of the word "derogate." *Webster's New Collegiate Dictionary* and the *Random House Dictionary of the English Language* gave us these definitions: "To lessen; to detract from; to take away a part.") Therefore, subject to one exception, the parties to a contract have a range of agreeing to the exclusion of from 0% to 100% of the text of the Convention, and, subject to the same exception, they are free to amend the effect of any part of it.

The one exception of this freedom to derogate or vary involves Articles 11 and 12. Article 11 does away with the Statute of Frauds, making a contract of sale enforceable without a writing. Article 12, however, permits any country who requires contracts of sale to be concluded in writing to make a declaration that Article 11 does not apply to contracts written by persons having their business within that state. Article 12 states "parties may not derogate from or vary the effect of this Article." (This explains our exception in the previous paragraph.) At this writing Argentina, Byelorussian Soviet Socialists Republic, Chile, China, Hungary, and the Ukranian Soviet Socialist Republic have taken advantage of Article 12. Therefore, if you are contracting with a person whose place of business is in one of these countries, and the two of you have agreed to apply the Convention, the contract must be in writing to be enforceable.

American purchasing officers should note that if you are contracting with someone whose place of business is in a country that has adopted the Convention, including Article 11, and the two of you have agreed to apply the Convention, the contract need not be in writing to be enforceable. This outcome results despite the fact that the U.C.C. requires the contract to be in writing. The Convention would over-ride the U.C.C. provision. One further note on this assumption. When the two of you are contracting the Convention is applicable to the two of you, unless you have *both agreed to avoid the Convention*.

Excluding the Convention. We reminded you previously that one must be very specific in excluding the Convention from an international sales contract since the Convention is now American law. A clause similar to the following should be adequate to substitute Missouri law, for example, in an international contract:

> The parties to this contract agree specifically that the laws of the State of Missouri, except for the Convention for the International Sale of Goods, shall be applicable to the formation and the interpretation and application of this contract.

This phraseology clearly shows that the parties want to exclude the Convention and apply the regular Missouri law to the contract.

Chapter II. General Provisions. Articles 7–13.

Interpretation of the Convention. The Convention provides its own rules for interpretation of itself in Article 7(1). The suggestion is made in this Article to keep in mind regard for three general principles: (1) the Convention's international character, (2) the need for uniformity in application, and (3) the observance of good faith.

> **(1) International character.** One must never forget, including the judiciary hearing cases under the C.I.S.G., that the Convention was written by a diverse group of legal professionals—scholars and practicing attorneys—from many countries. Each co-author no doubt had his or her own pet legal theories and approaches that they would liked to have seen legislated into the law. Compound that fact with the different principles and concepts prevailing in common law, civil law, and Third World countries, and one can readily understand that much of the Convention represents compromises and adjustments from prevailing legal principles in any of the authors' contracting countries. Therefore the Convention itself, in Article 7(1), attempts to give courts some idea of how it should be interpreted, at least in broad-brushed terms. First it reminds the courts of the "international character" of the Convention. Article 7(1) is telling the courts of all nations to interpret the Convention as it is written and not to attempt to bring into such interpretations the prevailing law of the country in which the court is located. Furthermore, the fact that it is international in character should emphasize the uniqueness of the law and that its terms are to be applied as written.
>
> **(2) Uniformity.** The article also reminds the courts that the Convention must be uniformly applied if it is to serve as a body of international law. In the translation from one of the six languages in which it is written, discrepancies could arise. Hopefully these discrepancies will be ferreted out and corrected. This and other types of possible variances will be discovered and corrected only when there is some reporting service developed to

uniformly report all cases decided under the law. Thus far there has been no public notice of such a service being developed.

(3) **Good faith.** Article 7(1) also reminds us of the need to observe good faith in the interpretation of the articles of the Convention. One wonders, though, why good faith in the Convention is limited only to the interpretation process? The Uniform Commercial Code, on the other hand, states in Section 1–203 "Every contract or duty within this Act imposes an obligation of good faith in its performance or enforcement." This is a broader expression of the need and the demand for good faith. It is hoped the courts, in their interpretation of the Convention, will expand its conception of good faith much farther. In some of the articles of the Convention that follow there are bits of evidence of its concern for good faith, such as in communication by the buyer of defects in delivered goods and in the requirement of a party to mitigate damages whenever possible. Would that there was a much more positive expression that good faith was essential to the performance and enforcement of any international contract!

Items Not Covered by the Convention. Article 7(2) gives direction to find answers for legal questions not answered in the Convention itself. The Article reads:

> (2) Questions concerning matters governed by this Convention which are not expressly settled in it are to be settled in conformity with the general principles on which it is based, or, in the absence of such principles, in conformity with the law applicable by virtue of the rules of private international law.

It is the opinion of your author that the two suggestions contained in Article 7(2) on how and where to resolve unanswered questions of matters governed by the Convention are non-productive; indeed they are counter-productive. After piously expressing the need to promote uniformity of interpretation in Article 7(1), the same law tells us in 7(2) to settle unanswered questions "in conformity with the general principles on which it is based . . ." ("It" refers to the Convention, one assumes.) One has difficulty visualizing jurists from tribunals in different countries agreeing in detail on what constitutes so expansive a concept as "general principles" of a term in a major treaty like the Sales Convention. The chances are very narrow that on any one given "unanswered question" two jurists could be found who would agree that the same general principle is applicable—and, even if they did agree on this, the chances of their interpreting that general principle uniformly is even more remote.

The second source that Article 7(2) suggests to find an answer to an unanswered question is in the domestic law of the jusridiction where the case is being tried. This suggestion is consistent with the directions given in Article 4 to use domestic law when a question is not covered by the Convention. Again, though, this obviously raises problems of uniformity in the application of the Convention. "Plugging the hole" under French law, for example, could give a different result than if U.S. law were used to fill the same gap. Where there is a possible wide variety of jurisdictions that might hear a case to be decided under the C.I.S.G., using domestic law can only create manifold interpretations of the same question. The Convention fails in Article 7 to be consistent and to provide properly for uniformity in the law.

Interpreting Statements or Conduct of a Party. One of the essentials of a valid contract is that there must be a "meeting of the minds." The parties must first agree to form a contract and then they must agree on the various aspects of that contract, including the terms and conditions. However, even after this is done, there will be occasions when there will be doubts that the parties did agree to agree because one party will not be in full accord with the other party's interpretation of the words or the conduct. This is not unusual because people do react differently to the same words or to the same phrases. Misunderstandings can and do arise.

In the event a court room trial results from failures of the parties to agree, and the problem stems from the interpretation of the contract or conduct of the party, Article 8 of the Convention provides some ground rules for the tribunal to follow in settling the dispute. Article 8(1) reads:

> (1) For the purposes of this Convention statements made by and other conduct of a party are to be interpreted according to his intent where the other party knew or could not have been unaware what that intent was.

Since questions of interpretation usually arise because the other party was not in agreement with the thinking of the first party, your author believes this article will be of little value in settling such disputes. The other party is contesting the interpretation because he or she had not followed the intent of the party making such statements.

Article 8(2) adds what could be termed the "prudent person" ground rule in divining what is a party's intent. It reads:

> (2) If the preceding paragraph is not applicable, statements made by and other conduct of a party are to be interpreted according to the

understanding that a reasonable person of the same kind as the other party would have had in the same circumstances.

Thus we have here the instruction to determine what should have been his intent if he or she were a reasonable person of the same kind. It appears this is getting closer to determining the intent in an objective fashion.

Article 8(3) gives us the rules of what may be used and considered in determining a party's intent under 8(1) and 8(2):

> (3) In determining the intent of a party or the understanding a reasonable person would have had, due consideration is to be given to all relevant circumstances of the case including the negotiations, any practices which the parties have established between themselves, usage, and any subsequent conduct of the parties.

This is a broad shopping list of sources to be used in interpreting a contract or portions of it, and is something every American purchasing officer should note. Before explaining the implications of the depth of the list of sources, let us first look at the similar provisions in U.S. law. United States contract law has long held to what is known as the "Parol Evidence Rule." Although this rule was not discussed in the original text we should become familiar with it now as well as with Article 8 of the Convention. Parol evidence is the term the legal community applies to verbal, word-of-mouth evidence. The Parol Evidence Rule, loosely stated, is that written contracts cannot be amended or altered by verbal testimony. The contract must be written and complete for this rule to apply. However, if a mistake occurred in the preparation of the written contract, or if fraud were involved in the construction of the contract, for example, verbal testimony can be offered to prove the extent of the original contract. This and other exceptions make the application of the rule somewhat discretionary by the courts.

Section 2–202 of the Uniform Commercial Code is now the governing statute in America on the parol evidence rule. The section is captioned "Final Written Expression: Parol or Extrinsic Evidence." It reads:

> Terms . . . which are otherwise set forth in a writing intended by the parties as a final expression of their agreement with respect to such terms as are included therein may not be contradicted by evidence of any prior agreement or of a contemporaneous oral agreement but may be explained or supplemented
>
> > (a) by course of dealing or usage of trade or by course of performance and

(b) by evidence of consistent additional terms unless the court finds the writing to have been intended also as complete and exclusive statement of the terms of the agreement.

A comparison of Article 8 of the Convention with Section 2-202 shows clearly that Article 8 is much more permissive of what may be used to interpret the communications and conduct of a party. Both the Article and the U.C.C. section allow evidence of course of dealing, usages, and course of performance to be used. And it is certain both would allow evidence of mistake or fraud although it is not explicitly stated. But there the similarity ends. The Convention permits evidence of the "negotiations" while the U.C.C. specifically prohibits the use of "any prior agreement or contemporaneous oral agreement." The Convention's Article 8 also allows evidence of "subsequent conduct of the parties" while the Code is silent on the topic, which makes subsequent conduct inadmissible as evidence.

It is apparent the Convention through its Article 8 clearly intends to allow the parties to make known their interpretation or understanding of the written contract. The Code, on the other hand, attempts to emphasize the written word and carefully limits any attempt to bypass the writing with verbal testimony. Keep in mind though that the court, under the Code, always maintains the discretion to declare the writing "incomplete" and thereby avoid the Parol Evidence Rule.

Nota Bene to the Purchasing Officer. We have devoted space in this supplement to explain the Parol Evidence Rule even though the purchasing officer is not particularly involved in its application in the court room. That is legal counsel's problem. Nonetheless the purchasing officer should discuss this topic with his or her counsel if any foreign sourcing is being done because Article 8 brings us some major changes in law. The legal rules you followed under the Uniform Commercial Code are changed drastically if you bring a purchase contract under the Convention. Article 8 really does away with all the customary limitations on evidence that are imposed by Section 2-202. Now that will not be all "bad" to some American counsel who dislike the limitations imposed by 2-202. On the other hand, many legal counsel not only applaud the limitations of Section 2-202 but insist purchasing officers include a merger clause in their contracts. A "merger clause" is a clause in the contract that brings all prior and contemporaneous agreements into the final written agreement. Such a merger clause should now include a reference to Article 8 if the contract is to be governed by the Convention. Here are suggested procedures for the purchasing officer to follow, depending upon whether you and your legal counsel are "in favor of" or "against" the Parol Evidence Rule:

(1) *You wish to maintain the Parol Evidence Rule even in international transactions.* A clause similar in content to the following should be included in all of your *international* contracts:

> The parties agree that this is the final and complete agreement between them; that it incorporates and replaces all of their prior and current formation statements and communications; and that they further agree that Articles 8(1), 8(2), and 8(3) of the C.I.S.G. are not applicable to this transaction.

The same clause, minus the reference to the Convention articles, should be included in all of your domestic contracts. (Despite the use of the merger clause, the purchasing officer is reminded that the court will continue to have discretionary power to declare whether a contract is complete, or whether mistake and/or fraud entered into its formation. Therefore, use of the merger clause is not absolutely foolproof.)

(2) *You welcome the freedom of evidenciary procedures in the Convention.* You will not require any merger clause in your purchase orders because the full freedom of use of prior, current, and future negotiations will be available to you in international contracts. This is what you have bargained for. Your only concern will be to record and to retain all communications and negotiations with your supplier. Your legal counsel will find them invaluable in the event of a court trial and you need to interpret an item in a contract by Article 8 law. Remember, however, this is only applicable to international contracts under the Convention. Section 2–202 of the Uniform Commercial Code will continue to control your domestic contracts.

Usages and Course of Dealing. Article 8(3) previously discussed, and now Article 9(1), binds the parties to any usages they have agreed to and also by any practices which they have established between themselves. The Uniform Commercial Code also recognizes usage of trade and course of dealing. In Section 1–205(3) both items are said to "supplement or qualify the terms of an agreement." An American purchasing officer should note particularly that Article 9(2) of the Convention makes applicable to any contract a usage widely known in international trade and regularly observed by parties in that type of industry. If the purchasing officer is not adept at international trade usages, it might be prudent to add the following clause to the suggested merger clause above:

The parties further agree they will not be bound by any international trade usages not repeated specifically in this contract despite the provisions of Articles 8 and 9 of the C.I.S.G.

The Need for a Writing. The Statute of Frauds. You are well aware of the fact that Section 2–201 of the Uniform Commercial Code requires that a contract for the sale of goods with a value of $500 or more must be in writing to be enforceable in a court of law. (See original text, pg. 265 et ff.) The Convention has taken the opposite approach in its Article 11. There it is stated that "a contract of sale need not be concluded in writing . . . It may be proved by any means, including witnesses."

American purchasing officers must be alert to this change. An acceptance of an offer need not be in writing. This could result in a contract being formed at the moment the offeree states "I accept your offer" during the negotiations. Modification and termination of contracts by mutual consent also can be accomplished and proven by the verbal route as well as by the more tangible evidence of a writing.

One troublesome exception in the Convention's approach to the enforceability of an oral contract lies in Article 12. Article 12 permits a "Contracting Country" whose domestic law requires a written contract for the sale of goods, to declare "Article 11 inoperative in our country." As an example of this, the United States could have declared Article 11 inoperative in the United States when it adopted the C.I.S.G. The United States had the right to do this under the Convention because of Section 2–201 of the Uniform Commercial Code which requires the written contract. Then any foreign supplier dealing with an American purchasing officer would have to be certain that any resulting contract was in writing to be enforceable. For the sake of consistency, we can be thankful of the fact that the United States *did not* avail itself of the opportunity to make this reservation when it ratified the Convention. But already other countries have made this reservation. If we are dealing with a supplier from any one of these countries, we must remember their verbal commitments are unenforceable. But if we are dealing with the other adoptees of the Convention, then verbal commitments are enforceable. What confusion!

Nota Bene to the Purchasing Officer. Purchasing officers should consider whether eliminating the requirement of a writing is "good" or "bad." There has been considerable discussion of the pros and cons of the Statute of Frauds in the United States. Legal commentaries have long taken stands against the Statute, claiming it is archaic in nature and slows down the pace of business. England, where our Statute of Frauds originated, abandoned it in 1954. Louisiana, the hold-out state on the Uniform Commercial Code, has long permitted oral contracts to be enforced in their courts. However, there are advantages to a writing that particularly serves the purchasing function well. You know what you are entitled to receive from your supplier when it is written. You avoid the age-old argument that begins with one party saying "But you said . . ." Yes, there are advantages of doing business in writing and we think it deeply applies in international trade.

PART II.
FORMATION OF THE CONTRACT. ARTICLES 14–24

(Part II treats of offer and acceptance under the Convention.)

Offer, Articles 14–17.

The Convention's Definition of an Offer. Article 14(1) gives us this definition of an offer:

> A proposal for concluding a contract addressed to one or more specific persons constitutes an offer if it is sufficiently definite and indicates the intention of the offeror to be bound in case of acceptance. A proposal is sufficiently definite if it indicates the goods and expressly or implicitly fixes or makes provision for determining the quantity and the price.

This definition coincides with the one we have been accustomed to using in America except for one major item—"price." Under the Convention, price is an essential term of any valid offer. Contract law in the United States, however, has never been particularly concerned about price and many contracts have been completed without it being mentioned. The prevailing market price at the time of delivery is used in such cases. Section 2–305 of the Uniform Commercial Code has codified this approach. It provides that the parties can conclude a contract even though the price is not settled. Subsection (a) of this section further provides that the price will be presumed to be a reasonable price at the time of delivery. We therefore have a major difference here between the Convention and the Code.

It should be pointed out that Article 55 of the Convention provides for a method of determining price where "a contract has been validly concluded." Some authorities believe Article 55 over-rides Article 14 and would thereby make an offer without a price a valid offer, because it makes provision for determining the price. It is difficult for your author to understand how a contract could be "validly concluded" through the offer and acceptance routine, when the offer by definition is invalid because of the lack of price. This will be explored further when we discuss Article 55 in numerical order. Now, though, the American purchasing officer is advised to make certain any offer being made includes a price. Also it is good advice to make any supplier's offer to you include the price. Without the mention of the price that offer may be only an invitation to do business, and your supplier could withdraw from entering into a contract upon your acceptance.

Other than on the subject of price, the Convention and American contract law are in remarkable agreement as to what constitutes a valid offer. Both emphasize the need for "intent" to make the offer and for the fact that communication of the offer is required before it is valid. Article 14(2) of the Convention continues this agreement with American contract law when it indicates that an advertisement or a catalog is only an invitation to do business. (See page 173 of the original text.)

Article 15(1) of the Convention also follows the American rule that an offer is effective when it reaches the offeree. (See page 167 of the original text.)

Revocable Offers. Article 15(2) leads off our discussion of revocable and non-revocable offers by providing that an irrevocable offer can be withdrawn by the offeror if the withdrawal reaches the offeree before the offer. This has never been codified, to the author's knowledge, in American law. However the result that the offer can be withdrawn seems equitable and provable because the intent to make the offer has disappeared before the time the offer first reaches the offeree.

The Convention codifies a point of law in Article 16(1) that is part of the common law and followed in the United States:

> 16(1) Until a contract is concluded an offer may be revoked if the revocation reaches the offeree before he has dispatched an acceptance.

(To avoid confusion, the reader should take special note of the fact that 16(1) deals with revocation *after* the offer has been received by the offeree. Article 15(2) deals with the situation where the offer is revoked *before* the offeree receives the offer.) That Article 16(1) agrees with the common law in its initial thrust is a well-known fact. The common law permitted an offeror to withdraw an offer at will because no consideration passed from the offeree to the offeror to support keeping the offer open.

The latter portion of Article 16(1) that reads ". . . before he (the offeree) has dispatched an acceptance" also "appears" to support the common law rule that an acceptance becomes effective when it is dispatched. On page 232 of the original text we presented the source of this common law rule in the case of Adams v. Lindsell decided in the English courts in 1818. Since that time most American jurisdictions have held fast to the notion that an acceptance is effective the moment it is mailed. (The only exceptions to this rule have been where the offeror has demanded acceptance to be made by telegram, telephone, or facsimile reproduction.)

Article 16(1) tricks its readers however. You will note that *it does not* state that an acceptance effectively creates a contract at the time it is dispatched. It merely states that an offer may be revoked before an acceptance is dispatched. A less than careful reader *will then assume* from this that a dispatched acceptance creates a contract. But alas! The Convention does not follow this assumption. It simply says that a dispatched acceptance only prevents a revocation from becoming effective. How do we know the Convention intends this? Because reading forward in the Convention we stumble upon Article 18(2) which tells us an acceptance ". . . becomes effective the moment the indication of assent reaches the offeror." Thus, under the Convention, receipt and not dispatch controls when an acceptance becomes effective.

If one follows Article 16(1) of the Convention to a logical conclusion, there is a period of time between the dispatch of an acceptance by the offeree and its receipt by the offeror when there is no contract. However during this time the offeror is bound to his offer because 16(1) will not allow him to revoke it. But during the same period of time the offeree remains free to change his mind about the contract. Article 22 permits an offeree to withdraw an acceptance any time before it becomes effective. In international trade it is not unusual for mail to take a week or more to be delivered. Thus an offeree under the Convention structure has an additional week to speculate on whether prices will increase or decrease. The offeree is free to act in his own best interest during that time. But the offeror is frozen to his offer.

Nota Bene to the Purchasing Officer. If you are the offeror make certain your offer contains a time limit to which you will be held. Then you will not be taken advantage of by an unscrupulous offeree as detailed above. Or if you want even more control over your offer you might consider spelling out "this offer is subject to revocation by the offeror any time before a bona fide acceptance is received."

Firm Offers. Firm offers under the Convention are presented in Article 16(2). The reader will find that the Convention's version of a firm offer differs somewhat from Section 2–205 of the Uniform Commercial Code, where firm offers are defined. One cannot compare Article 16(2) with the common law or general contract law prior to the Code because firm offers were not available to offerees at that time because of the lack of consideration. Here is the way 16(2) reads:

> (2) However, an offer cannot be revoked:
>> (a) if it indicates, whether by stating a fixed time for acceptance or otherwise, that it is irrevocable; or
>> (b) if it was reasonable for the offeree to rely on the offer as being irrevocable and the offeree has acted in reliance on the offer.

Article 16(2)(a) makes any offer a firm offer simply "if it indicates . . . it is irrevocable." The article suggests the offeror might make such an indication of irrevocability "by stating a fixed time for acceptance or otherwise." This simplified approach to the creation of a firm offer is enticing but at the same time dangerous. The use of certain verbiage may create a firm offer as long as it qualifies as "or otherwise," and, then again, the same words may not rise to be a firm offer. One assumes the authors of the Convention are looking more to the intention of the offeror, past practices, usages of the trade, etc., to make an independent judgment in each instance whether the offer is firm. That approach can be faulted only because it leaves the offeror and offeree "up in the air." Was there a firm offer made or not?

The answer to that question in the Convention comes after it is too late—the parties may have acted in the belief that the intention was read properly only to later discover they were incorrect. The law should be more precise so that the parties may read their position without having to resort to the courtroom to determine what was the intent of one or both of the parties. Such an approach does not aid in developing uniformity either, Article 7(1) notwithstanding.

Parties operating under the Uniform Commercial Code, on the other hand, will find a list of requirements they must meet to create a firm offer. Section 2–205 enumerates these conditions that must be met:

1. The offer must be made by a merchant.
2. The offer must be in writing.
3. The offer must be signed.
4. The offer must have a reasonable time limitation not over three months.

5. The offer must give assurance it will be held open.
6. If made on the offeree's form, the assurance must be separately signed by the offeror.

You will note on this list of Code requirements only #5 is matched by Article 16(2)(a) of the Convention. The balance of the list is conspicuous by its absence in the article. There is no need for the offer to be in writing (or signed) to be valid under the Convention and no time limits are imposed. No mention is made in the Convention of offers that are submitted on the offeree's Request for Quotation form. Therefore we must assume there is no need for a second signature by the offeror if the "R.F.Q." specifies that the bidder is submitting a firm quotation. The purchasing officer's only restraint here is his or her own good conscience. Even "good faith" is not mandated—though probably assumed by the Convention.

Nota Bene to the Purchasing Officer. The firm offer provision of the Convention, though loose and free, leaves much to be desired. Evidently it is another example of the many compromises that were made to get the Convention acceptable to all types and groups of countries. Your author suggests that the purchasing officer include in every request for quotation a statement similar to this:

> The supplier is required to submit this proposal to the buyer as a firm offer to sell. Supplier will complete the following statement:
>> Supplier agrees that this is a firm offer to sell and that it will be held firm and not be revocable until _____(date)_____.
>> Buyer has until and including that date to notify supplier of acceptance.
>
> _____
> (signed)

The purchasing officer is also advised that if the supplier insists on using his own form or letterhead to submit his proposal, and includes a clause making it a firm offer, be certain the firm offer is written in a straightforward manner. Do not accept statements that may seem to only "imply" the offer is firm. Make the supplier "stand up and be counted" as submitting a clear-cut, firm offer.

Firm Offers and the Doctrine of Promissory Estoppel. Article 16(2)(b) apparently codifies for international trade the doctrine of promissory estoppel (sometimes termed "detrimental reliance") in the United States. This topic is discussed in the original text on pages 208 et ff. It is pointed out there that an offeror who knew his offer was being relied upon by the offeree could not revoke the offer because he was estopped from doing so since he knew the offeree was depending on that offer. The doctrine of promissory estoppel is not recognized in all of the 50 states. Therefore, if an offeree is doing business in an industry where such protection of an offer is essential, use of the Convention is one way to be certain of the uniformity of application of this doctrine. The Convention would automatically be applied if the transaction occurred in international trade. The Convention, however, cannot be applied to domestic trade unless both parties expressly agree to be bound by it. The purchasing officer is advised to check with legal counsel to determine whether promissory estoppel is recognized under your state's laws.

Rejection of a Firm Offer. The Convention clarifies one issue about firm offers on which the Uniform Commercial Code is silent. Article 17 provides that an irrevocable offer is terminated when a rejection by the offeree reaches the offeror. Therefore, under the Convention, if a firm offer that is guaranteed firm until December 10 is rejected by the offeree on November 20, the offer is dead on November 20. The offeree cannot send an acceptance on December 1 and claim to have formed a contract. There was no offer alive on December 1 for the offeree to accept. By virtue of Article 17 the rejection killed the offer on November 20.

The same question is not covered by the Uniform Commercial Code and one would be required to apply general contract law to get the answer. Of course, under the common law there was no such thing as a "firm offer," unless consideration passed from the offeree to the offeror. If consideration did pass, then it was an option contract. Your author's opinion is that if this were an option contract then the offer would have had to be held open until December 10 unless the offeree signed some type of release, or the offeror returned the consideration and the offeree accepted its return. However, if the offer was a Section 2–205 firm offer where no consideration passed, then the answer would be the same as under the Convention. The offeror would not be bound to the offer after November 20. The rejection would kill the offer when it was communicated to the offeror.

Acceptance, Articles 18–24.

Acceptance Under the Convention. Article 18 gives us the Convention's definition of acceptance and the several methods by which acceptance may be accomplished. In several of these areas the Convention differs from our understanding of acceptance in contract law and under the Uniform Commercial Code. Article 18(1) reads:

> A statement made by or other conduct of the offeree indicating assent to an offer is an acceptance. Silence or inactivity does not in itself amount to acceptance.

It is clear the Convention expects that there will be some positive expression of acceptance coming from the offeree to the offeror. One assumes that means "notice"—notice that the offeree has accepted the offer.

Article 18(2) begins by affirming this need of "notice." It reads "An acceptance of an offer becomes effective at the moment the indication of assent reaches the offeror." Therefore an acceptance is not effective until some notice "indicating assent" reaches the offeror. This changes the rule of the common law as we know and practice it in the United States. Our rule which comes from Adams v. Lindsell in 1818 makes the acceptance effective the moment it is dispatched. The one exception to this occurs if the offeror specified in the offer that the acceptance must be in his or her hands before it becomes effective. Requiring a specific mode of acceptance is the offeror's prerogative as "master of the offer."

The requirement in the Convention of the receipt of the acceptance by the offeror is apparently part of the compromise procedures used in obtaining its adoption. We have already seen in our discussion of Article 16(1) that an offer cannot be revoked after an offeree has dispatched an acceptance. This dispatch of the offer has some legal significance in the Convention when we are involved in the revocation of offers but absolutely no legal power to effect an acceptance. The Convention has embraced 50% of the dispatch theory of acceptance and 50% of the receipt theory.

Does this inconsistency of the Convention make any difference? The offeree, be it the buyer or the supplier, assumes the responsibility of seeing to the safe delivery of the acceptance under the Convention. The offer might lapse before the acceptance arrives if the mail fails to deliver the acceptance in a timely fashion. (This favors the offeror.) However the offer cannot be revoked once the acceptance is dispatched. (This favors the offeree.) Since buyers and suppliers both act as offerees some of the time and act as offerors the other times, the scales of justice hang evenly here. But the inconsistency of the Convention on this point is another annoyance for those who use the Convention.

Article 18(3) is another part of the Convention that is not entirely crisp and clear. Eliminating some of its many words, the Article in effect states that "by virtue of the offer, or as a result of past practices, the offeree may indicate assent by performing an act." The Article provides that the act of the offeree can be accomplished without notice to the offeror and still be effective. The Article provides that the acceptance is effective the moment the act is performed provided it is performed within the time limit of the offer or within a reasonable time after the offer has been received, if it does not contain a time for acceptance. The two acts referred to specifically in the Article are (1) delivery of the goods if the offeree is the supplier, and (2) payment of the price if the offeree is the buyer.

These two avenues of acceptance are commonplace to the American buyer (see page 218 et ff in the original text), so we are not dealing with a new approach to acceptance. But the wording of Article 18(3) imposes a limitation on the use of these two acts of acceptance. For example, the supplier may use the delivery of the goods as acceptance only if:

1. the offer specifically invites delivery; or
2. the parties have established a practice of accepting in this manner; or
3. by usage between the parties or usage as well-known in the trade.

Thus, if there has been no usage or past practice established between the parties on delivery of the goods as a means of acceptance of an offer to buy, the only way it can be used is if the purchasing officer states on the offer to buy "You may accept this offer to buy by delivering the goods." Must we be that specific? The answer is "yes" if one reads the article carefully. Acceptance without notice to the buyer can only be accomplished by delivery of the goods if that action is authorized. The buyer cannot be surprised. When acceptance is accomplished in this manner, it is effective immediately. Without the prior authorization, though, delivery is not an acceptable means of acceptance and the buyer may return the goods.

This vagueness as to what the offeree is to do to accept is not present under the Uniform Commercial Code. Section 2–206 clearly states:

(a) an offer to make a contract shall be construed as inviting acceptance in any manner and by any medium reasonable . . .
(b) an order or other offer to buy goods for prompt or current shipment shall be construed as inviting acceptance either by a prompt promise to ship or by the prompt or current shipment of conforming. . . . goods.

Under the Uniform Commercial Code there is no doubt. The purchase order can be accepted by delivery of the goods or a written notice. Would that the Convention would take a stand instead of using "fiddle faddle" wording!

Nota Bene to the Purchasing Officer. To avoid any problem with the mischievous wording of Article 18, it is suggested a prompt written notice of acceptance be sent for every offer to sell that you accept. For those offers you have held for close to a "reasonable" length of time before you accept, you might consider accepting them with a telegram or facsimile and then confirm with your purchase order. Remember when you are operating under the Convention, acceptance *does not occur* when you dispatch your purchase order. The acceptance must be received by the supplier to be effective. International mail may take a good deal of time to deliver considering how long it takes the U.S. Mail to deliver a domestic letter. In any event, the monkey is on your back to get that acceptance to the supplier on time!

When you use your purchase order as an offer to buy in the international scene insist that the offeree put a written acceptance in your hands by a given date. Further the term on your order should specify "This offer remains revocable until your acceptance is in our hands, Article 16(1) of the C.I.S.G. notwithstanding." By using the latter, you avoid being locked in a firm offer after an acceptance has been dispatched.

Finally, remember that if your purchase order is an offer to buy, you may want delivery to occur as soon as possible. Then give your supplier the word: "This order may be accepted by delivery of the goods. No notice is required."

The "Battle of the Forms." The Convention's Article 19, in three parts, covers the "non-conforming acceptance" as does Section 2–207 of the Uniform Commercial Code. Both cover the same topic and both have three subsections. There the similarity ends.

Article 19(1) codifies the "mirror image" rule of the common law:

> (1) A reply to an offer which purports to be an acceptance but contains additions, limitations, or other modifications is a rejection of the offer and constitutes a counter-offer.

This is a recitation of the common law rule that requires an acceptance to be a mirror image of the offer to be effective. (See page 220 of the original text for a decision of the Minnesota court in 1951 which restated the rule in almost the identical terms of Article 19(1).) Subsection (1) of Section 2–207 of the Code was written in a deliberate attempt to end the legal problems created by application of the mirror image rule in a commercial world of buyers and sellers. The fact that these buyers and sellers have their own pre-printed forms that they use in the attempt to satisfy the mirror image rule creates what is termed the "Battle of the Forms." Article 19(1) does nothing to bring peace to the situation—in fact the article tends to exacerbate the battle.

Article 19(2) does attempt to "wring out" part of the mess created by non-conforming acceptances:

> (2) However, a reply to an offer which purports to be an acceptance but contains additional or different terms which do not materially alter the terms of the offer constitutes an acceptance, unless the offeror, without undue delay, objects orally to the discrepancy or dispatches a notice to that effect. If he does not so object, the terms of the contract are the terms of the offer with the modifications contained in the acceptance.

"But for a few words" this portion of the article seems to reach the same result as subsections (1) and (2) of Code Section 2–207. It makes an acceptance out of a non-conforming acceptance that contains additional or different terms. For it to be able to make the non-conforming acceptance effective, the changes from the offer must not be material—that is, they should not materially alter the offer. The other requirement for it to be operative is that the offeror must consent to the adoption of the inconsistencies contained in the non-conforming acceptance. Without offeror approval, Article 19(2) does not create a contract.

The prerequisites for Article 19(2) to be operative and make a non-conforming acceptance effective are also found in Code Section 2–207(1) and (2). Non-material additional terms become part of the final contract if both parties are merchants under 2–207(2)(b), and under Section 2–207(2)(c) the offeror is given the opportunity to object to any additional terms proposed by the offeror in the non-conforming acceptance. Thus the Convention and the Code, on the topic of non-conforming acceptances are closely aligned in procedure and result on this point, with one difference. "Different" terms in the non-conforming acceptance are treated differently under the two bodies of law. Under the Convention, "additional and different" terms are subject to approval of the offeror, and, if non-material, become part of the final contract. Under the Code only "additional" terms are considered and "different" terms are discarded. Non-material "additional" terms become part of the final contract if the parties are merchants.

The Convention goes the Code one step farther in its consideration of non-conforming acceptances. The Convention provides an official list of items "among other things" that are considered "material" in its Article 19(3):

> (3) Additional or different terms relating, among other things, to the price, payment, quality, and quantity of the goods, place and time of delivery, extent of one party's liability to the other, or the settlement of disputes are considered to alter the terms of the offer materially.

This is an extensive list of terms that are considered "material." It appears that the list covers most of the customary terms and conditions found in the contract for the purchase of goods. And when one considers the possibility of other non-listed terms being included under the phrase used in this article "among other things," we come to the conclusion most terms in a sales contract could be "material" under the Article 19(3) definition. The net result of this is that many non-conforming acceptances with different or additional terms will fall into the category of counter-offers under Article 19(1) because they are not "mirror images" of the original offers.

This result is not all bad if it will make the supplier and the buyer resume negotiations until all differences between the two conflicting contract forms are resolved. This is the true meaning of "agreement" in a contract—both parties understanding and agreeing to their respective duties, commitments, and rights without any qualification or reservation. "We are in total agreement and bound in contract."

Alas and alack! We fear that getting on with the negotiations as outlined above will not always occur to iron out the wrinkles between the purported acceptance and the offer. More than likely the parties will move forward to perform the contract they believe their forms created. The seller will deliver the goods and the buyer will accept and pay the agreed price. If no problems arise after delivery, both parties will close their files on the transaction. The seller made a successful sale and the buyer satisfied a need. So be it.

However, if something goes wrong with the transaction, the parties will get out their files and for the first time, read the form the other party sent. That is when they first realize the papers they interchanged do not form a contract! They did not agree on the term that their dispute involves. And to compound the problem, they also discover that the Convention, unlike the Uniform Commercial Code, has no provision to settle such a dispute. The parties are left to their own devices and the domestic law to find the answer. If the problem arose under the Uniform Commercial Code, the dispute would be settled by Subsection (3) of 2–207. Subsection (3) would say that the conduct of the parties created a contract and the final terms of this contract would be the terms on which the writings of the parties agree, plus any non-material additional terms in the acceptance and then plus any needed supplementary terms from the Code. Those terms on which the parties had differed would be stricken.

Under the Convention and Article 19, the non-conforming acceptance (because of different or additional material terms) becomes a counter-offer. If the supplier is the offeree and delivers the goods after sending the non-conforming acceptance, it is the replay of the old "last shot" principle. The goods are delivered under the supplier's counter-offer, and therefore the supplier's terms will be applied to the contract. The supplier fired the last shot with the counter-offer.

On the other hand, if the buyer is the offeree and after sending a non-conforming acceptance, receives the goods, it could be said that the supplier has accepted the buyer's counter-offer. This conduct puts us right back to the common law problems associated with the mirror image rule.

Such confusion has no place in modern business. The Convention is sadly deficient in not providing a solution to the problems created by the battle of the forms. One deduces that those who wrote the Convention are hoping purchasing officers and suppliers will thoroughly negotiate every term and condition when a purchase is made. Then there can be no non-conforming acceptances. But today—that is wishful thinking!

Nota Bene to the American Purchasing Officer. When operating under the Convention do not allow yourself to get trapped in a battle of the forms situation with a foreign supplier. A possible outcome of such an involvement could conclude by having the terms of your purchase contract determined by a foreign court applying foreign law. There follows here a few suggestions to assist you in avoiding such a trap.

1. Your first line of attack should be to send your foreign supplier two copies of your purchase order. One of these copies is an "Acceptance Copy" which the supplier is to accept by signing it and returning it to you. Your purchase order was an offer to buy when you sent it to the supplier. When it is signed by the supplier, your offer—and your terms and conditions—are accepted by him. (See pages 261-2 of the original text.)

2a. If your foreign supplier will not agree to doing business with you in the manner suggested in #1 above, then include the following clauses on your purchase order if it is an offer to buy:

> The supplier may only accept this offer to buy in writing or by delivering the goods ordered. By doing so the supplier accepts all of the terms and conditions set forth on the face and reverse side of this purchase

order. Any additional or different terms you may propose are rejected, unless they are accepted by the buyer in a separate writing.

2b. You can convert a supplier's offer to sell into an offer to buy from yourself by prefacing the above clause in this manner:

> Notwithstanding any prior negotiations, this is an offer to buy which you may accept only in writing or by delivering the goods ordered. By doing so the supplier accepts all of the terms and conditions set forth on the face and reverse side of this purchase order. Any additional or different terms you may propose are rejected, unless they are accepted by the buyer in a separate writing.

Please remember that in converting a supplier's offer to sell to your own offer to buy you run the risk of losing that supplier's proposition. You have rejected his offer to sell and that extinguishes that offer. The supplier does not have to accept your new offer to buy even though it is identical to his proposal which you just rejected with your purchase order. At this point it is in the supplier's discretion whether to move forward with the transaction or abandon it.

3. A purchasing officer has a better opportunity to control the direction of the negotiations under the Convention from the offeror's position. Article 19(2) for example gives the offeror the opportunity to approve or reject additional or different terms that appear in the acceptance. In addition the common law maxim, "The offeror is master of the offer," is generally recognized and does give the party in that position some opportunity to control the procedures. Should the purchasing officer be forced to be the offeree in the transaction, however, there is less that can be done to control your destiny. You are generally at the mercy of the offeror-supplier under the Article 19(2) approval procedure plus the fact that as the supplier in the transaction, the offeror can set into motion the "conduct" procedures by delivering the goods. That is always the first step in firing the "last shot."

The buyer-offeree can utilize a conditional acceptance clause to keep some semblance of control over the situation. Following is a typical conditional acceptance clause:

> This acceptance of your offer to sell is subject to your acceptance of the additional and different conditions shown on the face and reverse side of this purchase order. By delivering the goods ordered, you accept these different and additional terms from those shown on your offer to sell.

If your supplier delivers the goods to you after receiving this conditional acceptance, you have gotten your terms and conditions included in the contract.

However, once more you are risking loss of a favorable offer to sell.

Your supplier has every right to throw your conditional acceptance in the waste basket and sell the goods to another customer. That is the chance you take when you use a conditional acceptance.

4. If the purchasing officer does not want to risk this possible "walk away from it" by the supplier, you are at the bottom of the list of your alternatives to getting the goods on your terms and conditions. Now it is incumbent for you to decide how bad it would be for your organization to make the purchase under the supplier's terms and conditions. Attempt to negotiate any troublesome differences with the supplier. (As a matter of practicality, 90% of all terms and conditions are for the convenience and general good humor of the proposer and his or her counsel. Their use will cost the buyer nothing.)

Failing to "negotiate out" any unwelcome terms, your final option is to find another supplier. Alternate sourcing is always your last, but not insignificant, opportunity.

Some Acceptance "Housekeeping" Items. Articles 20 through 24 give us some of the rules of the Convention concerning acceptance. Article 20(1) states that a period of time fixed by the offeror for acceptance begins to run from the time (a) a telegram is handed in for dispatch, (b) the date is shown on a letter, or if none, (c) the date that is shown on an envelope. Article 20(2) states that holidays and non-business days during an acceptance period are counted. Only if a notice of acceptance cannot be delivered on the last day it is due because that is a holiday or a non-business day, does the period get extended to the first business day that follows.

Articles 21(1) and 21(2) deal with acceptances that are late. Both sections give options for consideration of the late acceptance to the offeror. Article 21(1) gives the offeror the option to regard a late acceptance as effective if he promptly notifies the offeree orally or in writing. Article 21(2) provides that if a late acceptance shows that if its transmission had been normal it would have reached the offeror in due time, it is effective *unless* the offeror, without delay, informs the offeree orally or by writing, that he considers the offer to have lapsed. This is in line with the Convention's approach to placing on the shoulders of the offeree the responsibility for the successful delivery of an acceptance.

Article 22 gives the offeree the right to withdraw an acceptance if it reaches the offeror before or at the same time as the acceptance would have been effective. Article 23 officially confirms that a contract is concluded when the acceptance becomes effective. The same pronouncement is contained in Article 18(2).

Article 24 defines when an offer or an acceptance officially "reaches" the addressee. The Article says this occurs when it is delivered to the addressee personally, to his mailing address, or to his place of habitual residence if he has no place of business. Any one of these three alternates constitute adequate delivery. This is similar to the definition of "receives" in Code Section 1–201 (26)(a) and (b). Article 24 concludes Part II of the Convention entitled "Formation of the Contract."

PART III.
SALE OF GOODS. ARTICLES 25–88

(Part III governs the rights and duties of the buyer and the supplier.)

Chapter I. General Provisions. Articles 25–29.

Fundamental Breach. This is a new term for American purchasing officers. The term is an important concept in Convention law. It is part of the system of remedies in the Convention.

"Fundamental breach" is a serious breach of contract in the Convention. The Convention recognizes more than one type of breach of contract because Article 25 defines a fundamental breach in this manner:

> A breach of contract committed by one of the parties is fundamental if it results in such detriment to the other party as substantially to deprive him of what he is entitled to expect under the contract, . . .

The only clue given in this definition on how to differentiate between a fundamental breach and other types of breach is that a fundamental breach "substantially deprives him of what he is entitled to expect." No definition is given of the word "substantially"—in fact, there are no word definitions given anywhere in the Convention. One can only assume that the phrase implies that the detriment to the other party must be really severe to merit the classification of a fundamental breach.

The degree of severity of breach necessary to be classified as fundamental under the Convention probably is comparable to the meaning of the same word "substantially" as used in Section 2–608(1) of the Uniform Commercial Code. The topic in the Code section is "revocation of acceptance" which is discussed on pages 370–72 of our original text. Section 2–608(1) allows the buyer to revoke his acceptance of the goods under certain circumstances. The section reads as follows:

> (1) The Buyer may revoke his acceptance of a lot or commercial unit whose non-conformity substantially impairs its value to him if he has accepted it . . .

You will recall that in the Code the buyer operates under the "perfect tender" rule when first receiving the goods. The buyer may reject the goods "if they fail in any respect to conform to the contract" when they are first delivered. But after the goods are once accepted by the buyer they can be returned to the seller under the Code only if the defects discovered after the original acceptance "substantially impairs their value to him."

Both the Convention and the Code use the word "substantially" to indicate a degree of severity. The Code uses it as a gradation of non-conformity of goods delivered by the supplier. The use of the word in Article 25 applies to deficient actions by either the buyer or the seller. However, nowhere is the word defined in either body of law and the decision would be made only in a lawsuit by the trier of fact. This makes it difficult for one who needs to know the precise meaning before taking action. One would like to determine it without the benefit of a lawsuit. All that can be said is for each purchasing officer confronted with the problem to be realistic in his or her appraisal of the severity of the breach.

"Foreseeability" is also included in Article 25 as one of the conditions for the breach to be fundamental. Article 25 concludes from that shown above with this:

> . . . unless the party in breach did not foresee and a reasonable person of the same kind in the same circumstance would not have foreseen such a result.

Thus a court, when determining whether a breach of contract is fundamental, must first ascertain "How bad was the breach?" If the court concludes it was "pretty bad" and deprived the aggrieved party of what he was entitled to expect under the contract, then it must go to the second question "Could the party who breached have foreseen what happened?" If the party who breached did not foresee what happened, and if the reasonably prudent person also could not have foreseen the event occurring, then one assumes there would be no fundamental breach. Then one must assume the injured party must be content with a smaller amount of damages or some other consolation because of the happening. This does not appear to bring a fair result to the party who is injured by the other party substantially breaching his or her obligations under the contract.

As a matter of interest there is no such requirement in the Code

Section 2–608 for the supplier to have foreseen the substantial impairment of value. If the impairment occurs, the supplier is responsible and answerable for damages or must accept the return of the goods. It is the author's opinion that this portion of the Convention is written "pro" supplier.

Avoidance of the Contract. We mentioned at the beginning of this discussion on the Convention that we would discuss its provisions in the numerical order they are presented. Article 25, defining fundamental breach, is shown as one of the general provisions that is applicable to several sections in Part III which covers the rights and duties of both buyers and sellers. It is possible for a buyer as well as a supplier to commit a fundamental breach under the Convention. We will discuss this later as the numerical progression gets to those articles.

And along this line of numerical progression, we now come to Article 26, again in the general provisions chapter. It surprises the reader by stating:

> A declaration of avoidance of the contract is effective only if made by notice to the other party.

The authors of the Convention assume we all know what is "avoidance of a contract." Using our command of the English language, we would assume avoidance implies "side-stepping" the contract or "getting out of our obligations of the contract." If we look forward in the Convention to Article 81, we get a better understanding of the term:

> (1) Avoidance of the contract releases both parties from their obligations under it, subject to any damages which may be due. Avoidance does not affect any provision of the contract for the settlement of disputes or any other provision of the contract governing the rights and obligations of the parties consequent upon the avoidance of the contract.

Thus the parties are released from any further duties under the contract if the contract is avoided. Perhaps we should add, however, that the parties are still obligated to pay damages that are due, and, if the contract has been partially or wholly performed, the other party is required to make restitution. Restitution is provided for in Article 81(2).

Back to our sequential study of the Convention, we note that Article 26 makes it quite clear that notice is essential to make an effective declaration of avoidance. "We can live with this requirement of notice" because a purchasing officer is accustomed to several sections in the Uniform Commercial

Supplement to Chap. 23 / Purchasing from Foreign Vendors

Code where notice is essential and, sometimes, penalties for failure to notify are particularly severe. Take for example Section 2–602(1) which states:

> (1) Rejection of goods must be within a reasonable time after their delivery or tender. It is ineffective unless the buyer seasonably notifies the seller.

Section 2–605(1) spells out the penalty for failure of the notice to the seller stating the defects that occasioned the rejection of the goods:

> (1) The buyer's failure to state in connection with rejection a particular defect which is ascertainable by reasonable inspection precludes him from relying on the unstated defect to justify rejection or to establish breach.

We gather from this that the notice given by the buyer to the supplier upon rejection must detail the defect that caused the buyer to reject. One assumes this is to give the supplier the opportunity to cure. (See pages 364–5 in the original text.) Section 2–608(2) is the section that requires notice to the supplier if the buyer revokes acceptance of the goods. Thus the Uniform Commercial Code parallels the Convention in requiring the buyer to notify the supplier promptly when something is wrong with the delivered goods. Probably the principal reason a buyer would seek avoidance of the contract is because of the failure of the goods to meet the contract description although the buyer could be concerned about the failure of the goods to be delivered seasonably. Keep in mind that under the Convention, avoidance of the contract may be an act of the supplier as well as the buyer. Avoidance of the contract will be discussed in more detail in succeeding sections.

When a Notice Is Effective. We must be careful to note that we are now discussing Part III of the Convention. Some of Part III's housekeeping rules are different than those in Part II. You will recall that in Article 18(2) of Part II the "receipt rule" is applied to acceptances. The offeror must be in receipt of an acceptance before it is effective. Now comes Article 27 in Part III where the "dispatch rule" is applied to notices we have been discussing as well as to other notices and communications required in most of Part III. The Article says that a delay in transmission of a notice or its failure to arrive does not deprive the party sending it of the right to rely upon it. Clearly Part III is embracing the "dispatch rule"—once mailed, it is effective. However, be on the alert because not all notices are treated in that manner.

Article 27 has a preamble that reads "unless otherwise expressly provided in this Part of the Convention . . ." We will call your attention to variations in the "dispatch rule" in Part III.

Applicability of the Remedy of Specific Performance. These first few articles that comprise Chapter I of Part III cover topics on a random basis and are in no apparent order. You are reminded these are General Provisions that relate to subsequent articles of the succeeding chapters of Part III.

One of the major remedies offered by the Convention is that of specific performance. We will discover later that the remedy is available to both parties under the Convention—in Article 46 for the buyer and in Article 62 for the supplier. One suspects that specific performance is a favorite remedy in some civil law and Third World countries. Common law countries recognize the remedy but limit its use. In the United States we much prefer to have monetary damages as a remedy. It is quicker and more direct. However, many countries opposed the inclusion of specific performance when the Convention was written, but its proponents won the battle.

A typical "olive branch" is offered to dissident countries who are not fond of the specific performance remedy. The olive branch is in the form of an article—Article 28—and is included here in the General Provisions of Chapter I. Article 28 provides that "a court is not bound to enter a judgment for specific performance unless the court would do so under its own law in respect of similar contracts of sale not governed by this Convention." You will note that the article does not direct the court to apply its own domestic law as it pertains to specific performance, but it simply states the court is "not bound" to order specific performance if its domestic law is different than the Convention.

Application of Article 28 will leave the parties in a quandary in many instances. One cannot be certain what a particular court will do when it finds itself "not bound" to follow the Convention. It seems a court would have four options: (1) apply the law of the Convention; (2) apply the law of the buyer's country; (3) apply the law of the supplier's country; and (4) apply the court's own domestic law if different from the first three alternatives. Which route the court will choose may seriously affect one or both parties' rights.

If one feels threatened by this, finding protection is no easy matter. A purchasing officer could see to it that a forum clause is included in the contract and the named forum would be the state court where his or her company is located. But there is no guarantee your own state court might not be inclined to apply the law of France where your supplier's office and manufacturing plant are located. Perhaps a clause whereby both parties agree not to seek the remedy of specific performance should a disagreement occur, might be more effective. When all the cards are down, not very many parties want the remedy of specific performance anyhow. While the civil law writers may be inclined to push for the remedy, it remains to be seen whether their constituents in the business world feel the same way. Finally, there is always the option of writing your contract outside of the Convention. That leaves you to the devices of the Uniform Commercial Code and its provisions for specific performance by the buyer or by the supplier!

Modification of the Contract. This is one topic that both the Convention and the Uniform Commercial Code agree upon. Article 29(1) of the Convention provides that a contract may be modified or terminated by the mere agreement of the parties. One assumes "mere agreement" means without having consideration passing. Section 2–209(1) of the Code does the same and asserts positively that no consideration is necessary to modify a contract.

The second subsections of Article 29 and Section 2–209 provide that parties who agree in their original contract that all modifications must be in writing cannot otherwise modify such a contract. Any modification must then be in writing and signed by both parties.

Nota Bene to the Purchasing Officer. One should consider having a clause to this effect in every international contract where the Convention is to be applied. Remember there is no need to have a writing for a contract to be enforceable under the Convention. An oral agreement is valid and enforceable. To make certain there is no opportunity for "misunderstood oral discussions" with foreign vendors, we believe it is prudent to include a clause such as "All modifications or any termination of this contract must be in writing and signed by both parties signing this original contract."

Chapter II. Obligations of the Seller. Articles 30–52.

This chapter spells out the specific obligations of the supplier in contracts for the sale of goods. It begins with Article 30 which repeats the customary obligations of the seller to: (1) deliver the goods, (2) hand over any documents relating to them, and (3) transfer the property (title) in the goods to the buyer. Section *I* of Chapter II following, discusses the first two of these obligations.

Section I. Delivery of the Goods and Handing over of Documents. Articles 31–34.

Delivery Terms. The Convention does not offer the variety of delivery terms as does the Uniform Commercial Code in Sections 2–319 to 2–324. It is apparent the Convention depends first on the parties to make the necessary provisions for delivery in their contract. And although not mentioned in the text of the Convention, one may safely assume that the predominant guide for acceptable delivery terms is the group known as "Incoterms." Incoterms has just been revised. The revised group of terms became effective June 1, 1990. Incoterms is a set of 13 different delivery terms that have a standard of meaning in international trade. These terms were developed, standardized, and promulgated by the International Chamber of Commerce. The 13 terms have a wide range from "Ex-Works" which means the seller makes the goods available at his factory or warehouse to "Delivered Duty Paid, Buyer's Receiving Dock, U.S.A.," which requires the supplier to put the goods at the designated destination. "Ex-Works" represents the supplier's minimum obligation and risk under delivery, and of course "Delivered Duty Paid" imposes the most obligations and expenses, and the most risk on the supplier. The other terms listed have intermediate duties and obligations assigned to the parties. Purchasing officers involved in foreign sourcing should have a copy of *Incoterms*. It can be obtained from:

> The I C C Publishing Company
> 156 5th Avenue
> New York, N.Y. 10010

The Convention relies heavily on the contract between the buyer and the supplier to spell out the details of the delivery arrangements, or to select an Incoterm. In a purchase from a foreign supplier there are many details to be agreed upon that are not customarily found in a domestic purchase. (See pages 397–8 in the original text for a general description of these types of items to be considered.) The necessary licenses, duties, and taxes must be paid at the exporting country's boundary; if passage is required through a third country at both that country's entry and exit border, the same routine must be followed; and, finally, this routine is again necessary at the importing country's border. It is a tedious process that must be attended to by one or both of the parties to the contract, and by their import and/or export agents.

Absent clear-cut terms in the agreement, or if there are vagaries requiring interpretation in the agreement, the Convention has drawn a few rules that can be applied. Article 31(a) covers the supplier's duty if a shipment contract is involved requiring the supplier to send the goods on their way:

> If the seller is not bound to deliver the goods at any other particular place, his obligation to deliver consists:
>
> (a) if the contract of sale involves carriage of the goods—in handing the goods over to the first carrier for transmission to the buyer.

One assumes the "carrier" mentioned in this article is the equivalent of a common carrier; that is, one capable of issuing a straight or order bill of lading at the time it accepts the goods from the supplier. Left "hanging" by this article is the question whether export licenses and fees must be satisfied by the buyer or the supplier. One would hope the two parties to the contract would be sufficiently cognizant of the need to make these arrangements and provide for the satisfaction of them in the original contract of sale. There will probably be times when such arrangements will be not made, and we then are left with the need to assign that responsibility. The Convention gives us no help. One can only suppose that the answer would be to lay such responsibility in the lap of the supplier. Since the supplier is the one who must hand over the goods to the carrier, it is doubtful the carrier would accept such goods for delivery to a foreign destination and issue a bill of lading unless all licenses, duties, and fees have been provided for by the shipper. Since the supplier is the shipper, we must assume he is left with this duty.

Article 32 requires the supplier to make certain shipping arrangements. 32(1) requires the supplier to clearly identify the goods shipped either by marking the goods, or identifying them in the shipping documents, or by giving the buyer notice of the consignment, specifying the goods. Article 32(2) places responsibility on the supplier for making proper contracts for the transportation of the goods, and to make any necessary special provisions for their transportation. This would include proper refrigeration if needed or protection against freezing and similar special provisions. This is similar to Section 2–504(a) and (b) of the Uniform Commercial Code. Article 32(3) calls for the cooperation of the seller if the buyer requests information and assistance in providing for insurance while the goods will be in transit. This would not be necessary if the original contract required the supplier to provide carriage insurance.

Time of Delivery of Goods. Article 33 (a) and (b) tells the supplier to deliver the goods on the date or within the period of time provided in the contract. If the contract does not specify the time for delivery, Article

33(c) says the goods must be delivered within a reasonable time after the contract is concluded. It is suggested that all contracts, whether international or domestic, contain some instructions for delivery and for the time of delivery. It is also suggested that phrases such as "deliver as soon as possible" or "please rush" are useless. Make a point to establish a specific date for delivery of the goods and add the phrase that "time is of the essence." (See pages 350–2 of the original text.)

Documents Required by the Contract. Article 34 provides that the supplier must hand over any required documents relating to the goods at the time and the place stated in the contract. If the documents are delivered ahead of schedule and there are defects in them, the seller may cure any such lack of conformity. However, in such cases, the article provides that the buyer retains his rights to any damages for which he might be entitled.

Section II. Conformity of the Goods and Third Party Claims. Sections 35–44.

Warranties in the Convention. The word "warranty" does not appear in the Convention. Nonetheless there are a full set of what we know as warranties contained in Article 35. The writers of the Convention elected to avoid the use of the term but provided the buyer with the same group of quality assurances under the caption of "Obligations of the Seller." Article 35(1) begins the grand pronouncement by reminding the supplier to live up to his contract:

> (1) The seller must deliver goods which are of the quantity, quality, and description required by the contract and which are contained or packaged in the manner required by the contract.

The "quality and description required by the contract" is what the Uniform Commercial Code elects to term "express warranties." Section 2–313(1)(b) states that an express warranty by the seller is "Any description of the goods made part of the basis of the bargain." However in 2–313(1)(a) The Code also states that "Any affirmation of fact or promise by the seller . . ." is also an express warranty. This type of express warranty is not specifically mentioned in the Convention. One assumes that such affirmations of fact and promises made by the supplier would be construed as part of the obligation of the seller under the Convention but we cannot allow ourselves to be lulled into believing this when we have the opportunity to make it a certainty.

The purchasing officer must make certain such affirmations and promises that he has relied on become part of the written contract. This will leave no doubt but that they will then be enforced as an obligation of the supplier under Article 35(1).

Article 35(2) gets on with what might be termed the implied obligations of quality placed on the supplier. This sub-article begins with the preamble "Except where the parties have agreed otherwise." This should remind the purchasing officer to beware of disclaimers by the supplier from responsibility for quality. Disclaimers of warranties (or of supplier's obligations under the Convention) are discussed below. However, you will note this preamble to Article 35(2) is the closest mention of a disclaimer in the Convention. There are no rules given on how to do it or instructions to make it "conspicuous" as in the Code. Full reliance for disclaimers is placed on the wording of the contract.

Each of the four sub-articles under Article 35(2) listed below begins with this full preamble:

> Except where the parties have agreed otherwise, the goods do not conform with the contract unless they:

It is interesting to note that this preamble ties each of the following four sub-articles to the contract itself. A breach of any of the four conditions will constitute a breach of contract.

> Article 35(2)(a): Are fit for the purposes for which goods of the same description would ordinarily be used;

This implied obligation attached to the seller's goods closely resembles the implied warranty of merchantability under the Code. (Section 2–314(2)(c).

> Article 35(2)(b): Are fit for any particular purpose expressly or impliedly made known to the seller at the time of the conclusion of the contract, except where the circumstances show that the buyer did not rely, or that it was unreasonable for him to rely, on the seller's skill and judgment;

This article is almost identical to the Uniform Commercial Code Section 2–315. The Convention seems to be less restrictive in applying this obligation than the Code because it states the particular purpose need be expressly or impliedly made known to the supplier. The Code phraseology is "Where the seller at the time of contracting has reason to know any particular purpose for which the goods are required . . ." Other than that slight difference which would make it easier for the buyer to establish a breach, the two sections are identical.

> Article 35(2)(c): Possess the qualities of goods which the seller has held out to the buyer as a sample or model;

This sub-article reverts back to what we know as express warranties under the Code and suggests the goods supplied must possess the qualities of any sample or model submitted. This is Section 2–313(c) of the Code, with the one difference that the Code refers to "any sample or model which is made part of the basis of the bargain." You will note Article 35(2)(c) refers to ". . . qualities of goods which the seller has held out to the buyer as a sample or model." Quite often it is the buyer who has the sample and submits it to the supplier to be matched. Will the fact that it is the buyer's sample make any difference in the supplier's obligation to match its qualities? The Uniform Commercial Code accepts any sample—the buyer's or the seller's. And it makes an express warranty that the sample's quality aspects will be matched by what the seller delivers. The same result should be reached under the Convention. It is the seller's obligation to match the qualities of the buyer's sample if he contracts to do so. This makes it a seller's obligation under Article 35(1)—a part of the contract requirements. The seller has taken the buyer's sample and contracted to supply copies of that sample. Matching the qualities of the buyer's sample then is the seller's obligation under the Convention. It is not an implied obligation under 35(2)(c) but a contract obligation under 35(1).

> Article 35(2)(d): Are contained or packaged in the manner usual for such goods, or, where there is no such manner, in a manner adequate to preserve and protect the goods.

This implied obligation of the seller to properly package the goods is unique—and welcome. Section 2–314(2)(e) of the Code requires the seller to adequately package and label the goods "as the agreement may require." This is part of the section describing the attributes of merchantable goods. Absent any provision in the contract, the seller has no obligation under the Code to adequately package. All the seller needs to do is contain the goods in some manner to be able to deliver them. The Convention, under Article 35(2)(d) makes proper packaging an implied duty of the supplier in every instance there is a sale. This is a "plus" for the Convention insofar as the buyer is concerned.

The question might be asked about quality statements that appear on labels or on containers when one is working under the rules of the Convention. Under the Uniform Commercial Code, the implied warranty of merchantability makes the promises and affirmations of fact made on the container or label implied warranties. The goods contained in such packages must conform to these representations. This is Section 2–314(2)(f). The Convention, on the other hand, is silent on the subject of promises on labels or containers. Would such affirmations have any value to a buyer seeking to hold his or her supplier to the quality assurances printed thereon?

We think that it does if one uses the Convention's rules of evidence. When we were discussing Article 8(3), we called your attention to the fact that "any subsequent conduct of the parties" was allowable evidence under the Convention to prove the intent of the parties. It appears to your author that affirmations of fact or promises on the containers or the labels are admissible evidence to determine the extent of the supplier's quality responsibilities. However, to make use of this evidence possible, there cannot be a merger clause confining the court to use of the final written contract only.

One final reminder for purchasing officers seeking to establish the equivalent of warranties under the Convention. All the details of a contract do not have to be in writing under the Convention to be enforceable in a court of law. This is true of warranties as well as other details. They may be proven by verbal testimony. Oral statements made by the representatives of the supplier can become the equivalent of warranties by being made part of the contract.

Disclaimer of Warranties Under the Convention. As mentioned previously, nowhere in the Convention is there any mention of how a supplier is to disclaim any particular obligations (warranties) imposed by Article 35(2). (A supplier cannot disclaim any obligations to deliver goods as described in the contract. These are the equivalents of express warranties.) Of course, Article 35(3) does give the seller an excuse from any of the implied obligations in Article 35(2)(a to d):

> . . . if at the time of the conclusion of the contract the buyer knew or could not have been unaware of such lack of conformity.

With characteristic lack of clarity and explanation, the Convention "drops this one on us" and goes no farther. There is no indication from the Convention of what situations the writers had in mind with this pronouncement. Probably this is intended to cover the situation where a buyer has had an opportunity to inspect, noted the item's defects, and, notwithstanding, elected to complete the purchase. It could also cover the situation where the product is being offered for sale on an "as is" basis, or under other circumstances that are spelled out in Code Section 2–316(3). In any event it is apparent that Article 35(3) is designed to relieve the supplier of his obligations under Article 35(2) when there is an indication the buyer has assumed part of these obligations. In short, the buyer is taking a calculated risk by completing the purchase. Please note that Article 35(3) applies only to the implied obligations of the supplier stated in Article 35(2). It does not touch the express type of warranty by description in the contract under Article 35(1).

There is only one other section in the Convention that tells how a supplier may transfer such quality obligations and risk to the buyer, and that is the preamble phrase in Article 35(2)—"Except where the parties have agreed otherwise . . ." This is the invitation to the supplier to attempt to contract away the usual risks of the Convention associated with warranting the product he is selling. It is the invitation to get the buyer to assume the risks associated with not warranting the product by the implied obligations imposed by Article 35(2).

Nota Bene to the Purchasing Officer. It makes no difference whether it is the Uniform Commercial Code's Section 2–316(2) telling the supplier the proper method of disclaiming implied warranties, or if the supplier must simply say in the contract with the buyer "I disclaim all of my implied obligations stated in Article 35(2) of the Convention." The result is the same—the risks are transferred to the buyer.

We have seen that there is a full set of the equivalent of express and implied warranties in the Convention. Recovery of all types of damages is also provided, including consequential damages that could be reasonably foreseen. Therefore, the purchasing officer is advised that any proposed disclaimers of warranties and/or limitations on damages are designed to take away from you and your organization benefits the Convention offers. It is to your advantage to strongly resist accepting any of such restrictions of your rights that might be proposed for inclusion in the contract with your supplier. Read carefully! Think carefully before you agree to such limitations and disclaimers!

Extent of Supplier's Quality Obligations. Article 36 contains two general rules concerning the period of time the seller is responsible for the quality of the goods.

Article 36(1) contains the well-known rule that the seller is responsible for any lack of conformity that exists in the goods at the time the risk passes to the buyer. The article reminds one that this responsibility continues even though the non-conformity is not discovered until after the risk has passed to the buyer. This obligation of the supplier extends not only to the non-conformity of the goods from the contract description that existed when the goods were appropriated to the contract, but also to any damage incurred in transportation of the goods to the point where the risk passes to the buyer. This is similar to the Code rules.

Article 36(2) simply reminds the supplier that the obligation for such non-conformity continues as long as the guarantee in the contract continues.

Supplier's Right to Cure. Article 37 is the first of two articles giving the supplier the right to cure defects in delivered goods. This article deals with the right to cure goods that were delivered before the required delivery date. (Article 48, to be discussed later in numerical order, covers cure after the delivery date.) This article suggests four methods by which the supplier may attempt to cure a non-conforming delivery:

a. Deliver any missing part.
b. Make up any deficiency in the quantity of goods supplied.
c. Deliver replacement goods for those deficient.
d. Remedy any lack of conformity in the goods delivered by repair.

Article 37 has one proviso in it that keeps the supplier's right to cure before delivery from being absolute. The proviso reads ". . . provided that the exercise of this right does not cause the buyer unreasonable inconvenience or unreasonable expense." Thus the purchasing officer can stop the supplier's attempts to cure even before delivery was due if he finds the "cure process" unreasonably interferes with his operations. In this respect the Convention rule is more restrictive on the supplier than is the Uniform Commercial Code. Under the Code, the supplier's right to cure before delivery is due is a "right" and cannot be interfered with by the buyer. See Section 2-508(1) of the Uniform Commercial Code.

Article 37 concludes with a general statement that the buyer retains the right to claim damages, notwithstanding the supplier's attempts to cure. We shall see later that the attempt to cure, if successful, denies the buyer the right to avoid the contract. All it states here is that it will not deny him the right to claim damages.

Nota Bene to the Purchasing Officer. One of the obstacles purchasing officers face in the Convention is that there is a strong effort to make a delivery "hold" regardless of the non-conforming condition of the goods.

The authors of the Convention recognize that much time, effort, and cost is involved in transportation of the goods from the supplier to the buyer in the international contract. Return of the goods, in most cases, would be sheer economic waste. It is much more practical to have the buyer "make do" with what was delivered—perhaps with some money allowance. This may be the reason why the right to damages clause is included in this article. Even though an attempt to cure might not be entirely successful to bring the goods to the condition demanded by the contract, it could make them useable enough to force the buyer to keep them and be satisfied by accepting some money damages.

Should a purchasing officer not be willing to accept goods under such conditions as above, it is suggested that the contract be taken out of the Convention and the Uniform Commercial Code be substituted as the applicable law. Remember, under the Uniform Commercial Code the buyer has the perfect tender rule going for him and can insist upon the delivery of goods that fully comply with the contract.

Time for Inspection of the Goods. The buyer is required to inspect the goods "within as short a period as practicable under the circumstances." This is Article 38(1). The second section in this article permits inspection to be accomplished after the goods have been delivered. The third section allows inspection to occur after the goods have arrived at their final destination, following redirection or redispatch by the buyer. This latter right applies only if the seller knew of the possibility the buyer might transship at the time of the conclusion of the original contract.

Notice of Non-Conformity of the Goods. Article 39(1) of the Convention should be placed before every purchasing officer:

> (1) The buyer loses the right to rely on a lack of conformity of the goods if he does not give notice to the seller specifying the nature of the lack of conformity within a reasonable time after he has discovered it or ought to have discovered it.

A supplier is entitled to assume that a sale is completed within a reasonable time after he has accomplished delivery. Further, the supplier is entitled to a prompt notice of any defects in the goods so he has a reasonable opportunity to "cure" the defects. It is with these thoughts in mind that Article 39(1) is included in the Convention.

You will note that the notice (1) must specify the lack of conformity the goods suffer, and (2) must be sent within a reasonable time after being discovered. The penalty the buyer suffers for failure to report the defect is that he or she is not entitled to rely on the defect by way of affirmative action against the supplier, or in defense of a supplier action against the buyer. It forces the buyer to act as if the goods were conforming from the beginning if no notice is given to the supplier. The consequences for failure to notify are severe.

However, the article is no more harsh on the buyer than the provisions in the three sections of the Uniform Commercial Code on the same topic. In the event of a rejection of goods, Section 2–602(1) requires that the rejection must be made within a reasonable time after the goods have been delivered. The rejection is ineffective unless the buyer seasonably notifies the seller. Section 2–605 requires the buyer to list all the defects ascertainable in the non-conforming goods that are rejected. Failure to list a defect precludes the buyer from relying on it to justify rejection. Section 2–607 applies after the buyer has accepted the goods and then discovers a defect. The buyer must then notify the seller within a reasonable time after discovering the breach. If the buyer fails to notify the seller he is barred from any remedy. Thus the Code as well as the Convention requires strict adherence to the need of notice to the supplier by the purchaser. And in both bodies of law, the penalty to the buyer is severe if he or she fails to notify promptly— that is, within a reasonable time.

Article 39(2) places an overall limitation of two years on the buyer to give notice, if that can be considered a reasonable time. That limit could be extended too, if the supplier has given the buyer a warranty that runs longer than two years.

Article 40 relaxes the rules against the buyer's failure to inspect promptly under Article 38 and to give notice of defects under Article 39. The relaxation occurs if the supplier knew of the defect or defects in the goods or "could not have been unaware" of such defects. Article 40 prohibits the seller from relying on Article 39's penalty against the buyer for failure to report defects of which the seller was cognizant.

The Warranty of Title—Third Party Claims. Another one of the supplier's obligations under the Convention is to deliver goods free from any right or claim of a third party, including rights or claims from patents or copyrights. The Convention distinguishes rights and claims arising from liens and encumbrances from those arising from patents and copyrights. Article 41 treats of third party claims arising from liens and encumbrances, and then specifically states that Article 42 governs claims from industrial property or other intellectual property.

The obligation of the supplier to deliver goods free of any right or claims of third parties seems to be absolute under Article 41. The only caveat to this is if the buyer "agreed to take the goods subject to that right or claim." One assumes a buyer might take goods subject to a lien only if the supplier gave the buyer a money allowance to be deducted from the cost of the goods to cover the lien.

The Uniform Commercial Code goes a bit farther in giving these types of assurances to the buyer than does the Convention. First, Section 2-312(1)(a) gives the buyer an express warranty that the title conveyed to the buyer shall be good. Then Section 2-312(1)(b) gives another express warranty that the goods shall be delivered "free from any security interest or other lien or encumbrance of which the buyer at the time of contracting has no knowledge." These are express warranties and not implied. Such warranties are not reached by the usual broad disclaimers of implied warranties that are so fluently given by some suppliers. The supplier here must disclaim this warranty by specific language.

Patent and Copyright Infringement. Finally, Section 2-312(3) of the Code makes the seller, if a merchant, warrant "that the goods shall be delivered free of the rightful claim of any third person by way of infringement or the like." As stated above, Convention Article 41 "hands over" claims of patent and trademark infringement to Article 42. Article 42 deals with the same subject matter as Code Section 2-312(2) but does not impose the obligations on the seller without giving him three rather significant exceptions. Because of the complexity of patent law generally, and of international patent law specifically, one can understand the desire to lighten this obligation from infringement claims on the international supplier. But that in itself does not justify transferring these risks to the innocent buyer. This is what Article 42 will do in many instances.

We will not repeat the entire Article 42 verbatim here, but will only synopsize the pertinent provisions for our discussion:

1. The article begins with the pronouncement that the seller must deliver goods free of any right or claim of a third party based on industrial property.

2. Then comes the first major caveat for the supplier: he must deliver goods free from any right or claim of a third party "of which at the time of the conclusion of the contract *the seller knew or could not have been unaware.*" The seller has no obligation if a patent infringement claim surprised him.

3. The second caveat is that the obligation of the supplier must be based upon the law of the State where the parties contemplated the

goods would be resold or used, or, in any other case, under the law of the State where the buyer has his residence.

4. And finally of course, this obligation of the seller does not extend to cases where the buyer knew or could not have been unaware of the right or claim of the third party.

You will note in point #2 above that for the seller to have the obligation for the penalties of a patent infringement, he must have known at the time of sale that the product he was selling did indeed infringe a patent. Article 42 states he has no obligation to the buyer if he did not know he was selling an infringement lawsuit to the buyer. One will challenge a supplier's good faith when he deliberately sells his customer a product that the supplier knows represents an infringement of a patent. But of course the Convention is not at all concerned about parties exercising good faith in their transactions; only in the interpretation process does the Convention suggest good faith. (See the discussion of Article 7(1).)

Article 42 is a supplier's dream world come true. He makes a sale of a product and has no responsibility to the buyer for the consequences if his product is proven to be one that infringes on a third party's patent, unless he knew from the beginning that it represents an infringement. A second caveat in this article limits the supplier's liability to the buyer for deliberate infringement only if it is an infringement under the country's laws where the product is to be used *and* if the supplier knew it was to be used in that country. If the supplier did not know in what country the product was to be used, then he is responsible to the buyer only if the product is an infringement in the country where the buyer has his place of business. Finally, Article 42(2)(a) presents a third caveat to allow a supplier to escape liability to the buyer for an infringement. That occurs when the buyer himself knew the product was an infringement. In such instances the supplier has no liability to the buyer but, of course, each of them individually and jointly have liability to the holder of the patent. This is when we like to observe that "it could not happen to a nicer pair of dishonest people" since both of them knowingly were involved in the infringement of a patent.

Article 42(2)(b) presents another instance where the supplier is relieved of infringement obligations. This is the situation where the buyer furnishes drawings or specifications which lead the supplier to infringement by compliance with such drawings or specifications. The article simply states the "obligation of the seller" does not extend to such a case. The buyer apparently incurs no liability for having given such specifications to his supplier even though they led the supplier down the primrose path to infringement.

Contrast this with the Uniform Commercial Code Sections 2–312(3) and 2–607(3), (4), (5), and (6). Here the merchant seller must warrant that the goods will be delivered free of the rightful claim of any third person by way of infringement. (Although the Uniform Commercial Code requires the seller to be a merchant to be responsible for infringement, remember that sales to consumers are not covered by the Convention. Therefore all suppliers under the Convention are the equivalent of merchants.) This subsection also says that a buyer who furnishes specifications to the seller must hold the seller harmless against any claim for infringement. Then Section 2–607(3 to 6) provides for notice to the other party when such a claim appears. It also provides that the infringing party (supplier or the buyer as the case may be) must defend the action, pay all expenses, and satisfy any judgment against the innocent party. This is good law and reaches an equitable result because it places the onus of the infringement upon the one who is in the best position to know most about the product.

Article 43(1) states the buyer loses the right to rely on the provisions of Article 41 (liens and encumbrances) or Article 42 (patent infringement) if he does not give notice to the seller specifying the nature of the right or claim of the third party within a reasonable time after he (the buyer) has became aware of it. Article 43(2) demonstrates that the authors of this portion of the Convention were "not with it" when writing it. 43(2) states the seller cannot rely on the provisions of 43(1) if he (the seller) knew of the right or claim of the third party. And yet, under Article 42(1) the seller has to know of the infringement claim at the time the contract is concluded if the buyer is to have a claim against the seller. It appears the writers of the Convention wasted the time of day by writing Article 43.

And now comes Article 44 which completes this discussion of notification of defects and liens and encumbrances. This article recognizes "reasonable excuses" which the buyer might claim prevented him from giving notice in a timely fashion. The article does not define what might be a reasonable excuse for failure to give the required notice. If the buyer can provide such a reason he is entitled to certain—but not all of—his remedies. Article 44 says "the buyer may reduce the price . . . or claim damages, except for loss of profit if he has a reasonable excuse . . ." Since we have not yet discussed damages, we must assume that some substantial types of damages are withheld from a buyer who has a reasonable excuse, chief among which is the right to avoid the contract.

Nota Bene to the Purchasing Officer. Article 42 does not represent the Convention's finest hour insofar as purchasing officers are concerned. But the same article certainly can endear the Convention to suppliers.

The possibilities of patent or copyright infringement claims in international trade are substantial. When one is purchasing a foreign-made product, the supplier and/or the manufacturer should know the most about the product, its derivation, and other related products in the industry classification. It would seem to be a logical *sequitur* that the buyer must depend upon the supplier for any patent knowledge pertaining to products in that field, because the supplier is the one who lives with the product and with the activities of competitors in the field. Yet the purchasing officer should not be required to depend solely upon the supplier's knowledge and good faith, whatever that might be under the Convention. Nor should the purchasing officer be required to live with the minimal protection against patent infringement given by the Convention. There are two suggestions we can give to add to the buyer's protection.

The first suggestion is to insert the following clause, or something similar, in every contract for goods that is covered by the Convention:

> The seller hereby agrees to defend and hold harmless the buyer should any claim of patent or copyright infringement be brought against the buyer because of the purchase, use, or resale of the goods or machinery purchased herein.

In all fairness, the buyer should give his or her foreign supplier the courtesy of the same protection if the supplier is furnished specifications developed by the buyer in the United States.

Of course, the second option available is to derogate 100% from the Convention and have the Uniform Commercial Code of your state become the applicable law for your international contracts.

Section III. Remedies for Breach of Contract by the Seller. Articles 45–52.

Index to Buyer's Remedies. Article 45 has three sub-sections. The first sub-section reads this way:

> (1) If the seller fails to perform any of his obligations under the contract or this Convention, the buyer may:
> (a) exercise the rights provided in articles 46–52;
> (b) claim damages as provided in articles 74–77.

The 'rights" mentioned in (1)(a) include the following:

1. The right to seek specific performance, require delivery of substitute goods, or to require the seller to repair the non-conforming goods. Article 46.

2. To fix an additional period of time for performance by the seller. Should the seller not perform within the additional period of time, the buyer may avoid the contract. Article 47.
3. Declare the contract "avoided." Article 49.
4. Reduce the price in the same proportion as the value of the goods had at the time of delivery to the value conforming goods would have had at that time. Article 50.
5. In the event of a partial delivery, to apply any of these rights to the quantity that has not been delivered. Article 51.
6. If the seller delivers before the due date, buyer may refuse to take delivery. If the seller delivers more than the contract total, the buyer may refuse to take more. Article 52.

Here are the list of damages provided in the Convention as mentioned in (1)(b):

1. For the loss suffered, including lost profits. Article 74.
2. For any costs arising from cover, including the difference between the contract price and the cover price. Article 75.
3. In the case of avoidance, the difference between market price at the time of avoidance and contract price if the party has not taken over goods; otherwise, at time of taking over goods. Article 76.

You will note the articles pertaining to damages are carried much later in the Convention. This is because the various types of damages are available to both the seller and the buyer. Part III of the Convention lists obligations of the seller first (this is what we are presently involved in), then the obligations of the buyer and finally provisions common to both the seller and the buyer. We shall continue our discussion in the numerical sequence of the articles as they appear in the Convention.

Specific Performance. The buyer's right to demand specific performance of the seller is one of the remedies the common law recognized. But it is not favored nor encouraged by the Uniform Commercial Code. Section 2–716(1) reads:

> (1) Specific performance may be decreed where the goods are unique or in other proper circumstances.

The fact that the remedy is confined mainly to those cases where "the goods are unique" limits its applicability. Apparently the Commissioners who wrote the Code believed the right to damages and the right to cover was all a buyer needed to be "made whole" by a defaulting supplier. And there never has been much complaint heard that the remedy has been that limited in scope.

The Convention, on the other hand, takes a more favorable approach to specific performance. Article 46(1) states that the buyer may require the supplier to perform his obligations "unless the buyer has resorted to a remedy which is inconsistent with this requirement." Nothing is said about the uniqueness of the goods—apparently it is a buyer's right to ask for specific performance. Later on we shall see in Article 62 that the seller has a similar right of specific performance against the buyer—that is, to make the buyer take the goods and pay the contract price for them. The Uniform Commercial Code does not give the supplier the same right in such precise terms.

One can only surmise that the right to specific performance is included in the Convention in such an unfettered state as a "sop" to civil law countries. Many civil law countries permit application of the remedy, although it is understood that not many buyers or suppliers avail themselves of this remedy. And, of course, Article 46(1) limits the application of the remedy if the buyer has resorted to an inconsistent remedy such as cover.

The reader is also reminded of our previous discussion of Article 28 at the beginning of Part III. Article 28 gives the court the opportunity of not following Article 46 and its specific performance remedy, if the court's own domestic law would not allow it to do so. While this is not a mandate to the court, it is an option some courts will have because of their own law. It places some vestige of ambiguity into the final disposition of such a case.

Two other possible remedies are given the buyer in Article 46. Subsection (2) gives the buyer the right to demand substitute goods from the supplier if the delivered goods' failure to conform to the contract is such as to constitute a fundamental breach of contract. (See the discussion of "fundamental breach at the beginning of Chapter I, Article 25.) If the purchasing officer is convinced the defects in the goods are severe enough, this is a possible remedy.

Subsection (3) of Article 46 gives the buyer the right to require the supplier to remedy the lack of conformity of the delivered goods "by repair unless this would be an unreasonable request." One surmises the authors of the Convention believed this was a much more favored remedy because the section does not require the buyer to treat the defect as a fundamental breach to request it. However the Convention does protect the supplier by stating that this is a right of the buyer "unless this is unreasonable having regard to all the circumstances." In an international sale buyer and supplier could be thousands of miles apart. If repairs to an item require the attention of an individual located in the supplier's plant, travel expenses for that individual would be heavy. Perhaps it is suggesting to both buyer and supplier to look around the buyer's locale for a suitable repair person to do the proper repair job on the supplier's goods. Of course such a repair would be at the supplier's expense. Furthermore, the supplier would have to assume full responsibility for the repair, since the repair person would be the supplier's agent or an independent contractor performing the repair for the supplier. The situation might occur where the buyer is asked by the supplier to recommend a "good" repair person to do the job. The buyer should be very careful in how this is done. Do not allow the supplier to make the repair person and the quality of the work the responsibility of the buyer.

An Additional Period of Time for Performance. The second "right" of a buyer listed in Article 45(1)(a) provides for a procedure that will be new to American purchasing officers. The Article reads this way:

> (1) The buyer may fix an additional period of time of reasonable length for performance by the seller of his obligations.

At first blush one may wonder how this action of fixing an additional period of time for the supplier to perform could possibly be related to a buyer's remedy against a breaching supplier. The truth of the matter is that this procedure is a preliminary step to securing one of the Convention's major remedies without taking some risk of falsely accusing a supplier of being in breach.

A bit later we shall discuss Article 49 which you will note from the list of remedies at the beginning of this section is "avoidance of the contract." Under Article 49 the buyer may declare the contract "avoided" if one of two possible events occur. The first of these is that the seller may commit a "fundamental breach" that will allow the buyer to avoid the contract. (Fundamental breach was defined previously in Article 25 above.) The other happening to trigger "fundamental breach action" occurs when the seller does not perform his obligations within an "additional time period" fixed by the buyer under Article 47(1). Therefore, if the buyer wants to avoid the contract without having to speculate on whether the supplier's delay in delivery is sufficiently gross enough to meet the undefined test of "substantially . . depriving him of what he is entitled to expect," the buyer has the "additional period notice" route as an alternative.

You will note that the buyer must fix the additional period of time at a "reasonable length." The "reasonableness" of the length of extension is one that is not spelled out in the Convention. One could refer to Article 7(1), which calls for good faith in international trading, as a guide. There are a myriad of different conditions that would need to be considered in each case before deciding whether any one extension is of reasonable length. For example, if the buyer is seeking the delivery of goods under an international contract, setting an additional period of three days beyond the contract date would not be reasonable unless the goods had already been shipped, or could be sent via air. Above all, when setting the additional period of time, the buyer should be specific on the closing date when delivery would be acceptable. "To be delivered no later than the close of business on June 10th" is being specific.

Perhaps the purchasing officer should also be reminded that a precise delivery date for delivery of all of the goods should be on the original purchase order, as well as the precise place where the goods are to be delivered. (This is good purchasing practice for every purchase, domestic or international.) This places the responsibility of getting the goods there on that date on the supplier's shoulders. Article 33(1), you will recall, mandates this obligation. If no date is mentioned, then Article 33(3) allows the supplier "a reasonable time" to get the goods to that location. "A reasonable time" is always open to argument as to when it expires. A precise date is not arguable.

Giving an extension of additional performance time can also be helpful to the buyer if the supplier is lagging on the delivery of substitute goods under Article 46(2). A similar extension of time can be given for cure by repair by the supplier under Article 46(3). Using the time extension as a "cutoff" on a supplier who prolongs the cure process is also helpful. We have read cases in the United States where a supplier takes as long as six months in attempting a repair without success. Having a "turn-off" valve will stand the buyer in good stead.

The final section of Article 47(2) prohibits the buyer from resorting to any remedy for breach of contract while the additional period of time that was fixed is "running." The buyer, in effect, invites the supplier to perform when giving this additional time period. He should not be permitted to take a diverse action that is inconsistent with such an invitation to the supplier. Once the extension of time is given, the buyer must be patient until the extension has run its full course. Such patience on the part of the buyer, however, does not deny the buyer of the rights he may have to claim damages against the supplier for delays in performance.

Seller's Right to Cure After Delivery. We previously discussed Article 37 wherein the supplier is given the opportunity to cure any defect if the goods have been delivered before the date for delivery. His right to cure in any manner "up to" the delivery date is almost unlimited, subject only to unreasonable inconvenience or expense to the buyer. Now comes Article 48 which gives the supplier some opportunity to cure "after the delivery date has passed," subject to some caveats:

> (1) Subject to article 49, the seller may even after the date for delivery, remedy at his own expense any failure to perform his obligations, if he can do so without unreasonable delay and without causing the buyer unreasonable inconvenience or uncertainty of reimbursement by the seller of expenses advanced by the buyer. However, the buyer retains any right to claim damages as provided for in this Convention.

Article 49, referred to in Article 48, covers "avoidance of the contract by the buyer." Since avoidance is mentioned in an article dealing with cure, one wonders if and how the two are related. Does this article imply the seller's right to cure is based upon the buyer not having avoided the contract as yet, or does the seller's right to cure delay the ability of the buyer to avoid the contract? This is like the proverbial chicken and the egg problem.

There has to be a relationship between "cure" and a "fundamental breach." One would assume a proper cure of non-conforming goods would make them conforming. And, if the goods are conforming to the contract, the buyer would be unable to claim they "substantially deprive him of what he is entitled to expect." Realizing this fact, then perhaps the chicken and the egg problem is solved. The cure rightfully should come first, because if the cure is successful the buyer will not have the right to avoid the contract.

Completion of a contract is particularly encouraged in international trade. One way to have a completed contract is to permit the seller to correct any defects in his product so that the product will be acceptable to the buyer. Therefore it is reasonable to permit an attempted cure under Article 48(1) before a buyer is permitted to exercise his right to avoid the contract under Article 49(1). This interpretation is particularly true when one notices the last sentence in Article 48(1) which retains the right to claim damages by the buyer in the event the cure process takes too long.

During our discussion of Article 37, which gives the supplier the right to cure defects in goods delivered before the required delivery date, we mentioned Section 2–508(1) of the Uniform Commercial Code. That Code section gives the supplier the same right to cure prior to the delivery date. Section 2–508(2) also gives the supplier a limited right to cure after the time for delivery has passed. However, the Code section seems to be more strict on the supplier than does the Convention:

> (2) Where the buyer rejects a non-conforming tender which the seller had reasonable grounds to believe would be acceptable with or without money allowance, the seller may if he seasonably notifies the buyer have a further reasonable time to substitute conforming tender.

Subsection (2) must be read in light of subsection (1) which gives the supplier the right to cure within the contract time. Subsection (2) gives the supplier "a further reasonable time" to cure—which means after the contract time has passed. Presumably this right of the supplier to cure is more limited under the Code than in the Convention. First off the supplier is allowed to cure only if there was a surprise rejection of the goods by the buyer. Then and only then is the supplier allowed the opportunity to cure after the contract time for performance has passed.

As a matter of actual practice, no reasonable purchasing officer would deny a supplier the opportunity to cure if it can be done promptly and quickly. However, buyers are also aware that a supplier can "string out" cure for a long period of time. Persistent repairs of the same type often indicate a product is not capable of maintaining the required operating level. The buyer should have the ability to draw a "finish" line, declare the product non-conforming and of no value to him, whether it is purchased in the international market or a local market. Because of the propensity of some suppliers to take long periods of time for cure, some purchasing officers put a "no-replacement" clause in a contract. This prevents the right of cure by the seller after the time for delivery has passed. One would assume a similar opportunity to use such a clause would be present under the Convention.

Seller's Notice of Intent to Cure. Articles 48(2 to 4) cover communication rules applicable to the seller's right to cure after the date of delivery. It is interesting to note that these rules are written so as to give the seller the right to cure in the event of no response by the buyer. Sub-article (2) states:

> (2) If the seller requests the buyer to make known whether he will accept performance and the buyer does not comply with the request within a reasonable time, the seller may perform within the time indicated in his request.

The article goes on to point out that if the buyer does not respond, the buyer cannot resort to any remedy inconsistent with the seller's attempts to cure. Sub-article (3) states:

> (3) A notice by the seller that he will perform within a specified period of time is assumed to include a request, under the preceding paragraph, that the buyer make known his decision.

These two sub-articles tell every purchasing officer to immediately respond to any supplier's request to cure if cure is not desired. Else, the buyer will get cure whether he really wanted it or not. About the only solace to the buyer is that sub-article (4) requires that the onus is on the seller to make certain such communications about cure are *received* by the buyer. The Convention does not apply the dispatch rule to such notices of intent to cure—the notice must be received by the buyer.

The Convention's Rules on Avoidance of Contract. Article 49 of the Convention sets out the general rules for avoidance under the Convention. 49(1) tells *when* the buyer may declare the contract avoided:

> (a) if the failure by the seller to perform any of his obligations under the contract or this Convention amounts to a fundamental breach of contract; or
> (b) in the case of non-delivery, if the seller does not deliver the goods within the additional period of time fixed by the buyer in accordance with paragraph (1) of Article 47 or declares that he will not deliver within the period so fixed.

The American purchasing officer should not be lulled into the belief that the right to avoid the contract under 49(a) is similar to the "perfect tender rule" of Code Section 2–601. In fact, there is no perfect tender rule for the buyer in the Convention. Under 49(1)(a) the buyer may avoid the contract only if the seller's breach is a fundamental breach. And a fundamental breach, you will recall, was defined in Article 25 of the Convention as one that "substantially deprives him of what he was entitled to expect under the contract." That wordage may be familiar to the American purchasing officer as coming from the Uniform Commercial Code. In fact, it is very similar to Section 2–608(1) of the Code which provides for revocation of acceptance by the buyer. Then the breach must be "substantial" to enable the buyer to revoke his acceptance of the goods. The buyer's right to avoidance under the Convention is based upon the same degree of substantial defect as is revocation of acceptance under the Code. That means there is no perfect tender rule in the Convention. The buyer must "make do" with less serious defects and does not have the option of rejecting such goods.

Article 49(1)(b) gives a buyer another opportunity to avoid a contract. This occurs only in cases of non-delivery of the goods. The occasion arises when the seller does not deliver the goods within an additional period of time for performance granted by the buyer under Article 47(1). Thus, even though failure to deliver promptly might not seriously injure the buyer, once the buyer gives the seller an additional period of time to perform under Article 47, the time of delivery becomes "of the essence" and goes to the core of the contract. (This is described in our original text on pages 350 and 351.) After that warning, if the seller does not then perform in a timely manner, the buyer may avoid the contract. This procedure codifies the approach we follow under general contract law to make "time of the essence" in a contract. The procedure under the Convention is to be preferred because the result then becomes automatic.

When Buyer Must Declare Avoidance Where Seller Has Delivered Goods. Subsection 2 of Article 49 gives us some rules as to when the buyer must declare a contract avoided in those cases where the supplier has delivered the goods. These rules are:

1) when delivery is late, within a reasonable time after the buyer has become aware the delivery has been made.
2) in respect to any other breach than late delivery, within a reasonable time after the buyer knew or ought to have known about the breach, or
3) where an additional period of time for delivery was given under Article 47(1), within a reasonable period of time after that performance date has passed, or
4) where the seller has not performed the cure he promised under an Article 48(2) notice within the time he stated, the buyer within a reasonable time must declare the contract avoided.

Failure of the buyer to act within the "reasonable time" allowed results in the buyer's loss of the right to declare the contract avoided.

Nota Bene to the Purchasing Officer. Your author would be remiss if he did not remind you at this point that Article 26 which follows the article on fundamental breach is a "two liner" that states "A declaration . . . of avoidance is effective only if made by notice to the other party." The message to you is to send notice if you avoid a contract!

Reduction of Price. Article 50 presents another right of the aggrieved buyer, although it appears to be a right of very doubtful value. The article states:

> If the goods do not conform with the contract and whether or not the price has already been paid, the buyer may reduce the price in the same proportion as the value of the goods actually delivered had at the time of delivery bears to the value that conforming goods would have had at that time.

This section has very limited use under narrow circumstances. It may be of advantage to the buyer if his opportunity to recover damages under Article 74 (which we will be discussing in numerical order) is limited because the seller is not at fault for the breach. This would be similar to a situation that develops under the Uniform Commercial Code's Section 2–615, which refers to failure of presupposed conditions. In such cases the buyer has no breach of contract action against the seller.

Part of the Goods Are Not Delivered or Part Are Non-Conforming. Article 51(1) covers the situation where the seller either does not deliver the complete contract quantity or a part of the delivered goods are non-conforming. The article provides that the remedies offered in Articles 46 to 50 can be applied to the missing part or to the non-conforming portion. Thus the buyer can ask for delivery of substitute goods to replace the non-conforming goods or avoid the contract with respect to the missing or non-conforming goods. The buyer may also seek damages.

The buyer's right to avoid the contract with respect to the non-conforming or missing goods does not allow the right to avoid the complete contract. Article 51(2) states:

> The buyer may declare the contract avoided in its entirety only if the failure to make delivery completely or in conformity with the contract amounts to a fundamental breach of contract.

Thus, only if the missing part of the delivery or the conforming goods could make the delivered portion useless may the buyer have the right to avoid the entire contract. But avoidance because part of the goods were non-conforming gives the buyer the right to avoid only that portion of the contract.

What Article 51(2) does is to make it difficult for a buyer to return the portion of the goods that are conforming. This is in line with the thought that pervades throughout the Convention that it is costly to deliver goods in international trade, and once delivered, every attempt is made to make that delivery "hold." The Uniform Commercial Code, in comparison, does not attempt to force the buyer to retain any portion of goods if another portion of them is non-conforming. Section 2–601 states:

> . . . the buyer may
>
> (a) reject the whole; or
> (b) accept the whole; or
> (c) accept any commercial unit and reject the rest
>
> if the goods or the tender of delivery fail in any respect to conform to the contract.

Thus the American buyer is able to dispose of any or all of the goods rather than being forced to accept "odd lots" as under the Convention or attempt to prove a partial non-delivery or a partial faulty delivery is a fundamental breach.

Nota Bene to the Purchasing Officer. Doing international business under the Convention may require you to accept something less than a complete delivery. A clause similar to the following could be inserted in your contract with the supplier to keep this from happening:

> Buyer insists on 100% delivery of conforming goods ordered under this purchase order, in one delivery. No over- or under-runs are acceptable. Buyer reserves the right to return the entire contract delivery if any portion of the goods are non-conforming.

Early Delivery and Over-Runs. Should a supplier deliver before the due date, the buyer has the right under article 52(1) to refuse to take delivery. It is suggested that unless the buyer has other requirements for the space where the goods are to be placed, delivery should be taken when tendered. Storage costs or demurrage could cause the seller to lose money on the contract.

Over-runs are covered in Article 52(2). The buyer is not required to accept any over-runs but may do so and pay the contract price for the excess quantity. No mention is made for exceptions to this rule where industry customs provide for over- or under-runs, as in cases of the printing, cannery, and foundry industries.

Chapter III. Obligations of the Buyer. Articles 53–65

The Convention presents the obligations of the seller in Chapter II. Now comes Chapter III which gives us the obligations of the buyer. We will not treat these in such detail unless the Convention makes unusual demands on the buyer.

Article 53 begins Chapter II by starting the fundamental obligations of the buyer:

> The buyer must pay the price for the goods and take delivery of them as required by the contract and this convention.

This comes as no surprise to purchasing officers. Section 2–301 of the Uniform Commercial Code places the same obligations on the buyer.

Section I. Payment of the Price. Articles 54–59.

Buyer—Get Prepared to Pay! The section leads off with a single-sentence article that reminds the buyer to make all of the necessary arrangements for payment to the supplier:

> The buyer's obligation to pay the price includes taking such steps and complying with such formalities as may be required under the contract or any laws or regulations to enable payment to be made.

We pointed out in our original text, beginning at page 400, that there are many details involved in arranging for credit and for payment when an international purchase is to be consummated. This can include clearance of government restrictions on money or goods going in and out of the parties' respective countries. Article 54 clearly reminds the buyer these are the buyer's obligations to handle. When the Convention does this it is also telling the supplier that any failure of the buyer to make these arrangements may be grounds for avoidance of the contract by the supplier.

Nota Bene to the Purchasing Officer. Credit terms and details of how the supplier is to be paid should be negotiated at the time the purchase is made. This is especially true for international purchases unless you and your foreign supplier have an established routine of doing business with each other.

Open Price Contracts. Once again we come upon an article dealing with open price contracts. This is Article 55 which is in the section dealing with the obligations of the buyer. You will remember that earlier in the Convention, in a section dealing with the Formation of a Contract, we found Article 14 which states that an offer "is sufficiently definite if it . . . expressly or impliedly fixes or makes provision for determining the quantity and the price." There we arrived at the conclusion that an offer under the Convention required a price in it to be valid.

Now comes Article 55 which states:

> Where a contract has been validly concluded but does not expressly or implicitly fix or make provision for determining the price, the parties are considered, in the absence of any indication to the contrary, to have impliedly made reference to the price generally charged at the time of the conclusion of the contract for such goods sold under comparable circumstances in the trade concerned.

Authorities who have written law review articles on the Convention are mixed in their opinion of whether Article 55 is to be believed or that Article 14 controls. Is a price necessary to form a contract as in Article 14 or can the parties be assumed to have conjured in their minds that the price which is "generally charged" would be applied? The latter assumption is rather difficult to believe but in the interest of making the Convention a better document with one less loose end, let us grant that thesis.

As a matter of fact, your author can see some relationship between Articles 14 and 55 of the Convention on the one hand, and Section 2–207(3) of the Uniform Commercial Code on the other. Article 55 begins with "Where a contract has been validly concluded. . ." We compare this with Section 2–207(3) "Conduct by both parties which recognizes the existence of a contract is sufficient to establish a contract for sale . . ." and we come to the conclusion it is similar logic that is "stretched a bit." Somehow the parties conclude a contract by performance and conduct. The Convention says "here is the manner in which we will determine the price of that contract in this instance." Article 55 assumes the parties meant to apply the price generally prevailing in the trade because they made the assumption they were in contract. While this may be placing words in the mouths of the writers of the Convention, it is one way to explain Article 55. We can certainly vouch that no self-respecting purchasing officer is going to purchase something and agree to pay a price that is considerably above the current market price. Likewise we know that no self-respecting supplier will be caught giving his product to the buyer.

You will note that Article 55 specifies the price to be applied is the one prevailing at the time "of the conclusion on the contract." Recall that the Uniform Commercial Code (Section 2–305) applies the price prevailing at the time of delivery.

Manner of Payment—Place. The settlement of the amount owing the seller is usually spelled out in a contract involving the international sale of goods. Both buyer and seller could face governmental obstacles in the settlement of their debt and usually will face up to the problem at the time they are contracting. Should there be no provision for the place where settlement is to be made, the following rules are set by Article 57:

(1)(a) if no place for payment is provided, the buyer must pay at the seller's place of business;
(1)(b) if payment is to be made against the handing over of the goods or documents, the buyer must pay where the handing over occurs.

Time for Payment and Inspection of Goods. Article 58 spells out the rules of the Convention about time of payment and the inspection of the goods when the contract is silent on these issues. Here again the parties are free to agree on such issues in their contract. The Uniform Commercial Code usually preambles a section with "Unless otherwise agreed, . . ." The Convention does much the same by stating "if the buyer is not bound to pay the price . . .", so under either codified law, the parties are first given the opportunity to establish their own rules on time for payment and where inspection is to occur. If they do not take advantage of this invitation, then the Convention, in Article 58, provides these guides to time of payment and time of inspection:

(1) If the buyer is not bound to pay the price at any other specific time, he must pay it when the seller places either the goods or documents controlling their disposition at the buyer's disposal . . .
(2) If the contract involves carriage of the goods, the seller may dispatch the goods on terms whereby the goods, or documents controlling their disposition, will not be handed over to the buyer except against payment of the price.
(3) The buyer is not bound to pay the price until he has had an opportunity

to examine the goods, unless the procedures for delivery or payment agreed upon by the parties are inconsistent with his having such an opportunity.

We can put 57(1)(a) together with 58(1) and assert with some authority that the Convention requires the buyer to pay for the goods at the seller's place of business when the seller makes the goods available to the buyer. We can also assert that where the goods are to be shipped by the seller, the seller can ship the goods against documents of title that require the buyer to pay for the goods in exchange for the title documents. Article 58(3) spells out the fact that the buyer is not bound to pay the price until he has had an opportunity to inspect the goods, unless the payment procedures agreed upon in the buyer-seller contract prevent this from happening. And this usually happens to the buyer—the buyer waives the right to inspect before paying for the goods when agreeing to allow the seller to ship against documents of title.

The provisions of Article 58 are similar to those in the Uniform Commercial Code—Sections 2-310(1) and (2). Sub-section 2-310(2) repeats the buyer's right to inspect before payment, but Section 2-508(3) specifically states that:

> . . . the buyer is not entitled to inspect the goods before payment of the price when the contract provides
> (b) for payment against documents of title . . .

Therefore under both the Convention and the Code the buyer waives the right of inspection before payment when the contract provides for shipment against documents of title.

We discussed the problems of payment and inspection in foreign purchases on pages 402 to 404 of the original text. In every purchase, whether domestic or international, there is always the desire to protect oneself against the other party. The buyer does not want to pay for the goods until the goods have been inspected and are known to conform to the contract. On the other hand, the supplier is not willing to release the goods before the buyer has paid the price. The Convention and the Code, in general, provides for the *exchange* of the price and the goods. These acts are supposedly simultaneous so that neither the buyer nor the supplier have any advantage or take any unusual risk.

Variations from this "exchange" pattern are manifold. The seller will sell on credit and the buyer is thereby given time to inspect the goods before payment. On the other hand, arrangements could be made for the seller to "ship against documents" which results in the buyer having to pay for the goods long before ever laying eyes upon them. In domestic transactions, either of these assumptions are a relatively safe and conservative procedure for the parties; that is, if the buyer and the seller have both done their "homework" and verified each other's credit standing.

International trade presents more problems that are not as easily solved. Greater distances between buyer and seller means that transportation costs are greater, cure costs of the supplier are greater, and the supplier's ability to dispose of unwanted goods is much more limited. In addition, there may be governmental restrictions on currency transactions. Determining the credit standings of the buyer and the seller are also more difficult. Therefore there is less willingness by either party to place as much trust in each other, and substitute procedures must be found.

We suggested one method for American buyers to follow in the original text. The funds are made available to the seller in the seller's country via a letter of credit or some similar financing device. This can be arranged for through the buyer's local bank and its correspondent banks that have a branch in the seller's country. When the seller ships the goods, the money can be obtained from the correspondent bank in the seller's country. When the seller ships the goods to the buyer, the seller can obtain his money from the bank in his country by presenting the order bill of lading the seller received from the transportation company. This bill of lading should show that conforming goods have been sent by the seller. Remember that the bank in the seller's country, who has the buyer's letter of credit, is a representative or agent of the buyer's bank. That bank is under the duty not to release the funds to the seller without receiving in return a proper bill of lading showing that conforming goods have been sent. This is some protection for the buyer, but it is not a real substitute for inspection. Of course, the buyer could go the full step and employ someone in the supplier's country to make the inspection for the buyer.

Nota Bene to the Purchasing Officer. You will find that the Convention tries very hard to protect both parties in an international sale, but when that is impossible to accomplish, the nod then seems to go to the supplier. Here in Article 58, the buyer's right of inspection first is lost so that the seller can be properly protected.

Section I of Chapter III of the Convention concludes with Article 59. This article makes the simple observation and rule that the buyer must pay for the goods on the due date without any "demand for payment" being made by the supplier. Your author is unaware of any similar section in the Uniform Commercial Code except for Section 2–511(2) which permits the seller to demand payment in legal tender if sufficient time is given the buyer to obtain legal tender.

Section II. Taking Delivery. Article 60.

Section II consists of one article—60—which states that the buyer's obligation to take delivery consists of doing all the acts which could reasonably be expected of him in order for the seller to make delivery and for the buyer to take over the goods. There is no section of the Uniform Commercial Code exactly like this, although Section 2–319(3) requires the buyer to give the seller any needed instructions for making delivery. Failure of the buyer to do this could render the buyer in default under Section 2–311(3)(b), which gives the seller certain rights to complete or avoid the contract.

Section III. Remedies for Breach of Contract by the Buyer. Articles 61–65.

Remedies Available to the Seller. Section III of this chapter, (which is III), is almost a mirror image of Section III in Chapter II. The difference is that Chapter II covered the remedies available to the buyer, and Chapter III, Section III deals with the remedies of the seller. Article 61 indexes the remedies available to the seller. Its first subsection reads this way:

> (1) If the buyer fails to perform any of his obligations under the contract or this Convention, the seller may
>
> (a) exercise the rights provided in Articles 62 to 65;
> (b) claim damages as provided in Articles 74 to 77.

The "rights" mentioned in 61(1)(a) include the following:

1. The right to require the buyer to pay the price, take delivery, or perform his other obligations. Article 62.
2. To fix an additional period of time of reasonable length for performance by the buyer of his obligations. Article 63.
3. To declare the contract avoided. Article 64.
4. To supply missing specifications that the buyer fails to supply. Article 65.

The list of damages provided for the seller in the Convention are the same as those provided the buyer in Article 45. This is one of the fine features of the Convention—damages are the same for the buyer and for the seller.

Seller's Right to the Equivalent of Specific Performance. Article 62 states:

> The seller may require the buyer to pay the price, take delivery, or perform his other obligations.

The seller will probably use this article only to enforce payment by the buyer if the buyer has already received and accepted the goods. Although the article is basically the seller's right to obtain and enforce specific performance (to parallel the buyer's right under Article 46), its use to enforce specific performance will seldom be used. Section 2–709(1) of the Uniform Commercial Code gives the seller the same opportunity to claim the price if the goods have been delivered and accepted by the buyer.

Additional Period of Time for Buyer to Perform. Article 63 gives the seller the right to grant buyer a reasonable amount of additional time to perform his or her obligations. If after the expiration of that additional time the buyer has not performed, the seller may declare the contract avoided. This is similar to the buyer's right to do this in Article 47. You will recall that we said that right was needed if the buyer wanted to declare the contract avoided and was not certain the seller's breach was deep enough to warrant an outright declaration of avoidance. By giving the additional period of time to perform, the party giving that time is assured of the right to declare the contract avoided if the other party does not perform within that time period.

Seller's Right to Avoid the Contract. Article 64 spells out the seller's right to avoid the contract if the failure of the buyer to perform his obligations under the contract amounts to a fundamental breach of contract. It also provides the seller with the opportunity to avoid as we pointed out in the previous paragraph. These provisions for the seller are the same as were given the buyer in Article 49.

Supplying Missing Specifications. Article 65 gives the seller the right to supply missing specifications for the goods if the buyer fails to do so. The seller is required to inform the buyer what he has done in this respect. The Uniform Commercial Code in Section 2–311 gives the party awaiting such instructions the right to supply the instructions or they have the right to declare the other party to be in breach.

Chapter IV. Passing of Risk. Articles 66 to 70.

Damage After Risk Passed to Buyer. The first basic rule we encounter is in Article 66:

> Loss of or damage to the goods after the risk has passed to the buyer does not discharge him from his obligation to pay the price, unless the loss or damage is due to an act or omission of the seller.

This article is self-explanatory and within our understanding of the risk of loss as it is applied under the Uniform Commercial Code.

Risk of Loss When Goods Are in Transit. The general rule of the Convention concerning risk of loss while the goods are in transit is contained in Article 67:

> (1) If the contract of sale involves carriage of the goods and the seller is not bound to hand them over at a particular place, the risk passes to the buyer when the goods are handed over to the first carrier for transmission to the buyer in accordance with the contract of sale. If the seller is bound to hand the goods over to a carrier at a particular place, the risk does not pass to the buyer until the goods are handed over to the carrier at that place. The fact that the seller is authorized to retain documents controlling the disposition of the goods does not affect the passage of the risk.

You will note the risk of loss passes to the buyer "when the goods are handed over to the first carrier for transmission to the buyer." To your author this appears to be much more precise than the Uniform Commercial Code's expression in Section 2–509(1)(a) "when the goods are duly delivered to the carrier . . ." The Code's definition lacks the preciseness of exactly when in "delivery" does the risk pass to the buyer.

The reader will note that even though the seller makes the shipment under reservation, as with documents, the risk of loss still passes to the buyer at the time the goods are handed over to the first carrier. This is in line too with section 2–509(1)(a).

Miscellaneous Rules Regarding Breach. The final three articles in this chapter on the passage of the risk contain miscellaneous rules involved in the action. Article 68 presents a special rule where the goods are sold while in transit. Article 69(2) covers the case where the buyer is to take over the goods at a place other than the seller's place of business. This sub-article states that the risk passes to the buyer when delivery is due and the buyer has been made aware that his goods are available to him.

Article 69(2), by the process of elimination, also points out that Article 69(1) refers to the situation where the buyer is to take over the goods at the seller's place of business. The rule states the risk passes to the buyer when he takes the goods or when he breaches his contract by failing to take delivery. These rules are the same as in the Uniform Commercial Code.

Article 70 covers the situation when the seller hands over non-conforming goods to the carrier. If the non-conformity is such as to give the buyer the right to avoid the contract, that right continues despite the fact that the goods may be damaged in transit. Though technically the damaged goods were the buyer's goods, the fundamental breach of the seller causes the loss to fall back on him. Section 2–510(1) of the Uniform Commercial Code protects the buyer in the same fashion—except that the seller's default need not be such a serious breach to enable the buyer to reject or revoke his acceptance of the goods.

Chapter V. Provisions Common to the Obligations of the Seller and the Buyer. Articles 71–88.

Section I. Anticipatory Breach and Installment Contracts Articles 71–73.

Article 71 provides some general rules regarding anticipatory breach. Sub-article (1) states that:

> (1) A party may suspend the performance of his obligations if, after the conclusion of the contract, it becomes apparent that the other party will not perform a substantial part of his obligations as a result of:
>
> (a) a serious deficiency in his ability to perform, or in his creditworthiness; or
> (b) his conduct in preparing to perform or in performing the contract.

Note the permissive words ". . . may suspend performance . . .", which implies the party may only temporarily interrupt his or her performance because the other party, under sub-article (3), may provide adequate assurance of his ability to perform. 71(3) makes it mandatory that the party suspending performance must notify the other party of his action. The Uniform Commercial Code has a similar provision in Section 2–609(1).

Nowhere in these articles is there any definition of what is adequate notice of suspension, whether it has to be in writing, and who is responsible for its delivery. The suggestion to the American purchasing officer is (1) put it in writing, (2) give all of the necessary facts of why you are questioning the possibility of performance, and (3) make certain that your message is delivered to your supplier by sending it via "return receipt requested" mail.

You will also note that sub-article (2) of Article 71 provides for stoppage of delivery when the goods are in transit and the buyer is proven to be insolvent. A similar section 2–705(1), is in the Uniform Commercial Code.

Avoidance of Contract Prior to Date of Performance. Article 72 goes one step farther than Article 71. It provides the aggrieved party may declare the contract avoided if it is clear the other party "will commit a fundamental breach of contract." The aggrieved party must give notice to the other party if time allows. No notice is required if the breaching party has declared he will not perform his obligations.

Avoidance in Installament Contracts. Article 73 of the Convention provides that the failure of one party to perform any of his obligations in respect to any installment constitutes a fundamental breach in respect to that installment. Sub-article (2) provides that if this gives the aggrieved party good grounds to conclude future installments will likewise be violated, the aggrieved party may declare all future installments avoided. Sub-article (3) provides for the aggrieved party to declare the entire contract avoided if each installment is interdependent of the other. This is all similar to Section 2–612 of the Uniform Commercial Code.

Section II. Damages. Articles 74–77.

Article 74 begins Section II on damages. This article states the general rule for damages under the Convention, and with one caveat, coincides with the Uniform Commercial Code:

> Damages for breach of contract by one party consist of a sum equal to the loss, including loss of profit, suffered by the other party as a consequence of the breach.

The caveat, if it may be called that, is found in the second sentence of Article 74:

> Such damages may not exceed the loss which the party in breach foresaw or ought to have foreseen at the time of the conclusion of the contract, in the light of the facts and matters of which he then knew or ought to have known, as a possible consequence of the breach of contract.

The basic rule of damages included in the first sentence is incontrovertible. Note particularly that loss of profit is specifically mentioned as an element of damages for either party. Also note that the Uniform Commercial Code does not permit the buyer to receive damages for loss of profit. This is a plus for the Convention, although your author can see some difficulties of proof for a buyer seeking to collect loss of profit as damages. We have had cases in the United States under the Uniform Commerical Code where the courts have specifically denied recovery for the buyer's overhead or profits.

The second sentence of the article places a strong limit on the amount of consequential damages that can be recovered by an aggrieved party. This article requires the breaching party to have some knowledge of the possibility of the occurrence before he can be held liable for the consequences. We believe this is a bit of a hardship on the buyer particularly.

Those knowledgeable in matters of the Convention, with some manner of correctness, will say this necessary foreseeability of the consequence is written into Section 2–715 of the Code. This subsection reads:

> (2) Consequential damages resulting from the seller's breach include:
>> (a) any loss resulting from general or particular requirements and needs of which the seller at the time of contracting had reason to know and which could not reasonably be prevented by cover or otherwise; and
>> (b) injury to person or property proximately resulting from any breach of warranty.

Section 2–715 makes only the seller liable for consequential damages. (2)(a) says the seller is liable only if he had reason to know the consequence and it could not be prevented by cover or otherwise. However (2)(b) says that where an injury to a person or property is involved because of a breach of warranty, no such knowledge requirement is imposed on the seller before being found liable for the damage.

Damages Where Buyer Has Executed a Cover. Article 75 deals with the damages due where the seller has resold the goods or the buyer has executed a "cover" purchase. In such instances the damages are the difference between the contract price and the price in the substitute transaction as well as any further damages recoverable under Article 74. While the phrase "further damages under Article 74" is not explained, one assumes it has reference to regaining the full measure of profits lost. This would be of advantage to the supplier, although it may be possible for the buyer to prove lost profits too.

Damages Where Contract Is Avoided and There Is No Cover Transaction. Article 76 covers this topic. The measure of damages in such instances is the difference between the contract price and the current price at the time of avoidance, plus anything more that might be recoverable under Article 74. Again, that probably refers to lost profits. Although this article is written for both buyers and sellers, one would assume the seller will derive the most advantage from it.

The section concludes with Article 77, which imposes upon either party claiming under Articles 74 to 76, the duty to mitigate damages, including loss of profit, wherever possible. Failure of the aggrieved party to do so gives the other party the right to claim an equivalent reduction in damages recoverable.

Section III. Interest. Article 78.

Interest is provided as a penalty against any party who fails to pay the price or any other sum that is in arrears. This is Article 78. No rate of interest is specified. There is no similar provision in the Uniform Commercial Code although interest may be awarded by the Court in appropriate circumstances.

Section IV. Exemptions. Articles 79–80.

The Convention, under the caption of "Exemptions," presents its version of the Uniform Commercial Code's Section 2–615 which the American purchasing officer knows as "Failure of Pre-Supposed Conditions." There is some difference in the approaches the Convention follows versus the Code.

The Convention, in the first sub-article of Article 79, details the circumstances that must exist for either party to be given an exemption:

- a) The failure is due to an impediment beyond his control.
- b) He could not have been expected to take the impediment into account at the time of contracting.
- c) He could not have avoided its consequences.

Sub-article (2) gives the defaulting party another exemption. Here the rule is that if the party in default was depending on a third person's performance to complete his own performance, and if the third person could not perform because of an impediment described in sub-article (1), the defaulting party then has an exemption. In other words, the third party's exemption becomes the defaulting party's exemption too.

Sub-article (3) provides that the exemption lasts as long as the impediment lasts. One assumes the defaulting party must perform after the impediment is removed if the other party continues to demand performance. One also assumes the defaulting party would be given an extension of his or her performance date equal to the length the impediment continues.

The fourth sub-article requires the defaulting party to give notice to the injured party within a reasonable time after the impediment appears. Failure to give such notice or failure of the injured party to receive such notice, subjects the defaulting party to exposure for damages.

Finally, sub-article (5) makes it quite clear that the exemption exempts the defaulting party from payment of damages only. The injured party may pursue any other right available under the Convention. This might be the right to avoid the contract so that the injured party will not have to await removal of the impediment. Such party can go elsewhere, if desired, to fulfill the need, such as having the right to cover.

There are differences between Article 79 and the applicable Code sections. The basic Code section on this topic is 2–615 and it is written only as an exemption for the supplier. The buyer has none. We will not go into discussions of the differences between the Convention and the Code on this topic, since 2–615 is discussed in the original text on pages 373–74.

Article 80 simply prevents an injured party from relying on the failure of the other party to perform if such delay has been occasioned by the aggrieved party.

Section V. Effects of Avoidance. Articles 81–84.

These four sections give miscellaneous rules concerning the effects of avoidance of a contract. We will simply enumerate such rules and show the appropriate article in parentheses.

1. Avoidance releases both parties from their obligations under the contract. Of course, this does not apply to any damages that may have accrued. (81)
2. Avoidance does not affect any other provision of the contract that governs the rights and obligations of the parties, or how disputes are to be settled. (81)

3. A party who has performed may claim restitution from the other party. (81)
4. The buyer loses the right to declare the contract avoided or to require the seller to deliver substitute goods if it is impossible for him to make restitution of the goods substantially in the condition in which he received them. This does not apply if the impossibility of making restitution is not due to the buyer's act, or if the goods have perished, or if the goods have been sold in the normal course of business. (82)
5. A buyer who has lost the right to declare the contract avoided or to require the seller to deliver substitute goods in accordance with Article 82, retains all other remedies under the convention. (83)
6. If the seller is bound to refund the price, he must also pay interest on it. (84)

Nota Bene to the Purchasing Officer. The manner in which this section is written poses some interesting questions about breaches of warranty that are discovered after the goods have gone into production. The American buyer should protect against the need to return goods after having worked them partially, by including a clause in the contract giving the buyer the opportunity to return any goods at any point in production when a breach from the contract description is discovered.

Section VI. Preservation of the Goods. Articles 85–88.

These are four articles at the conclusion of the Convention that require the party in possession to take reasonable care of the goods even though the other party has defaulted in one manner or another. These rules are similar to those in the Uniform Commercial Code in Sections 2–603 and 2–515. See pages 365–66 in the original text.

The C.I.S.G. and the American Purchasing Officer. Now that we have dissected the Convention as well as compared its major provisions with the Uniform Commercial Code, the next questions to be faced are "Can we live with it?" and "Should we contract under its principles of law?" The answer to the first question would be affirmative. We can live with the Convention. Although it is not a perfect law by any measure of the imagination, it is not all "bad." It has some good features going for it that the purchasing officer will find advantageous. But there are also places in the Convention where its laws are written in favor of the supplier and against the buyer. Before making a final decision on "good or bad," let us enumerate the advantages and disadvantages in the use of the Convention, and then point out where the Convention can be said to be written against the best interests of the purchasing officer.

The Good Word About the Convention. Perhaps the finest thing that can be said about the Convention is that it is now a uniform law in 32 different countries of the world, including the United States. That is a sizeable portion of the world. There must be merit in the Convention because it enables us to sit in our office located in any one of the 50 United States and contract under the same body of law with suppliers in any one of 31 foreign countries. The fact that there is "one law" that governs all of us in that circle helps us considerably. The possibility of either party acting in ignorance of the applicable law is minimized.

The Bad Piece of Business About the Convention. Perhaps the most worrisome feature about the Convention is the fact that it may not be uniformly interpreted and applied. The probability that the Courts of 32 different countries will interpret each section of the Convention in identically the same manner is remote. If it does happen, it will be a huge surprise. There are two major problems that militate against uniformity. The first is the fact that some articles in the Convention depend upon the application of domestic law to the problem in litigation. We all know that domestic law varies. We also know that the domestic law to be applied can be the law of the plaintiff's country or that of the defendant's. So there is a built-in possibility of diversity of application.

The other factor pointing to non-uniformity is that at the present time there is no centralized reporting service that brings together in one place all of the decisions rendered under the Convention. It is essential that jurists, attorneys, and all parties involved in litigation, have the opportunity to learn how other countries, as well as their own country, have applied specific articles of the Convention. Without such experiences, each party and their legal counsel begin a transaction in uncharted seas. Such a situation also limits the ability of legal counsel to give proper legal advice on how to proceed. Your author feels certain there will be some reporting service developed in the not too distant future.

The Major Differences Between the Convention and the Uniform Commercial Code. Before itemizing these major differences between these two bodies of law, your author wishes to make one general observation. The American purchasing officer is advised to expect in the Convention a great desire to have the contract completed without too many, if any, adjustments being made. Some of the articles are written with the deliberate intent to place responsibility for safe transportation of the goods on the shoulders of the buyer. Another article wants to make certain the buyer accepts non-conforming goods if they are at all useable regardless of their deviation from the contract description.

The general thrust of the Convention is that it recognizes that there is considerable effort and expense expended by the supplier in preparing the goods for shipment and forwarding them. Because of that fact the Convention wants to exert every pressure possible on the buyer to accept and utilize the goods if at all possible, no matter whether the goods are conforming or non-conforming. Of course all buyers subscribe to the general approach that economic waste should be avoided whenever possible. Therefore it is good business to try to "make do" with what has been delivered by a supplier, but particularly by a foreign supplier. On the other hand, the American purchasing officer does not want to be forced into accepting goods that will result in his or her company's product not being up to acceptable standards. It is in this area that we should be concerned about the effect of the Convention on the quality of our products. In any event the American purchasing officer can protect against such eventualities by appropriate clauses in the purchase contract. But then, that is not living totally within the Convention.

There follows here a list of major differences in the Convention. We have listed them by their appropriate article numerical sequence.

1. Article 2(a) states the Convention does not apply to consumer purchases and sales. This difference does not affect purchasing officers in their daily routine.

2. Article 3(2) codifies in the Convention that if the predominant part of a contract is for services, the Convention is not applicable. This is not so stated in the Code but is now generally applied by the courts. The clarification of this point in the Convention enures to the benefit of both buyer and supplier.

3. Article 8(3) overturns the parol evidence rule of the Code by providing, *inter alia,* that ". . . the negotiations, . . . usages, and any subsequent conduct of the parties" may be used in determining the intent of a contracting party. Both buyer and supplier are equally affected by this change.

4. Article 9(2) brings "international usages" into any contract unless excluded by agreement of the parties. Although this affects both parties, caution should tell the American purchasing officer to "beware."

5. Article 11 does away with the Statute of Frauds as we know it in the Code. An oral contract for the sale of goods is now possible. Your author believes this is a disadvantage to the purchasing officer.

6. Article 12 permits Article 11 from becoming effective in any country that requires a writing (such as in the United States) for an enforceable contract. The United States did not take advantage of this caveat but other countries did. This makes another non-uniform application of the Code.

7. Article 14(1) requires a price to be included in a valid offer. This may prolong negotiations between the buyer and the supplier.

8. Article 16(2)(a) apparently makes it more simple for a firm offer to be created than under the Code. This is a plus for the buyer.

9. Article 16(2)(b) codifies the doctrine of promissory estoppel in the topic on revocation of an offer. This is a plus for the buyer, since the Code is silent on the doctrine and some states recognize it while others do not.

10. Article 17 provides that a rejection terminates a firm offer. The Code is silent on this. Probably it is an assist to the supplier.

11. Article 18(2) changes the dispatch rule for acceptances. It demands the acceptance be received by the offeror before becoming effective. It is your author's opinion this change works to the detriment of the buyer because more acceptances come from the buyer. Whomever accepts an offer is at the mercy of the postal service unless facsimiles are utilized.

12. Article 19(1) restates the mirror image rule for acceptance of an offer. The Code in Section 2–207 attempted to eliminate this. A backward step for both the buyer and the supplier.

13. Article 19(2) restates the Code's Section 2–207(1) but adds "subject to the offeror's approval." This is a detriment to the buyer who more often sends the acceptance. Should it be delayed, the buyer should not be required to depend upon the supplier to decide whether it will be accepted. This gives the supplier the opportunity to speculate on "up and down" prices.

14. Article 19(3) does the buyer and supplier a favor by spelling out what different or additional terms will be considered "material." This is an improvement over Section 2–207, which lets one guess. However, Article 19(3) lists so many items that it makes most additional or different terms "material," thereby losing the 19(2) rule of contract completion.

15. Article 25, defining a fundamental breach, requires the breach to "substantially deprive the other party . . ." This works against the buyer because it impliedly does away with the perfect tender rule and gives redress only when there is a substantial defect.

16. Article 25 also favors the supplier by giving him the right to a fundamental

breach only if the results could have been "foreseen" by him. This works against the buyer in many instances.

17. Article 29 on modification of a contract follows the Code by not requiring consideration to pass for a contract modification. But because of Article 11 (abandoning the Statute of Frauds), the amended contract does not have to be in writing.

18. The Convention contains no delivery terms, depending entirely on Incoterms. This is not all bad except that Incoterms are amended from time to time with little or no notice.

19. Article 35 gives a full set of Code warranties to each contract and makes these warranties part of the contract. This is definitely a buyer's advantage. However, nowhere in the Convention is there any prescribed method of disclaiming warranties. The buyer must be alert to the wording the supplier gives concerning warranties.

20. Article 37 gives the supplier the opportunity to "cure" defects before the time for delivery has passed. Article 48 gives the seller the same opportunity to "cure" after the time for delivery has passed. The latter right generally prevents the buyer from declaring a fundamental breach until the rites of "cure" have been exhausted. All of this works against the buyer.

21. Article 42 gives the buyer protection against patent infringement but only if the supplier knew of the possible infringement suit. This is definitely against the buyer.

22. Article 47(1) allows the buyer to grant the supplier additional time for performance of his obligations under the contract. This is new to the American purchasing officer. It gives a precise time to declare a fundamental breach but it prolongs completion of the contract.

23. Article 52(2) prohibits the supplier from delivering and charging for "overruns." An advantage for buyers.

24. Article 54 emphasizes the buyer's payment problems of foreign sourcing by making the buyer alert to "being prepared to pay" and comply with all formalities of import and export.

25. Article 55 applies a price where the contract is silent. It applies the price prevailing at the time of contracting; not at the time of delivery as does the Code. It works for and against both parties.

26. Article 74 makes the supplier liable for consequential damages only if he could have foreseen them. This definitely works against the buyer.

Conclusion for the American Purchasing Officer. It is apparent that the price you pay for foreign sourcing is not overwhelming. If contracting and performing under the Convention is the only way your supplier will do business—and you want to do business with that supplier—then attempt to protect yourself as we have indicated in the body of this text.

Since most purchasing officers do more domestic than foreign sourcing, they live under the Uniform Commercial Code daily. One can only ask the question "Is it essential to also learn the confusing vagaries of the Convention?" to do business with some foreign suppliers. Hopefully most of your suppliers will agree to do business on your terms and under your state's version of the Uniform Commercial Code. Then you will have the best of both worlds.

Nota Bene to the Purchasing Officer. It is suggested that before the first negotiation with any supplier occurs which might be covered by the Convention, the two parties sign an agreement as to which law will be applicable. Perhaps you, the purchasing officer, should take the offensive on this and hand the supplier a paper making your own state law (the Uniform Commercial Code and not the Convention) applicable to any business you might do. Furthermore, if you do a continuing business with a supplier, why not execute one "Overriding Agreement for All Purchases" agreement with that supplier. Settle your problems once and for all time with such an overriding agreement.

Appendix C
UNITED NATIONS CONVENTION ON CONTRACTS FOR THE INTERNATIONAL SALE OF GOODS (1980)*

The States Parties to This Convention,

BEARING IN MIND the broad objectives in the resolutions adopted by the sixth special session of the General Assembly of the United Nations on the establishment of a New International Economic Order,

CONSIDERING that the development of international trade on the basis of equality and mutual benefit is an important element in promoting friendly relations among States,

BEING OF THE OPINION that the adoption of uniform rules which govern contracts for the international sale of goods and take into account the different social, economic and legal systems would contribute to the removal of legal barriers in international trade and promote the development of international trade,

HAVE AGREED as follows:

PART I

SPHERE OF APPLICATION AND GENERAL PROVISIONS

Chapter I
Sphere of Application

ART. 1. Parties to whom applicable.

* [**Editor's Note:** The boldface captions of ART.1 through ART.101 are not part of the official text of the Convention but are provided by the author for the convenience of the reader. "ART." refers to Articles of the Convention.]

(1) This Convention applies to contracts of sale of goods between parties whose places of business are in different states:
- (a) when the States are Contracting States; or
- (b) when the rules of private international law lead to the application of the law of a Contracting State.

(2) The fact that the parties have their places of business in different States is to be disregarded whenever this fact does not appear either from the contract or from any dealings between, or from information disclosed by, the parties at any time before or at the conclusion of the contract.

(3) Neither the nationality of the parties nor the civil or commercial character of the parties or of the contract is to be taken into consideration in determining the application of this Convention.

ART. 2. Types of sales not applicable.

This Convention does not apply to sales:
- (a) of goods bought for personal, family or household use, unless the seller, at any time before or at the conclusion of the contract, neither knew nor ought to have known that the goods were bought for any such use;
- (b) by auction;
- (c) on execution or otherwise by authority of law;
- (d) of stocks, shares, investment securities, negotiable instruments or money;
- (e) of ships, vessels, hovercraft or aircraft;
- (f) of electricity.

ART. 3. Not applicable where buyer supplies materials for manufacture nor when preponderant part of sale is for services.

(1) Contracts for the supply of goods to be manufactured or produced are to be considered sales unless the party who orders the goods undertakes to supply a substantial part of the materials necessary for such manufacture or production.

(2) This Convention does not apply to contracts in which the preponderant part of the obligations of the party who furnishes the goods consists in the supply of labour or other services.

ART. 4. Applies to formation of contract and rights and obligations of parties; not concerned with validity of property in goods.

This Convention governs only the formation of the contract of sale and the rights and obligations of the seller and the buyer arising from such a contract. In particular, except as otherwise expressly provided in this Convention, it is not concerned with:
- (a) the validity of the contract or of any of its provisions or of any usage;
- (b) the effect which the contract may have on the property in the goods sold.

ART. 5. Not applicable for personal injury or death caused by goods.

This Convention does not apply to the liability of the seller for death or personal injury caused by the goods to any person.

ART. 6. Parties may derogate from part or all.

The parties may exclude the application of this Convention or, subject to article 12, derogage from or vary the effect of any of its provisions.

Chapter II
General Provisions

ART. 7. Need for uniformity and good faith in interpretation; domestic law to be applied for topics not covered herein.

(1) In the interpretation of this Convention, regard is to be had to its international character and to the need to promote uniformity in its application and the observance of good faith in international trade.

(2) Questions concerning matters governed by this Convention which are not expressly settled in it are to be settled in conformity with the general principles on which it is based or, in the absence of such principles, in conformity with the law applicable by virtue of the rules of private international law.

ART. 8. Statements to be interpreted by intent; what a reasonable party would understand; or by negotiations, practices, and subsequent conduct of parties.

(1) For the purposes of this Convention statements made by and other conduct of a party are to be interpreted according to his intent where the other party knew or could not have been unaware what that intent was.

(2) If the preceding paragraph is not applicable, statements made by and other conduct of a party are to be interpreted according to the understanding that a reasonable person of the same kind as the other party would have had in the same circumstances.

(3) In determining the intent of a party or the understanding a reasonable person would have had, due consideration is to be given to all relevant circumstances of the case including the negotiations, any practices which the parties have established between themselves, usages and any subsequent conduct of the parties.

ART. 9. Parties bound by agreed-to and well-known international usages.

(1) The parties are bound by any usage to which they have agreed and by any practices which they have established between themselves.

(2) The parties are considered, unless otherwise agreed, to have impliedly made applicable to their contract or its formation a usage of which the parties knew or ought to have known and which in international trade is widely known to, and regularly observed by, parties to contracts of the type involved in the particular trade concerned.

ART. 10. Place of business is one that has closest relationship to contract; if none, party's residence.

For the purposes of this Convention:
(a) if a party has more than one place of business, the place of business is that which has the closest relationship to the contract and its performance, having regard to the circumstances known to or contemplated by the parties at any time before or at the conclusion of the contract;
(b) if a party does not have a place of business, reference is to be made to his habitual residence.

ART. 11. No need for writing to prove contract of sale.

A contract of sale need not be concluded in or evidenced by writing and is not subject to any other requirement as to form. It may be proved by any means, including witnesses.

ART. 12. Rule of Article 11 may be overcome by statement of Contracting Country under Article 96.

Any provision of article 11, article 29 or Part II of this Convention that allows a contract of sale or its modifications or termination by agreement or any offer, acceptance or other indication of intention to be made in any form other than in writing does not apply where any party has his place of business in a Contracting State which has made a declaration under article 96 of this Convention. The parties may not derogate from or vary the effect of this article.

ART. 13. "Writing" includes telegram and telex.

For the purposes of this Convention "writing" includes telegram and telex.

PART II

FORMATION OF THE CONTRACT

ART. 14. Valid offer must contain quantity and price; must be communicated.

(1) A proposal for concluding a contract addressed to one or more specific persons constitutes an offer if it is sufficiently definite and indicates the intention of the offeror to be bound in case of acceptance. A proposal is sufficiently definite if it indicates the goods and expressly or implicitly fixes or makes provision for determining the quantity and the price.

(2) A proposal other than one addressed to one or more specific persons is to be considered merely as an invitation to make offers, unless the contrary is clearly indicated by the person making the proposal.

ART. 15. Offer effective when reaches offeror; irrevocable offer may be withdrawn if withdrawal reaches offeree before offer.

(1) An offer becomes effective when it reaches the offeree.
(2) An offer, even if it is irrevocable, may be withdrawn if the withdrawal reaches the offeree before or at the same time as the offer.

ART. 16. Offer may be revoked before offeree has dispatched an acceptance; offer irrevocable if it states fixed time for acceptance or if offeree has acted in reliance thereon.

(1) Until a contract is concluded an offer may be revoked if the revocation reaches the offeree before he has dispatched an acceptance.

(2) However, an offer cannot be revoked:
    (a) if it indicates, whether by stating a fixed time for acceptance or otherwise, that it is irrevocable; or
    (b) if it was reasonable for the offeree to rely on the offer as being irrevocable and the offeree has acted in reliance on the offer.

ART. 17. Any offer terminated at time of rejection.

An offer, even if it is irrevocable, is terminated when a rejection reaches the offeror.

ART. 18. Acceptance must be communicated and received by offeror; parties can agree to make performance an acceptance.

(1) A statement made by or other conduct of the offeree indicating assent to an offer is an acceptance. Silence or inactivity does not in itself amount to acceptance.

(2) An acceptance of an offer becomes effective at the moment the indication of assent reaches the offeror. An acceptance is not effective if the indication of assent does not reach the offeror within the time he has fixed or, if no time is fixed, within a reasonable time, due account being taken of the circumstances of the transaction, including the rapidity of the means of communication employed by the offeror. An oral offer must be accepted immediately unless the circumstances indicate otherwise.

(3) However, if, by virtue of the offer or as a result of practices which the parties have established between themselves or of usage, the offeree may indicate assent by performing an act, such as one relating to the dispatch of the goods or payment of the price, without notice to the offeror, the acceptance is effective at the moment the act is performed, provided that the act is performed within the period of time laid down in the preceding paragraph.

ART. 19. Acceptance must be mirror image or is counter-offer; non-material additions or differences may be objected to by offeror; list of items deemed to be material.

(1) A reply to an offer which purports to be an acceptance but contains additions, limitations or other modifications is a rejection of the offer and constitutes a counter-offer.

(2) However, a reply to an offer which purports to be an acceptance but contains additional or different terms which do not materially alter the terms of the offer constitutes an acceptance, unless the offeror, without undue delay, objects orally to the discrepancy or dispatches a notice to that effect. If he does not so object, the terms of the contract are the terms of the offer with the modifications contained in the acceptance.

(3) Additional or different terms relating, among other things, to the price, payment, quality and quantity of the goods, place and time of delivery, extent of one party's liability to the other or the settlement of disputes are considered to alter the terms of the offer materially.

ART. 20. Time runs from dispatch of telegram or letter; official holidays and non-business days included in time count.

(1) A period of time for acceptance, fixed by the offeror in a telegram or a letter begins to run from the moment the telegram is handed in for dispatch or from the date shown on the letter or, if no such date is shown, from the date shown on the envelope. A period of time for acceptance fixed by the offeror by telephone, telex or other means of instantaneous communication, begins to run from the moment that the offer reaches the offeree.

(2) Official holidays or non-business days occurring during the period for acceptance are included in calculating the period. However, if a notice of acceptance cannot be delivered at the address of the offeror on the last day of the period because that day falls on an official holiday or a non-business day at the place of business of the offeror, the period is extended until the first business day which follows.

ART. 21. Late acceptance valid if offeror so notifies offeree.

(1) A late acceptance is nevertheless effective as an acceptance if without delay the offeror orally so informs the offeree or dispatches a notice to that effect.

(2) If a letter or other writing containing a late acceptance shows that it has been sent in such circumstances that if its transmission had been normal it would have reached the offeror in due time, the late acceptance is effective as an acceptance unless, without delay, the offeror orally informs the offeree that he considers his offer as having lapsed or dispatches a notice to that effect.

ART. 22. **Acceptance may be withdrawn anytime before becoming effective.**

An acceptance may be withdrawn if the withdrawal reaches the offeror before or at the same time as the acceptance would have become effective.

ART. 23. **Contract concluded at moment acceptance effective.**

A contract is concluded at the moment when an acceptance of an offer becomes effective in accordance with the provisions of this Convention.

ART. 24. **Communication reaches person when delivered personally or at place of business or mailing address.**

For the purposes of this Part of the Convention, an offer, declaration of acceptance or any other indication of intention "reaches" the addressee when it is made orally to him or delivered by any other means to him personally, to his place of business or mailing address or, if he does not have a place of business or mailing address, to his habitual residence.

PART III

SALE OF GOODS

Chapter 1
General Provisions

ART. 25. **Definition of fundamental breach.**

A breach of contract committed by one of the parties is fundamental if it results in such detriment to the other party as substantially to deprive him of what he is entitled to expect under the contract, unless the party in breach did not foresee and a reasonable person of the same kind in the same circumstances would not have foreseen such a result.

ART. 26. **Notice required for declaration of avoidance.**

A declaration of avoidance of the contract is effective only if made by notice to the other party.

ART. 27. **Communications in Part II effective when dispatched.**

Unless otherwise expressly provided in this Part of the Convention, if any notice, request or other communication is given or made by a party

Appendix C

in accordance with this Part and by means appropriate in the circumstances, a delay or error in the transmission of the communication or its failure to arrive does not deprive that party of the right to rely on the communication.

ART. 28. Specific performance available only if is domestic law of country.

If, in accordance with the provisions of this Convention, one party is entitled to require performance of any obligation by the other party, a court is not bound to enter a judgment for specific performance unless the court would do so under its own law in respect of similar contracts of sale not governed by this Convention.

ART. 29. Modification requires no writing unless otherwise agreed.

(1) A contract may be modified or terminated by the mere agreement of the parties.

(2) A contract in writing which contains a provision requiring any modification or termination by agreement to be in writing may not be otherwise modified or terminated by agreement. However, a party may be precluded by his conduct from asserting such a provision to the extent that the other party has relied on that conduct.

Chapter II
Obligations of the Seller

ART. 30. Seller's duties.

The seller must deliver the goods, hand over any documents relating to them and transfer the property in the goods, as required by the contract and this Convention.

Section I.
Delivery of the goods and handing over of documents

ART. 31. Seller bound to hand over goods to first carrier if carriage is required; otherwise buyer takes where goods located.

If the seller is not bound to deliver the goods at any other particular place, his obligation to deliver consists:

(a) if the contract of sale involves carriage of the goods—in handing the goods over to the first carrier for transmission to the buyer;
(b) if, in cases not within the preceding subparagraph, the contract relates to specific goods, or unidentified goods to be drawn from a specific stock or to be manufactured or produced, and at the time of the conclusion of the contract the parties knew that the goods were at, or were to be manufactured or produced at, a particular place—in placing the goods at the buyer's disposal at that place;
(c) in other cases—in placing the goods at the buyer's disposal at the place where the seller had his place of business at the time of the conclusion of the contract.

ART. 32. Seller must mark goods clearly for carrier or give buyer notice; if seller bound to arrange for carriage must make proper contract; if not bound to insure, must provide buyer with information.

(1) If the seller, in accordance with the contract or this Convention, hands the goods over to a carrier and if the goods are not clearly identified to the contract by markings on the goods, by shipping documents or otherwise, the seller must give the buyer notice of the consignment specifying the goods.

(2) If the seller is bound to arrange for carriage of the goods, he must make such contracts as are necessary for carriage to the place fixed by means of transportation appropriate in the circumstances and according to the usual terms for such transportation.

(3) If the seller is not bound to effect insurance in respect of the carriage of the goods, he must, at the buyer's request, provide him with all available information necessary to enable him to effect such insurance.

ART. 33. Seller must deliver on proper date or within reasonable time.

The seller must deliver the goods:
(a) if a date is fixed by or determinable from the contract, on that date;
(b) if a period of time is fixed by or determinable from the contract, at any time within that period unless circumstances indicate that the buyer is to choose a date; or

(c) in any other case, within a reasonable time after the conclusion of the contract.

ART. 34. Seller must hand over documents as required by contract.

If the seller is bound to hand over documents relating to the goods, he must hand them over at the time and place and in the form required by the contract. If the seller has handed over documents before that time, he may, up to that time, cure any lack of conformity in the documents, if the exercise of this right does not cause the buyer unreasonable inconvenience or unreasonable expense. However, the buyer retains any right to claim damages as provided for in this Convention.

Section II.
Conformity of the goods and third party claims

ART. 35. Seller must deliver proper goods; goods must meet normal warranties.

(1) The seller must deliver goods which are of the quantity, quality and description required by the contract and which are contained or packaged in the manner required by the contract.

(2) Except where the parties have agreed otherwise, the goods do not conform with the contract unless they:
   (a) are fit for the purposes for which goods of the same description would ordinarily be used;
   (b) are fit for any particular purpose expressly or impliedly made known to the seller at the time of the conclusion of the contract, except where the circumstances show that the buyer did not rely, or that it was unreasonable for him to rely, on the seller's skill and judgment;
   (c) possess the qualities of goods which the seller has held out to the buyer as a sample or model;
   (d) are contained or packaged in the manner usual for such goods or, where there is no such manner, in a manner adequate to preserve and protect the goods.

(3) The seller is not liable under subparagraphs (a) to (d) of the preceding paragraph for any lack of conformity of the goods if at the time of the conclusion of the contract the buyer knew or could not have been unaware of such lack of conformity.

ART. 36. Seller liable for any lack of conformity existing when risk passes to buyer; also liable if defects occur after because of breach of obligation.

(1) The seller is liable in accordance with the contract and this Convention for any lack of conformity which exists at the time when the risk passes to the buyer, even though the lack of conformity becomes apparent only after that time.

(2) The seller is also liable for any lack of conformity which occurs after the time indicated in the preceding paragraph and which is due to a breach of any of his obligations, including a breach of any guarantee that for a period of time the goods will remain fit for their ordinary purpose or for some particular purpose or will retain specified qualities or characteristics.

ART. 37. Seller may cure defects before time of delivery has passed.

If the seller has delivered goods before the date for delivery, he may, up to that date, deliver any missing part or make up any deficiency in the quantity of the goods delivered, or deliver goods in replacement of any non-conforming goods delivered or remedy any lack of conformity in the goods delivered, provided that the exercise of this right does not cause the buyer unreasonable inconvenience or unreasonable expense. However, the buyer retains any right to claim damages as provided for in this Convention.

ART. 38. Buyer must inspect promptly.

(1) The buyer must examine the goods, or cause them to be examined, within as short a period as is practicable in the circumstances.

(2) If the contract involves carriage of the goods, examination may be deferred until after the goods have arrived at their destination.

(3) If the goods are redirected in transit or redispatched by the buyer without a reasonable opportunity for examination by him and at the time of the conclusion of the contract the seller knew or ought to have known of the possibility of such redirection or redispatch, examination may be deferred until after the goods have arrived at the new destination.

ART. 39. Buyer must give seller notice of lack of conformity or lose right; final deadline two years from date goods handed over.

(1) The buyer loses the right to rely on a lack of conformity of the goods if he does not give notice to the seller specifying the nature of the

lack of conformity within a reasonable time after he has discovered it or ought to have discovered it.

(2) In any event, the buyer loses the right to rely on a lack of conformity of the goods if he does not give the seller notice thereof at the latest within a period of two years from the date on which the goods were actually handed over to the buyer, unless this time-limit is inconsistent with a contractual period of guarantee.

ART. 40. Seller must not have known of defects to rely on Articles 38 and 39.

The seller is not entitled to rely on the provisions of articles 38 and 39 if the lack of conformity relates to facts of which he knew or could not have been unaware and which he did not disclose to the buyer.

ART. 41. Seller must deliver free of any right or claim of third party.

The seller must deliver goods which are free from any right or claim of a third party, unless the buyer agreed to take the goods subject to that right or claim. However, if such right or claim is based on industrial property or other intellectual property, the seller's obligation is governed by article 42.

ART. 42. Seller must deliver goods free of any claim based on industrial property; seller must have known of such claims to be liable.

(1) The seller must deliver goods which are free from any right or claim of a third party based on industrial property or other intellectual property, of which at the time of the conclusion of the contract the seller knew or could not have been unaware, provided that the right or claim is based on industrial property or other intellectual property:
    (a) under the law of the State where the goods will be resold or otherwise used, if it was contemplated by the parties at the time of the conclusion of the contract that the goods would be resold or otherwise used in that State; or
    (b) in any other case, under the law of the State where the buyer has his place of business.

(2) The obligation of the seller under the preceding paragraph does not extend to cases where:
    (a) at the time of the conclusion of the contract the buyer knew or could not have been unaware of the right or claim; or
    (b) the right or claim results from the seller's compliance with technical drawings, designs, formulae or other such specifications furnished by the buyer.

ART. 43. Buyer must notify seller of claims under Articles 41 and 42.

(1) The buyer loses the right to rely on the provisions of article 41 or article 42 if he does not give notice to the seller specifying the nature of the right or claim of the third party within a reasonable time after he has become aware, or ought to have become aware, of the right or claim.

(2) The seller is not entitled to rely on the provisions of the preceding paragraph if he knew of the right or claim of the third party and the nature of it.

ART. 44. Buyer may reduce price if has excuse for no notice.

Notwithstanding the provisions of paragraph (1) of article 39 and paragraph (1) of article 43, the buyer may reduce the price in accordance with article 50 or claim damages, except for loss of profit, if he has a reasonable excuse for his failure to give the required notice.

Section III.
Remedies for breach of contract by the seller

ART. 45. Remedies of buyer.

(1) If the seller fails to perform any of his obligations under the contract or this Convention, the buyer may:
    (a) exercise the rights provided in articles 46 to 52;
    (b) claim damages as provided in articles 74 to 77.

(2) The buyer is not deprived of any right he may have to claim damages by exercising his right to other remedies.

(3) No period of grace may be granted to the seller by a court or arbitral tribunal when the buyer resorts to a remedy for breach of contract.

Appendix C

ART. 46. Buyer may require specific performance; may require substitute goods if lack of conformity a fundamental breach; or request repair.

(1) The buyer may require performance by the seller of his obligations unless the buyer has resorted to a remedy which is inconsistent with this requirement.

(2) If the goods do not conform with the contract, the buyer may require delivery of substitute goods only if the lack of conformity constitutes a fundamental breach of contract and a request for substitute goods is made either in conjunction with notice given under article 39 or within a reasonable time thereafter.

(3) If the goods do not conform with the contract, the buyer may require the seller to remedy the lack of conformity by repair, unless this is unreasonable having a regard to all the circumstances. A request for repair must be made either in conjunction with notice given under article 39 or within a reasonable time thereafter.

ART. 47. Buyer may fix additional period of time for performance.

(1) The buyer may fix an additional period of time of reasonable length for performance by the seller of his obligations.

(2) Unless the buyer has received notice from the seller that he will not perform within the period so fixed, the buyer may not, during that period, resort to any remedy for breach of contract. However, the buyer is not deprived thereby of any right he may have to claim damages for delay in performance.

ART. 48. Seller may cure after date of delivery.

(1) Subject to article 49, the seller may, even after the date for delivery, remedy at his own expense any failure to perform his obligations, if he can do so without unreasonable delay and without causing the buyer unreasonable inconvenience or uncertainty of reimbursement by the seller of expenses advanced by the buyer. However, the buyer retains any right to claim damages as provided for in this Convention.

(2) If the seller requests the buyer to make known whether he will accept performance and the buyer does not comply with the request within a reasonable time, the seller may perform within the time indicated in his

request. The buyer may not, during that period of time, resort to any remedy which is inconsistent with performance by the seller.

(3) A notice by the seller that he will perform within a specified period of time is assumed to include a request, under the preceding paragraph, that the buyer make known his decision.

(4) A request or notice by the seller under paragraph (2) or (3) of this article is not effective unless received by the buyer.

ART. 49. When buyer may declare contract avoided; limitations thereon.

(1) The buyer may declare the contract avoided:
   (a) if the failure by the seller to perform any of his obligations under the contract or this Convention amounts to a fundamental breach of contract; or
   (b) in case of non-delivery, if the seller does not deliver the goods within the additional period of time fixed by the buyer in accordance with paragraph (1) of article 47 or declares that he will not deliver within the period so fixed.

(2) However, in cases where the seller has delivered the goods, the buyer loses the right to declare the contract avoided unless he does so:
   (a) in respect of late delivery, within a reasonable time after he has become aware that delivery has been made;
   (b) in respect of any breach other than late delivery, within a reasonable time:
      (i) after he knew or ought to have known of the breach;
      (ii) after the expiration of any additional period of time fixed by the buyer in accordance with paragraph (1) of article 47, or after the seller has declared that he will not perform his obligations within such an additional period; or
      (iii) after the expiration of any additional period of time indicated by the seller in accordance with paragraph (2) of article 48, or after the buyer has declared that he will not accept performance.

ART. 50. Buyer may reduce price if delivered goods non-conforming.

If the goods do not conform with the contract and whether or not the price has already been paid, the buyer may reduce the price in the same proportion as the value that the goods actually delivered had at the time of the delivery bears to the value that conforming goods would have had at that time. However, if the seller remedies any failure to perform his obligations in accordance with article 37 or article 48 or if the buyer refuses to accept performance by the seller in accordance with those articles, the buyer may not reduce the price.

ART. 51. Articles 46–50 apply to part of goods not delivered; buyer may avoid contract only if partial delivery amounts to fundamental breach.

(1) If the seller delivers only a part of the goods or if only a part of the goods delivered is in conformity with the contract, articles 46 to 50 apply in respect of the part which is missing or which does not conform.

(2) The buyer may declare the contract avoided in its entirety only if the failure to make delivery completely or in conformity with the contract amounts to a fundamental breach of the contract.

ART. 52. Buyer may refuse early delivery or excess quantity.

(1) If the seller delivers the goods before the date fixed, the buyer may take delivery or refuse to take delivery.

(2) If the seller delivers a quantity of goods greater than that provided for in the contract, the buyer may take delivery or refuse to take delivery of the excess quantity. If the buyer takes delivery of all or part of the excess quantity, he must pay for it at the contract rate.

Chapter III
Obligations of the Buyer

ART. 53. Buyer must pay price and take delivery.

The buyer must pay the price for the goods and take delivery of them as required by the contract and this Convention.

Section I.
Payment of the price

ART. 54. Buyer must take steps to comply with payment formalities.

The buyer's obligation to pay the price includes taking such steps and complying with such formalities as may be required under the contract or any laws and regulations to enable payment to be made.

ART. 55. **Price of completed unpriced contract may be implied from prevailing price at time of contracting.**

Where a contract has been validly concluded but does not expressly or implicitly fix or make provision for determining the price, the parties are considered, in the absence of any indication to the contrary, to have impliedly made reference to the price generally charged at the time of the conclusion of the contract for such goods sold under comparable circumstances in the trade concerned.

ART. 56. **Net weight to apply.**

If the price is fixed according to the weight of the goods, in case of doubt it is to be determined by the net weight.

ART. 57. **Payment due at seller's place of business or where documents handed over.**

(1) If the buyer is not bound to pay the price at any other particular place, he must pay it to the seller;
    (a) at the seller's place of business; or
    (b) if the payment is to be made against the handing over of the goods or of documents, at the place where the handing over takes place.

(2) The seller must bear any increase in the expenses incidental to payment which is caused by a change in his place of business subsequent to the conclusion of the contract.

ART. 58. **Payment due when goods placed at buyer's disposal; payment against documents must be made before goods handed over; buyer has right to inspect before payment unless terms are inconsistent.**

(1) If the buyer is not bound to pay the price at any other specific time, he must pay it when the seller places either the goods or documents controlling their disposition at the buyer's disposal in accordance with the contract and this Convention. The seller may make such payment a condition for handing over the goods or documents.

(2) If the contract involves carriage of the goods, the seller may dispatch the goods on terms whereby the goods, or documents controlling their

disposition, will not be handed over to the buyer except against payment of the price.

(3) The buyer is not bound to pay the price until he has had an opportunity to examine the goods, unless the procedures for delivery or payment agreed upon by the parties are inconsistent with his having such an opportunity.

ART. 59. Seller need not make demand for payment.

The buyer must pay the price on the date fixed by or determinable from the contract and this Convention without the need for any request or compliance with any formality on the part of the seller.

Section II.
Taking delivery

ART. 60. Buyer's obligation to take delivery.

The buyer's obligation to take delivery consists:
    (a) in doing all the acts which could reasonably be expected of him in order to enable the seller to make delivery; and
    (b) in taking over the goods.

Section III.
Remedies for breach of contract by the buyer

ART. 61. Remedies for breach of contract by buyer.

(1) If the buyer fails to perform any of his obligations under the contract or this Convention, the seller may:
    (a) exercise the rights provided in articles 62 to 65;
    (b) claim damages as provided in articles 74 to 77.
(2) The seller is not deprived of any right he may have to claim damages by exercising his right to other remedies.
(3) No period of grace may be granted to the buyer by a court or arbitral tribunal when the seller resorts to a remedy for breach of contract.

ART. 62. Seller may require specific performance.

The seller may require the buyer to pay the price, take delivery or perform his other obligations, unless the seller has resorted to a remedy which is inconsistent with this requirement.

ART. 63. Seller may fix additional period of time for performance.

(1) The seller may fix an additional period of time of reasonable length for performance by the buyer of his obligations.

(2) Unless the seller has received notice from the buyer that he will not perform within the period so fixed, the seller may not, during that period, resort to any remedy for breach of contract. However, the seller is not deprived thereby of any right he may have to claim damages for delay in performance.

ART. 64. When seller may declare contract avoided.

(1) The seller may declare the contract avoided:
 (a) if the failure by the buyer to perform any of his obligations under the contract or this Convention amounts to a fundamental breach of contract; or
 (b) if the buyer does not, within the additional period of time fixed by the seller in accordance with paragraph (1) of article 63, perform his obligation to pay the price or take delivery of the goods, or if he declares that he will not do so within the period so fixed.

(2) However, in cases where the buyer has paid the price, the seller loses the right to declare the contract avoided unless he does so:
 (a) in respect of late performance by the buyer, before the seller has become aware that performance has been rendered; or
 (b) in respect of any breach other than late performance by the buyer, within a reasonable time:
  (i) after the seller knew or ought to have known of the breach; or
  (ii) after the expiration of any additional period of time fixed by the seller in accordance with paragraph (1) of article 63, or after the buyer has declared that he will not perform his obligations within such an additional period.

ART. 65. Seller may specify features of goods if buyer fails to do so.

(1) If under the contract the buyer is to specify the form, measurement or other features of the goods and he fails to make such specification either on the date agreed upon or within a reasonable time after receipt of a request from the seller, the seller may, without prejudice to any other rights he may have, make the specification himself in accordance with the requirements of the buyer that may be known to him.

(2) If the seller makes the specification himself, he must inform the buyer of the details thereof and must fix a reasonable time within which the buyer may make a different specification. If, after receipt of such a communication, the buyer fails to do so within the time so fixed, the specification made by the seller is binding.

Chapter IV
Passing of Risk

ART. 66. Buyer must pay for goods if damaged after risk has passed.

Loss of or damage to the goods after the risk has passed to the buyer does not discharge him from his obligation to pay the price, unless the loss or damage is due to an act or omission of the seller.

ART. 67. Risk passes to buyer when goods handed over to first carrier on shipment contract.

(1) If the contract of sale involves carriage of the goods and the seller is not bound to hand them over at a particular place, the risk passes to the buyer when the goods are handed over to the first carrier for transmission to the buyer in accordance with the contract of sale. If the seller is bound to hand the goods over to a carrier at a particular place, the risk does not pass to the buyer until the goods are handed over to the carrier at that place. The fact that the seller is authorized to retain documents controlling the disposition of the goods does not affect the passage of the risk.

(2) Nevertheless, the risk does not pass to the buyer until the goods are clearly identified to the contract, whether by markings on the goods, by shipping documents, by notice given to the buyer or otherwise.

ART. 68. Risk passes to new buyer when sold in transit.

The risk in respect of goods sold in transit passes to the buyer from the time of the conclusion of the contract. However, if the circumstances so indicate, the risk is assumed by the buyer from the time the goods were handed over to the carrier who issued the documents embodying the contract of carriage. Nevertheless, if at the time of the conclusion of the contract of sale the seller knew or ought to have known that the goods had been lost or damaged and did not disclose this to the buyer, the loss or damage is at the risk of the seller.

ART. 69. Risk passes to buyer when takes over goods in other situations than in Articles 67–69.

(1) In cases not within articles 67 and 68, the risk passes to the buyer when he takes over the goods or, if he does not do so in due time, from the time when the goods are placed at his disposal and he commits a breach of contract by failing to take delivery.

(2) However, if the buyer is bound to take over the goods at a place other than a place of business of the seller, the risk passes when delivery is due and the buyer is aware of the fact that the goods are placed at his disposal at that place.

(3) If the contract relates to goods not then identified, the goods are considered not to be placed at the disposal of the buyer until they are clearly identified to the contract.

ART. 70. Articles 67–69 do not apply if seller has committed fundamental breach.

If the seller had committed a fundamental breach of contract, articles 67, 68 and 69 do not impair the remedies available to the buyer on account of the breach.

Chapter V
Provisions Common to the Obligations of the Seller and of the Buyer

Section I.
Anticipatory breach and instalment contracts

Appendix C

ART. 71. Party may suspend performance if apparent other party will not perform; seller may stop goods in transit.

(1) A party may suspend the performance of his obligations if, after the conclusion of the contract, it becomes apparent that the other party will not perform a substantial part of his obligations as a result of:
- (a) a serious deficiency in his ability to perform or in his creditworthiness; or
- (b) his conduct in preparing to perform or in performing the contract.

(2) If the seller has already dispatched the goods before the grounds described in the preceding paragraph become evident, he may prevent the handing over of the goods to the buyer even though the buyer holds a document which entitles him to obtain them. The present paragraph relates only to the rights in the goods as between the buyer and the seller.

(3) A party suspending performance, whether before or after dispatch of the goods, must immediately give notice of the suspension to the other party and must continue with performance if the other party provides adequate assurance of his performance.

ART. 72. Party may declare contract avoided if other party committing fundamental breach.

(1) If prior to the date for performance of the contract it is clear that one of the parties will commit a fundamental breach of contract, the other party may declare the contract avoided.

(2) If time allows, the party intending to declare the contract avoided must give reasonable notice to the other party in order to permit him to provide adequate assurance of his performance.

(3) The requirements of the preceding paragraph do not apply if the other party has declared that he will not perform his obligations.

ART. 73. In instalment contract, any failure a fundamental breach for that instalment; may declare balance avoided if one failure gives grounds for future.

(1) In the case of a contract for delivery of goods by instalments, if the failure of one party to perform any of his obligations in respect of any instalment constitutes a fundamental breach of contract with respect to that instalment, the other party may declare the contract avoided with respect to that instalment.

(2) If one party's failure to perform any of his obligations in respect of any instalment gives the other party good grounds to conclude that a fundamental breach of contract will occur with respect to future instalments, he may declare the contract avoided for the future, provided that he does so within a reasonable time.

(3) A buyer who declares the contract avoided in respect of any delivery may, at the same time, declare it avoided in respect of deliveries already made or of future deliveries if, by reason of their interdependence, those deliveries could not be used for the purpose contemplated by the parties at the time of the conclusion of the contract.

Section II.
Damages

ART. 74. Damages for breach of contract.

Damages for breach of contract by one party consist of a sum equal to the loss, including loss of profit, suffered by the other party as a consequence of the breach. Such damages may not exceed the loss which the party in breach foresaw or ought to have foreseen at the time of the conclusion of the contract, in the light of the facts and matters of which he then knew or ought to have known, as a possible consequence of the breach of contract.

ART. 75. Damages where cover occurs.

If the contract is avoided and if, in a reasonable manner and within a reasonable time after avoidance, the buyer has bought goods in replacement or the seller has resold the goods, the party claiming damages may recover the difference between the contract price and the price in the substitute transaction as well as any further damages recoverable under article 74.

ART. 76. Recovery of difference between contract price and current price at time of avoidance.

(1) If the contract is avoided and there is a current price for the goods, the party claiming damages may, if he has not made a purchase or resale under article 75, recover the difference between the price fixed by the contract and the current price at the time of avoidance as well as any further damages recoverable under article 74. If, however, the party claiming damages has avoided the contract after taking over the goods, the current price at the time of such taking over shall be applied instead of the current price at the time of avoidance.

(2) For the purpose of the preceding paragraph, the current price is

the price prevailing at the place where delivery of the goods should have been made or, if there is no current price at that place, the price at such other place as serves as a reasonable substitute, making due allowance for differences in the cost of transporting the goods.

ART. 77. Duty to mitigate loss.

A party who relies on a breach of contract must take such measures as are reasonable in the circumstances to mitigate the loss, including loss of profit, resulting from the breach. If he fails to take such measures, the party in breach may claim a reduction in the damages in the amount by which the loss should have been mitigated.

Section III.
Interest

ART. 78. Arrears carries interest.

If a party fails to pay the price or any other sum that is in arrears, the other party is entitled to interest on it, without prejudice to any claim for damages recoverable under article 74.

Section IV.
Exemptions

ART. 79. Exempt if impediment beyond control; third party failure to perform.

(1) A party is not liable for a failure to perform any of his obligations if he proves that the failure was due to an impediment beyond his control and that he could not reasonably be expected to have taken the impediment into account at the time of the conclusion of the contract or to have avoided or overcome it or its consequences.
(2) If the party's failure is due to the failure by a third person whom he has engaged to perform the whole or a part of the contract, that party is exempt from liability only if:
    (a) he is exempt under the preceding paragraph; and
    (b) the person whom he has so engaged would be so exempt if the provisions of that paragraph were applied to him.
(3) The exemption provided by this article has effect for the period during which the impediment exists.

(4) The party who fails to perform must give notice to the other party of the impediment and its effects on his ability to perform. If the notice is not received by the other party within a reasonable time after the party who fails to perform knew or ought to have known of the impediment, he is liable for damages resulting from such non-receipt.

(5) Nothing in this article prevents either party from exercising any right other than to claim damages under this Convention.

ART. 80. Must not cause other party's failure to perform.

A party may not rely on a failure of the other party to perform, to the extent that such failure was caused by the first party's act or omission.

Section V.
Effects of avoidance

ART. 81. Effect of avoidance.

(1) Avoidance of the contract releases both parties from their obligations under it, subject to any damages which may be due. Avoidance does not affect any provision of the contract for the settlement of disputes or any other provision of the contract governing the rights and obligations of the parties consequent upon the avoidance of the contract.

(2) A party who has performed the contract either wholly or in part may claim restitution from the other party of whatever the first party has supplied or paid under the contract. If both parties are bound to make restitution, they must do so concurrently.

ART. 82. Buyer loses right of avoidance if cannot return goods.

(1) The buyer loses the right to declare the contract avoided or to require the seller to deliver substitute goods if it is impossible for him to make restitution of the goods substantially in the condition in which he received them.

(2) The preceding paragraph does not apply:
    (a) if the impossibility of making restitution of the goods or of making restitution of the goods substantially in the condition in which the buyer received them is not due to his act or omission;
    (b) if the goods or part of the goods have perished or deteriorated as a result of the examination provided for in article 38; or
    (c) if the goods or part of the goods have been sold in the normal course of business or have been consumed or transformed by

the buyer in the course of normal use before he discovered or ought to have discovered the lack of conformity.

ART. 83. Buyer who loses right of avoidance or to get substitute goods, has all other remedies.

A buyer who has lost the right to declare the contract avoided or to require the seller to deliver substitute goods in accordance with article 82 retains all other remedies under the contract and this Convention.

ART. 84. Refund must include interest.

(1) If the seller is bound to refund the price, he must also pay interest on it, from the date on which the price was paid.

(2) The buyer must account to the seller for all benefits which he has derived from the goods or part of them:
- (a) if he must make restitution of the goods or part of them; or
- (b) if it is impossible for him to make restitution of all or part of the goods or to make restitution of all or part of the goods substantially in the condition in which he received them, but he has nevertheless declared the contract avoided or required the seller to deliver substitute goods.

Section VI.
Preservation of the goods

ART. 85. Seller must preserve goods if buyer in default.

If the buyer is in delay in taking delivery of the goods or, where payment of the price and delivery of the goods are to be made concurrently, if he fails to pay the price, and the seller is either in possession of the goods or otherwise able to control their disposition, the seller must take such steps as are reasonable in the circumstances to preserve them. He is entitled to retain them until he has been reimbursed his reasonable expenses by the buyer.

ART. 86. Buyer must preserve goods he may not accept.

(1) If the buyer has received the goods and intends to exercise any right under the contract or this Convention to reject them, he must take such steps to preserve them as are reasonable in the circumstances. He is entitled to retain them until he has been reimbursed his reasonable expenses by the seller.

(2) If goods dispatched to the buyer have been placed at his disposal at their destination and he exercises the right to reject them, he must take possession of them on behalf of the seller, provided that this can be done without payment of the price and without unreasonable inconvenience or unreasonable expense. This provision does not apply if the seller or a person authorized to take charge of the goods on his behalf is present at the destination. If the buyer takes possession of the goods under this paragraph, his rights and obligations are governed by the preceding paragraph.

ART. 87. Responsible party may warehouse goods.

A party who is bound to take steps to preserve the goods may deposit them in a warehouse of a third person at the expense of the other party provided that the expense incurred is not unreasonable.

ART. 88. Responsible party may sell goods if unreasonable delay by owner.

(1) A party who is bound to preserve the goods in accordance with article 85 or 86 may sell them by any appropriate means if there has been an unreasonable delay by the other party in taking possession of the goods or in taking them back or in paying the price or the cost of preservation, provided that reasonable notice of the intention to sell has been given to the other party.

(2) If the goods are subject to rapid deterioration or their preservation would involve unreasonable expense, a party who is bound to preserve the goods in accordance with article 85 or 86 must take reasonable measures to sell them. To the extent possible he must give notice to the other party of his intention to sell.

(3) A party selling the goods has the right to retain out of the proceeds of sale an amount equal to the reasonable expenses of preserving the goods and of selling them. He must account to the other party for the balance.

PART IV

FINAL PROVISIONS

ART. 89. Secretary General designated depository.

The Secretary-General of the United States is hereby designated as the depository for this Convention.

Appendix C

ART. 90. Convention does not over-rule other international agreements.

This Convention does not prevail over any international agreement which has already been or may be entered into and which contains provisions concerning the matters governed by this Convention, provided that the parties have their places of business in States parties to such agreement.

ART. 91. Convention open for ratification.

(1) This Convention is open for signature at the concluding meeting of the United Nations Conference on Contracts for the International Sale of Goods and will remain open for signature by all States at the Headquarters of the United Nations, New York until 30 September 1981.
(2) This Convention is subject to ratification, acceptance or approval by the signatory States.
(3) This Convention is open for accession by all States which are not signatory States as from the date it is open for signature.
(4) Instruments of ratification, acceptance, approval and accession are to be deposited with the Secretary-General of the United Nations.

ART. 92. Option of Country not to be bound by Part II or Part III.

(1) A Contracting State may declare at the time of signature, ratification, acceptance, approval or accession that it will not be bound by Part II of this Convention or that it will not be bound by Part III of this Convention.
(2) A Contracting State which makes a declaration in accordance with the preceding paragraph in respect of Part II or Part III of this Convention is not to be considered a Contracting State within paragraph (1) of article 1 of this Convention in respect of matters governed by the Part to which the declaration applies.

ART. 93. Contracting State may designate where Convention applicable.

(1) If a Contracting State has two or more territorial units in which, according to its constitution, different systems of law are applicable in relation to the matters dealt with in this Convention, it may, at the time of signature, ratification, acceptance, approval or accession, declare that this Convention is to extend to all its territorial units or only to one or more of them,

and may amend its declaration by submitting another declaration at any time.

(2) These declarations are to be notified to the depositary and are to state expressly the territorial units to which the Convention extends.

(3) If, by virtue of a declaration under this article, this Convention extends to one or more but not all of the territorial units of a Contracting State, and if the place of business of a party is located in that State, this place of business, for the purposes of this Convention, is considered not to be in a Contracting State, unless it is in a territorial unit to which the Convention extends.

(4) If a Contracting State makes no declaration under paragraph (1) of this article, the Convention is to extend to all territorial units of that State.

ART. 94. Contracting State with similar laws may declare Convention inapplicable.

(1) Two or more Contracting States which have the same or closely related legal rules on matters governed by this Convention may at any time declare that the Convention is not to apply to contracts of sale or to their formation where the parties have their places of business in those States. Such declarations may be made jointly or by reciprocal unilateral declarations.

(2) A Contracting State which has the same or closely related legal rules on matters governed by this Convention as one or more non-Contracting States may at any time declare that the Convention is not to apply to contracts of sale or to their formation where the parties have their places of business in those States.

(3) If a State which is the object of a declaration under the preceding paragraph subsequently becomes a Contracting State, the declaration made will, as from the date on which the Convention enters into force in respect of the new Contracting State, have the effect of a declaration made under paragraph (1), provided that the new Contracting State joins in such declaration or makes a reciprocal unilateral declaration.

ART. 95. Contracting State may avoid Article 1(1)(b).

Any State may declare at the time of the deposit of its instrument of ratification, acceptance, approval or accession that it will not be bound by subparagraph (1)(b) of article 1 of this Convention.

ART. 96. Contracting State that requires writing may declare Article 11 not effective.

A Contracting State whose legislation requires contracts of sale to be concluded in or evidenced by writing may at any time make a declaration in accordance with article 12 that any provision of article 11, article 29, or Part II of this Convention, that allows a contract of sale or its modification or termination by agreement or any offer, acceptance, or other indication of intention to be made in any form other than in writing, does not apply where any party has his place of business in that State.

ART. 97. Declarations made under the Convention.

(1) Declarations made under this Convention at the time of signature are subject to confirmation upon ratification, acceptance or approval.

(2) Declarations and confirmations of declarations are to be in writing and be formally notified to the depositary.

(3) A declaration takes effect simultaneously with the entry into force of this Convention in respect of the State concerned. However, a declaration of which the depositary receives formal notification after such entry into force takes effect on the first day of the month following the expiration of six months after the date of its receipt by the depositary. Reciprocal unilateral declarations under article 94 take effect on the first day of the month following the expiration of six months after the receipt of the latest declaration by the depositary.

(4) Any State which makes a declaration under this Convention may withdraw it at any time by a formal notification in writing addressed to the depositary. Such withdrawal is to take effect on the first day of the month following the expiration of six months after the date of the receipt of the notification by the depositary.

(5) A withdrawal of a declaration made under article 94 renders inoperative, as from the date on which the withdrawal takes effect, any reciprocal declaration made by another State under that article.

ART. 98. No reservations permitted except those expressly authorized.

No reservations are permitted except those expressly authorized in this Convention.

ART. 99. When Convention enters into force.

(1) This Convention enters into force, subject to the provisions of paragraph (6) of this article, on the first day of the month following the expiration of twelve months after the date of deposit of the tenth instrument of ratification, acceptance, approval or accession, including an instrument which contains a declaration made under article 92.

(2) When a State ratifies, accepts, approves or accedes to this Convention after the deposit of the tenth instrument of ratification, acceptance, approval or accession, this Convention, with the exception of the Part excluded, enters into force in respect of that State, subject to the provisions of paragraph (6) of this article, on the first day of the month following the expiration of twelve months after the date of the deposit of its instrument of ratification, acceptance, approval or accession.

(3) A State which ratifies, accepts, approves or accedes to this Convention and is a party to either or both the Convention relating to a Uniform Law on the Formation of Contracts for the International Sale of Goods done at The Hague on 1 July 1964 (1964 Hague Formation Convention) and the Convention relating to a Uniform Law on the International Sale of Goods done at The Hague on 1 July 1964 (1964 Hague Sales Convention) shall at the same time denounce, as the case may be, either or both the 1964 Hague Sales Convention and the 1964 Hague Formation Convention by notifying the Government of the Netherlands to that effect.

(4) A State party to the 1964 Hague Sales Convention which ratifies, accepts, approves or accedes to the present Convention and declares or has declared under article 92 that it will not be bound by Part II of this Convention shall at the time of ratification, acceptance, approval or accession denounce the 1964 Hague Sales Convention by notifying the Government of the Netherlands to that effect.

(5) A State party to the 1964 Hague Formation Convention which ratifies, accepts, approves or accedes to the present Convention and declares or has declared under article 92 that it will not be bound by Part III of this Convention shall at the time of ratification, acceptance, approval or accession denounce the 1964 Hague Formation Convention by notifying the Government of the Netherlands to that effect.

(6) For the purpose of this article, ratifications, acceptances, approvals and accessions in respect of this Convention by States parties to the 1964 Hague Formation Convention or to the 1964 Hague Sales Convention shall not be effective until such denunciations as may be required on the part of those States in respect of the latter two Conventions have themselves become effective. The depositary of this Convention shall consult with the Government

of the Netherlands, as the depositary of the 1964 Conventions, so as to ensure necessary co-ordination in this respect.

ART. 100. Effective date of applicability of Convention.

(1) This Convention applies to the formation of a contract only when the proposal for concluding the contract is made on or after the date when the Convention enters into force in respect of the Contracting States referred to in subparagraph (1)(a) or the Contracting State referred to in subparagraph (1)(b) of article 1.

(2) This Convention applies only to contracts concluded on or after the date when the Convention enters into force in respect of the Contracting States referred to in subparagraph (1)(a) or the Contracting State referred to in subparagraph (1)(b) of article 1.

ART. 101. Contracting State may denounce this Convention.

(1) A Contracting State may denounce this Convention, or Part II or Part III of the Convention, by a formal notification in writing addressed to the depositary.

(2) The denunciation takes effect on the first day of the month following the expiration of twelve months after the notification is received by the depositary. Where a longer period for the denunciation to take effect is specified in the notification, the denunciation takes effect upon the expiration of such longer period after the notification is received by the depositary.

DONE at Vienna, this day of eleventh day of April, one thousand nine hundred and eighty, in a single original, of which the Arabic, Chinese, English, French, Russian and Spanish texts are equally authentic. IN WITNESS WHEREOF the undersigned plenipotentiaries, being duly authorized by their respective Governments, have signed this Convention.

Cumulative Index

(Note: References to the Supplement are preceded by "S" and are in boldface.)

A

Acceptance of goods, 361–363
  revocation of, 370–372
  See also under Offers
Accountability, duty of, 59–60
Agency contract, breach of, 73–74
Agency/employer relationship:
  appointment of agent, 17–18
  definition of, 14–15
  definition of purchasing agent, 15
  role of agent, 16–17
  termination of agency relationship, 20
  See also under Agent; Principal
Agency law:
  apparent authority in, 29–31
  description of, 14–15
  types of authority and, 22
Agent:
  appointment of an, 17–18
  ascertaining authority of an, 40–43
  other titles for, 15
  principal's duty to compensate the, 66–67
  principal's duty to indemnify the, 67
  principal's duty not to interfere with the work of an, 67–68
  principal's duty to reimburse the, 67
  principal's liability for criminal acts of the, 79–83
  purchase orders and authority of the, 79–83
  role of the, 13–14, 15–17
  termination of the agency relationship, 20
  See also Liabilities, agent
Agent, duties of:
  accountability, 59–60
  confidentiality, 61–63

Agent (*cont'd.*)
  to exercise reasonable care, 56–58
  to keep the employer informed, 60–61
  loyalty, 52–55
  obedience to instructions, 55–56
  to possess necessary skills and training, 63
American Law Institute, 145, 146, 150
Antitrust legislation, 101–102
  See also under specific acts
Apparent authority:
  in agency law, 29–31
  description of, 27
  unauthorized procurement and, 31–32
Association meetings, antitrust and, 123–125
Authority:
  advantages of written, 23–24, 27–28
  apparent, 27, 29–32
  ascertaining, of an agent, 40–43
  ascertaining, of a purchasing officer, 48–49
  ascertaining, of a supplier, 43–48
  definition of, 21
  delegating order-signing, 77–79
  duty of principal regarding, 65–66
  emergency, 26
  express/actual, 22–23
  implied, 25–26
  purchase orders and agent's, 79–83
  of subagents and buyers, 28–29
  types of, in agency law, 22
Automobile, liability. *See* Liability, automobile

B

Bid bonds, 205–208
Blanket orders, 296

Index

Bribery, 136–140
Buyers:
  appointment of, 19
  authority of, 28–29
  performance and the responsibilities of, 357–363

C

Certified Purchasing Manager (C.P.M.), 15, 63, 128–129
Clayton Act, 103
Collision damage waiver insurance, 95
Commercial law, 143–144
Common law, description and sources of, 3–6
Comparative liability, 86–87
Compensation, duty of principal to compensate the agent, 66–67
Confidentiality, duty of, 61–63
Conflict of interest, 53–55
Contract law, traditional, 240–245
Contracts. *See* and under type of; Purchase orders
Convention for the International Sale of Goods (CISG), S3–114, S172
  acceptance under convention, S22–30, S119–121
  and American purchasing officer, S171–172
  anticipatory, S166–167
  breach, S198–200
  avoidance of contract, S32–34, S55–56, S130–131, S154–156, S164, S167
  battle of forms, S25–28, S122
  breach of contract, remedies for, S49–58, S147–158, S163–164
  breach of seller, S65–66
  buyer's obligations, S58–65, S158–164
  conformity of goods, S136–147
  cover purchase and damages, S68
  cure after delivery by seller, S53–55
  damages, S68–70, S167–169, S200–201
  delivery terms, S36–38, S134–135, S156–157
  disclaimer of warranties, S41–42, S139–140
  early delivery, S58, S157–158
  effects of avoidance, S170–171, S202–203
  elimination from contracts, S5–6
  equivalence of specific performance, S64
  exemptions, S201–202
  final provisions, S204–209
  formation of contracts, S17–22, S114–128, S181–184
  fundamental breach, S30–32, S128–130
  general provisions, S10–17, S107–108, S179–181
  inspection of the goods, S142
  installment contracts, S67–68, S166–167
  intent to cure, notice of, S153–154
  interest, S201
  interpretation issue, S12–14, S109–S111
  items not covered by, S11–12, S108–109
  manner/time of payment, S60–62, S160–162
  missing specifications, supplying, S64–65, S164
  modifications to contract, S35, S133
  negative aspects of, S71–72
  non-conformity of goods, S44–45, S57–58, S142–143, S156–157
  offers
    definition of, S17–18, S114–115
    firm offers, S19–22, S117–119
    revocable offers, S18–19, S115–116
  open price contracts, S59–60, S159–160
  origin of, S3–4
  over-runs, S58, S157–158
  passing of risk, S65–66, S165–166, S197–198
  patent/copyright infringement, S45–48, S144–146
  payment of price, S158–163
  preservation of the goods, S171–176, S203–204
  price reduction, S156
  provisions common to obligations of seller/buyer, S66–75, S166–176, S198
  quality obligations, S42, S140–141
  remedy of specific performance, S34–35, S132–133, S164
  right to cure by supplier, S42–43, S141, S152–153
  risk of loss, S65
  sale of goods, S30–48, S128–133, S184–197
  seller's obligations, S133–136
  sphere of application, S7–10, S104–107, S177–179
  taking delivery, S163
  text of (Appendix A), S79–114
  time for inspection, S44
  time for performance, S51–53, S64, S135–136, S164
  compared to UCC, S72–75
  U.S. Constitution and, S4–5
  "unless otherwise agreed," S9–10
  usages and course of dealing, S15–16

Convention for the International Sale of Goods (*cont'd.*)
    warranties, **S38–41, S136–139, S143–144**
    written contracts, **S16**
Counteroffers, 175–176
Credit terms:
    cash discounts and, 331–332
    code provisions for, 329–331
    counting the days for, 331
Criminal acts of the agent, principal's liability for, 70–71
Criminal liabilities, 98–100

D

Damages. *See* Remedies
Deep-pocket principle, 85–86
Defects in goods, 368–370
Delivery:
    C. & F. destination, 346–347
    C.I.F. or C. & F. net landed weights, 347
    C.I.F. destination, 345–346
    damages for non-, 383
    defects in goods and, 368–370
    definition of, 336–337
    duties of seller under a shipment contract, 341–342
    ex-ship, 347–348
    F.A.S. vessel, 345
    F.O.B. place of destination, 342–343
    F.O.B. place of shipment, 339–341
    F.O.B. vessel, car or other vehicle, 343–345
    foreign vendors and, 397–398
    methods of enforcing, 350–352
    no arrival, no sale, 348
    place of, 338
    in single of several lots, 349
    tender of, 337–338
    time for, 349–350
Detrimental reliance, **S21**
Disclaimer of warranties, CISG, **S41–42**
Doctrine of promissory estoppel, **S21–22**

E

Electronic Data Interchange (EDI), **S57–67,** 79
    Trading Partner Agreement, **S68**
        Section 1.2, **S74**
        Section 1.2.1, **S73, S74–75**
        Section 1.2.2, **S75–77**
        Section 1.3, **S74, S77**
        Section 1.4, **S77, S78, S79, S80**
        Section 1.5, **S78, S79–80, S91**

Electronic Data Interchange (EDI) (*cont'd*)
    Section 3.3, **S73, S77, S78, S79, S89**
    Section 3.3.1, **S89, S90**
Electronic Messaging Task Force, **S58**
Emergency authority, 26
Emergency purchasing, 36–38
Environmental hazards, 99–100
Environmental laws, **S2–4**
Ethics:
    accepting gifts, 59–60, 133–139
    definition of, 127, 128
    of the National Association of Educational Buyers, 129–132, 136, 137
    of the National Association of Purchasing Management, 132–133, 136
    purchasing codes of, 128
    exemptions, **S169–170**
Excess personal liability, 91
Express/actual authority, 22–23
Express warranties:
    advantages of, 311–312
    affirmation of fact or promise, 307–308
    description of goods as, 309–310
    sample/model of, 310–311
    types of, 306
    wording used in, 311

F

Federal Rules of Evidence (FRE), **S62**
    Section 1001(1), **S62**
    Section 1001(3), **S62**
    Section 1002, **S91**
Federal Trade Commission Act, 103
Foreign vendors, purchasing from:
    American v. foreign laws, 405
    American regulations, 408
    conducting business in buyer's state, 405–406
    Convention for the International Sale of Goods (CISG), **S3–114, S99–100, S101, S103–1**
    delivery considerations, 397–398
    determining final cost, 399–400
    escrow accounts, 406
    excuses for late delivery or nondelivery, 407–408
    letter of credit, 407
    payment options, 400–404
    performance bonds, 406
    problems with, 392–397, 404
    retaining part of purchase price, 407
    selection of suppliers, 404
    transit financing, 398–399

Index

G

Gifts, accepting, 59–60, 133–139
Government agencies, purchasing for, 408–413
Government procurement officers, liability and, 97–98

I

Implied authority, 25–26
Indemnify the agent, principal's duty to, 67
Installment contracts, 296
    interest, **S169**
Invitations to do business, 172–175

J

Joint and several liability, 86
Jurisdiction, definition of, 6–7

L

Law Merchant, 4, 152
Legal counsel, role of, 9–10
Liabilities, agent:
    breach of agency contract, 73–74
    execution of contracts and purchase orders, 74–83
    tort, 83–98
Liabilities, criminal, 98–100
Liabilities, principal:
    for criminal acts of the agent, 70–71
    vicarious, 68–70
Liability:
    automobile, 89, **S1**
    comparative, 86–87
    excess personal, 91
    factors you should know about your employer's liability insurance, 96–97
    government procurement officers and, 97–98
    using a company-owned automobile, 92–95
    using a rental automobile, **S1**, 95–96
    using your own automobile, 90–92
    See also Tort
Libel, 88
Licensed products, purchasing, 98–99
Liquidated damages, 352
Loyalty, duty of, 52–55

M

Marshall, John, 17
Merchantability, implied warranty of, 312–316

Mirror image rule, **S25**
Misfeasance, 84–85
Model Agreements, **S61**, **S68–69**
    Section 1, **S82**
    Section 1.1, **S70**, **S71**, **S77**, **S81**, **S83**, **S84**, **S89**
    Section 1.2.3, **S73**, **S76**, **S94**
    Section 2, **S80–86**
    Section 2.1, **S70**, **S73**, **S77**, **S80**, **S85**
    Section 2.2, **S65**, **S80**, **S81**, **S82**
    Section 2.3, **S65**, **S70**, **S74**, **S80**, **S83**, **S85**, **S89**
    Section 2.4, **S80**, **S81**, **S82**, **S84–86**
    Section 3, **S70**, **S86–91**
    Section 3.1, **S70**, **S84**, **S86–S89**, **S90**
    Section 3.2, **S79**, **S89**
    Sec. 3.3.2, **S66**, **S71**, **S90**, **S91**
    Section 3.3.3, **S61**, **S70**, **S71**, **S90**
    Section 3.3.4, **S78**, **S90**, **S91**
    Section 4, **S91–97**
    Section 4.1, **S91–92**
    Section 4.2, **S64**, **S92**
    Section 4.3, **S92**, **S93**
    Section 4.4, **S93**
    Section 4.5, **S76**, **S93**, 94
    Section 4.6, **S73**, **S76**, **S79**, **S94**
    Section 4.7, **S94**, **S95**

N

National association of Educational Buyers (N.A.E.B.), 129–132, 136, 137
National Association of Purchasing Management, 15, 63, 128, 132–133, 136
National Conference of Commissioners on Uniform State Laws, 144–146, 150
National emergencies, procurement during, 100
Negligence:
    duty to exercise reasonable care, 56–58
    See also under Liabilities
New York Times, 140
Nonfeasance, 84–85

O

Obedience to instructions, duty of, 55–56
Occupational Safety and Health Administration (OSHA), 100, **S2**
Offers:
    bid bonds and, 205–208
    definition of, 165
    essentials of valid, 167–172

Offers (cont'd)
  lapses of, 176–181
  legal implications of, 166–167
  promissory estoppel and, 208–210
  rejection of, 181–184
  revocation of, 184–188
  securing firm, 202–204
  sources of, 165–166
  See also Uniform Commercial Code, Section 2-205; Uniform Commercial code, Section 2-207
Offers, acceptance of, 186
  contract formation by conduct of both parties, 228–230
  controlling the manner of, 233–235
  definition of, 213–216
  proof of mailing an, 235–238
  source of, 216–217
  when does acceptance become effective, 230–233
Offers, buyer's methods of accepting:
  advance payment and, 233–234
  in blank, 218
  receipt and, 221–223
  repeat terms of offer, 219–221
Offers, supplier's methods of accepting:
  begins to manufacture and, 227–228
  in blank, 224–225
  delivery of goods, 226–227
  repeat terms of offer, 225–226
Official Comment, **S61**
Option contracts, 204–205
Oral contracts:
  origin of, 266
  Statute of Frauds, 24, 266–267
  See also Uniform Commercial Code, Section 2-201
Over-runs, CISG, **S58**

P

Payment, 374–375
  foreign vendors and, 400–404
Performance:
  bonds, 406
  buyer's responsibilities in, 357–363
  definition of, 355–356
  duty to exercise reasonable care, 56–58
  right to adequate assurance of, 373–374
  right to specific, 385–386
  steps in, 357
Pocket Code of the Rules of Evidence, 236

Price:
  escalation clauses, 325–327
  how to express, 324–325
  legality of a contract and, 323
  open-price orders, 327–329
Pricing arrangements, quantity and, 296–297
Principal:
  definition of, 14
  See also Liabilities, principal
Principal, duties of:
  to compensate the agent, 66–67
  to indemnify the agent, 67
  not to interfere with the work of an agent, 67–68
  to possess the authority delegated to the agent, 65–66
  to reimburse the agent, 67
Promissory estoppel, doctrine of, 208–210
Protecting whistle blowers, 98
Prudent person rule, 56
Purchase, definition of, 157–158
Purchase contract/order, essentials of, 158–163
Purchase orders, execution of:
  agent's authority and, 79–83
  delegating order-signing responsibility, 77–79
  format for signing, 74–75
  legal signature for, 75–77
Purchasing agent. See Agent
Purchasing officer:
  appointment of a, 18–19
  ascertaining authority of a, 48–49
  foreign sourcing, **S102**
  other titles for a, 15
  role of a, 13–14, 15–17
  torts and the responsibility of a, 87–98
  See also Agent
Purchasing subagents, appointment of, 19

Q

Quality, definition of, 299–300
Quantity:
  blanket orders and, 296
Quantity (cont'd.)
  how to express, 282–283
  installment contracts and, 296
  need for specification of, 281–282
  pricing arrangements and, 296–297
  requirements contracts and, 281–282, 283–295

R

Reimburse the agent, principal's duty to, 67
Rejection of goods, 363–368

Index

Remedies:
    buyer's, 380–390
    cover and, 381–382
    damages for breach in accepted goods, 383–384
    damages for nondelivery, 383
    importance of documentation, 380–381
    incidental and consequential damages, 384–385
    limitations on, 386–390
    liquidated damages, 386
    right to specific performance, 385–386
    seller's, 390–391
Remedy of specific performance, CISG, S34–35
Requirements contracts:
    definition of, 281–282
    drafting of, 286–295
    one-time, 295
    purpose of, 283–285
    Uniform Commercial Code, Section 2–306 and, 285–286
Robinson-Patman Act:
    description of, 103–105, 113–115
    "discrimination in price" and, 116–117
    "discrimination in price prohibited" by, 117–118
    exemption to, 125
    "knowingly to induce or receive a discrimination in price" and, 120–123
    "price discrimination permitted" by, 118–119
    section 2(c) of, 115
    section 2(f) of, 115–116

S

Sherman Antitrust Act:
    boycotts and, 110
    collusion, 110
    description of, 102, 105–106
    group buying, 111–113
    reciprocity and, 106–110
Signatures, legal, 75–77
Skills and training, duty to possess necessary, 63
Slander, 88
Statute of Frauds, 24, 266–267, S61
Subagents:
    appointment of, 19
    authority of, 28–29
Supplier, ascertaining authority of a, 43–48

T

Task Force Committee of ABA, S63
Third party, definition of, 14

Tort:
    business use of an automobile and, 89–97
    comparative liability, 86–87
    deep-pocket principal, 85–86
    defining wrongful acts, 84–85
    definition of a, 83–84
    joint and several liability, 86
    libel, 88
    purchasing officer's responsibility for, 87–98
    responsibility and, 85
    slander, 88
Tort-feasor, 84
Trade secrets, 61–63
Trading Partner Agreement, *see* Electronic Data Interchange

U

Unauthorized procurement:
    cooperation from suppliers and, 38
    dealing with an occasional, 39–40
    description of, 31–32
    eliminating, 34–38
    problems created by, 33–34
Uniform Bill of Lading Act, 145
Uniform Commercial Code:
    applicability of the, 147–148
    compared to CISG, S72–75, S172–175
    code references in the, 150
    content of the, 146–147
    contract law and the, 245
    course of dealings defined in the, 154
    definitions in the, 149–150
    delivery terms and the, 336–350
    genesis of the, 145–146
    good faith defined in the, 155–156
    goods defined in the, 151–152
    merchants defined in the, 152–153
    purposes and policies of the, 148–149
    Section 1–102, S70
    Section 1–102(1), S50, S70
    1–102(2), S59, S70
    Section 1–102(2)(b), S59
    Section 1–102(3), S49, S60, S70, S90
    Section 1–103, S71, S78, S85
    Section 1–201(26), S84
    Section 1–201(37), S7, S10–12
    Section 1–201(39), S62, S79
    Section 1–201(46), S90
    Section 1–203(3), S49, S53
    Section 1–204 of the, 364
    Section 1–204, S84
    Section 1–204(2), S78

Uniform Commercial Code (cont'd)
  Section 1–205, **S61**, **S91**
  Section 1–205(1), **S61**
  Section 1–205(2), **S74**
  Section 1–206(1), **S83**
  Section 1–206(1)(b), **S84**
  Section 2–103(1)(a), **S16**
  Section 2–103(1)(b), **S16**
  Section 2–103(1)(c), **S16**
  Section 2–103(1)(d), **S16**
  Section 2–104(1), **S16**, **S70**
  Section 2–104(3), **S16**, **S70**
  Section 2–106(1), **S16**
  Section 2–201, description of, 267–268, **S91**
  Section 2–201(1), **S58**
  Section 2–202(a), **S91**
  Section 2–204 of the, 228–230, **S70**
  Section 2–204(3), **S88**
  Section 2–206 of the, 233–235
  Section 2–207, **S65**, **S88**
  Section 2–207(3), **S91**
  Section 2–208, **S72**, **S91**
  Section 2–209, **S72**, **S91**
  Section 2–301 of the, 336, 355
  Section 2–305 of the, 327–329, **S85**, **S88**
  Section 2–306 of the, 285–286
  Section 2–306, **S87**
  Section 2–307 of the, 349
  Section 2–308 of the, 338
  Section 2–308, **S88**
  Section 2–309 of the, 349, **S88**
  Section 2–309, **S88**
  Section 2–310 of the, 329–333, 375
  Section 2–311 of the, 344
  Section 2–312 of the, 301–305
  Section 2–313 of the, 306–312
  Section 2–314 of the, 312, 314–315
  Section 2–315 of the, 316
  Section 2–316 of the, 318–321
  Section 2–319 of the, 339–341, 342–343, 344, 345
  Section 2–320 of the, 345–346
  Section 2–321 of the, 347
  Section 2–322 of the, 347–348
  Section 2–323 of the, 343, 344
  Section 2–324 of the, 348
  Section 2–326, **S10**, **S16**
  Section 2–401, **S10**
  Section 2–403(3), **S16**
  Section 2–503 of the, 337, 343–345, 356
  Section 2–504 of the, 341
  Section 2–507 of the, 337, 356–357

Uniform Commercial Code (cont'd)
  Section 2–508 of the, 368–369, 375
  Section 2–509 of the, 338
  Section 2–510 of the, 372, 375
  Section 2–511 of the, 374–375
  Section 2–512 of the, 360, 375
  Section 2–513 of the, 359–360, 375
  Section 2–515 of the, 359
  Section 2–601 of the, 363, 375
  Section 2–602 of the, 364, 365–366, 375
  Section 2–603 of the, 366, 375
  Section 2–604 of the, 366–367, 375
  Section 2–605 of the, 364–365, 375
  Section 2–606 of the, 361–362, 375
  Section 2–607 of the, 362, 375
  Section 2–608 of the, 371, 375
  Section 2–609 of the, 373, 375
  Section 2–610 of the, 373, 375
  Section 2–613 of the, 373, 375
  Section 2–615 of the, 373–374, 375
  Section 2–706 of the, 367, 375
  Section 2–711 of the, 367, 375, 381
  Section 2–712 of the, 381–382
  Section 2–713 of the, 383
  Section 2–714 of the, 364, 375, 383–384
  Section 2–715 of the, 382, 384
  Section 2–716 of the, 386
  Section 2–718 of the, 352, 386
  Section 2–719 of the, 385, 386–389
  Section 2–721 of the, 390
  Section 2–725 of the, 389, **S60**
  Section 9–105(1)(b), **S16**
  Section 9–105(1)(f), **S16**
  Section 9–105(1)(i), **S16**
  Section 9–105(1)(j), **S16**
  Section 9–105(1)(k), **S16**
  Section 9–106, **S16**
  Section 9–109(1), **S16**
  Section 9–402, **S16**
  Statute of Frauds in the, 24
  usage of trade defined in the, 154–155
Uniform Commercial Code, Article 2A, **S5–9, S14–56, S115–183**
Uniform Commercial Code, Section 2–201:
  subsection (2) of, 269–274
  subsection (3) of, 274–276
  summary of, 276–277
  description of, 267–268
  subsection (1) of, 268–269
Uniform Commercial Code, Section 2–205:
  description of, 188–189
  must assure that it will be held open, 195–196
  must be to buy or sell goods, 193–194

Index

Uniform Commercial Code, Section 2–205 (cont'd)
    must be made by a merchant, 191–193
    must be signed, 195
    must be a valid offer, 191
    must be in writing, 194–195
    must contain a reasonable time limitation, 196–199
    offeree's form and separately signed, 199–201

Uniform Commercial Code, Section 2–207:
    additional terms in, 247–248
    credit terms and, 331
    criticism of, 245–246
    purpose of, 246–247
    subsection (1) of, 248–251
    subsection (2) of, 251–257
    subsection (3) of, 257–259
    summary of, 260–263
    the title in, 248
    warranties and, 313

Uniform Commercial Code Official Text, 150

Uniform Negotiable Instruments Law, 145
Uniform Sales Act, 145
United Nations Convention on Contracts for the International Sale of Goods, **S177–209**

V

Vicarious liabilities, 68–70

W

Wall Street Journal, 53, 54, 140
Warranties:
    against infringement, 302–305
    CISG, **S38–41**
    definition of, 300
    exclusion of, 317–321
    express, 305–312
    implied, of fitness for a particular purpose, 316–317
    implied, of merchantability, 312–316
    of title, 301–302